Upside Down and
Inside Out

Upside Down and Inside Out

The 1992 Elections and American Politics

James Ceaser
Andrew Busch

Littlefield Adams Quality Paperbacks

LITTLEFIELD ADAMS QUALITY PAPERBACKS

Published in the United States of America
by Rowman & Littlefield Publishers, Inc.
4720 Boston Way, Lanham, Maryland 20706

British Cataloging in Publication Information Available

Library of Congress Cataloging-in-Publication Data

Ceaser, James W.
Upside down and inside out : the 1992 elections and American
politics / James Ceaser, Andrew Busch.
p.   cm.
Includes bibliographical references and index.
1. Presidents—United States—Election—1992. 2. United States
Congress—Elections, 1992. 3. Elections—United States. 4. United
States—Politics and government—1989- I. Busch, Andrew.
II. Title
JK1968   1992c   324.973'0928—dc20   93-9292   CIP

ISBN 0-8226-3023-0 (paper : alk. paper)

Printed in the United States of America

The paper used in this publication meets the minimum requirements of
American National Standard for Information Sciences—Permanence of
Paper for Printed Library Materials, ANSI Z39.48–1984.

To
Adeline Maedler
Ruby Busch
and
Helen Ceaser

Contents

Acknowledgments

We would like to thank Andrew Hall, George Monsivais, Brad Watson, and above all Brian Menard for their assistance in preparing this manuscript. Brian proved to be a source of endless knowledge and ideas about American elections. As many of our closest contacts were inside the Bush administration, we owe a special debt of gratitude to all the colleagues and graduate students who claimed to be Friends of Bill, of which, it goes without saying, there are too many to mention. The editors of Rowman and Littlefield Publishers, Jonathan Sisk and Lynn Gemmell, provided welcome assistance and advice. Support in typing the manuscript was provided by the Salvatori Center at Claremont McKenna College. Last, but certainly not least, Ms. Blaire French lent her usual sharp pencil and warm encouragement to the enterprise.

CHAPTER ONE

American Politics in Another Dimension

George Bush is wrong about most things, but he is
right when he said this is a "weird year."
—Bill Clinton, July 27, 1992[1]

November 3, 1992 marked the end of an Alice in Wonderland year
in which American politics seemed to be turned upside down and
inside out. A President boasting victory in one of the nation's most
successful wars was rejected for reelection with the lowest percentage of the popular vote of any incumbent since William Howard
Taft. A Governor from Arkansas began as the Democrats' frontrunner,
was nearly knocked out of the race by a series of scandalous revelations, then rebounded to win. An idiosyncratic Texas billionaire
"ran" without declaring, withdrew, changed his mind again, and ended
with a higher percentage of the popular vote than any third-party
candidate since Teddy Roosevelt in 1912.

The key to understanding the topsy-turvy 1992 national election lies in the emergence of a new dimension of American politics
that combined and interacted with the traditional dimension. The
traditional dimension is made up of the familiar axes of partisanship
(Democratic, Independent, and Republican) and issue positioning or
ideology (liberal, moderate, and conservative). These two axes tend
to coincide with and reinforce each other, with Republicans being
more on the conservative side of the political spectrum and Democrats more on the liberal side. The fit is far from perfect, however,
as political leanings on different issues provoke cross-pressures. These
cross-pressures produce the conflicted voter groups known by such

1

hybrid labels as "Reagan Democrats," "liberal Republicans," "pro-life Democrats," and "pro-choice Republicans."

The new, second dimension of politics that emerged in 1992 has no single recognized name, hardly any institutionalized form, and—because this plane is devoid of conventional ideology—no clear left-right significance. As far as partisanship is concerned, Republicans and Democrats are as likely to be found at one end of this dimension as at the other. Yet there is a vigorous, if curious, kind of politics at work on this plane. The defining cleavage is variously referred to by the distinction of amateur versus professional, the unconventional versus the conventional, the people versus the establishment, life beyond the beltway versus life within the beltway, and—perhaps most commonly—outsider versus insider.

In one of the first essays ever written on political parties, the British philosopher David Hume identified the underlying division in Great Britain in his age as one between the court and the country parties. The court party backed the monarchy inside the moatway, while the country party claimed to stand for the great bulk of the people beyond.[2] If one substitutes "Washington" for the court, something of the spirit of the second dimension of American politics begins to come into focus. America's court party in 1992 was the "party" of insiders, while her country party was the "party" of outsiders.

Outsiderism as a theme of American politics in one sense has roots as old as the republic itself. The outsider appeal, which relies heavily on a down-home commonsense populism, resonates with fundamental elements of the American tradition that can be traced back to certain themes of the revolutionaries, the anti-federalists, the Jeffersonians, and the Jacksonians. (In fact, if one wished to make a long academic detour, it would probably be possible to locate the roots of the lineage of outsiderism directly with the "country" party in Britain, from which Americans early on borrowed a whole discourse of anti-insider thought.[3]) Outsiderism declaims against the overblown perquisites and privileges of those in office, against the systematic use of political power to keep and maintain power (creating a "political class"), against corruption and an easy reliance by those in office on double standards. Outsiderism as a theme seeks a government that is somehow "in touch" with the people.

In another sense, however, outsiderism as we know it today originated in the 1976 presidential campaign of Jimmy Carter, when the term "outsider" began to acquire wide currency. Not by accident, perhaps, three of the major strategists of that campaign (Patrick Caddell, Gerald Rafshoon, and Hamilton Jordan) all were active for a time as advisers to "outsider" candidates in 1992. And Jerry Brown, who jumped in late in the 1976 nomination campaign and ran to the outside of Carter's outsider campaign (nearly derailing it), reappeared in 1992 to push the appeal further, only to be superseded by a yet higher form of outsiderism in the person of Ross Perot.

The modern variant of outsiderism, while it incorporates many of the earlier elements, adds something new. It functions almost entirely as a symbol, devoid of any specific content. Its essence is the appeal of being "not part of," and thus not tainted by, the inside, or the establishment, or the way things are done. Outsiderism is used in the first instance to distance oneself from the corruption of the court—that "little group of Washington insiders, lobbyists, and professional politicians who think of the national government as their own private playground."[4] Outsiderism is then employed to "tap into" the anger that exists against Washington, which in turn is connected to a more diffuse resentment of the conditions of society. Once this act of distancing has been accomplished and the bond of common sentiment forged, outsiderism is then used to lay a claim to putting one "in touch" with some deeper and purer wellspring of the American spirit. Outsiderism is a moral as well as political category.

One may object to this idea of symbolism by citing the case of Ronald Reagan. Reagan managed to appropriate much of the appeal of outsiderism, both while running for office and while governing, but Reagan tied outsiderism, at least some of the time, to a more specific meaning. For Reagan, being against the "inside" or Washington meant getting government "off of our backs and out of our lives," which is to say reducing the scope of government. Insofar as Reagan and the Republicans linked outsiderism to this specific program, rather than relying on pure form, it may be said that they deviated from the development of strict modern outsiderism. The proof of this last point is found in the character of outsiderism in 1992, which had no clear connection to Reagan's views and proved broad enough to hold a David Duke, a Ross Perot, and a Jerry Brown, as well as congressional candidates of virtually every political stripe.

Outsiderism has a powerful attraction in part because it is so amorphous and multifaceted. It is like an empty box with a false bottom from which most anything can be pulled. Some outsider positions may be serious and thoughtful, others meaningless or downright dangerous. But much of the time, it is not a question of position, but merely of positioning. What strategists and candidates understand is that with the use of a vague symbol, they can appeal to diverse positions united only by a common mood or discontent.

The hope is that everything that is mixed up in this vast vessel of discontent will somehow hold together long enough to get one to the next stage of the campaign.

Being against "politics as usual," outsiderism quite naturally stresses what is wrong with how things are done in Washington. Failures of policy are often ascribed to defects of process, ranging from charges that the electoral process is corrupted by money and special interests to criticisms that the institutions have fallen under control of one elite group or another. In the wake of the savings and loan debacle and the House bank scandal, 1992 proved an especially appropriate time to raise an outsider appeal against court politics, especially against Congress. Few citizens could close their ears to complaints against "our elected officials who have allowed this great system to be mired in the mud of special interests, who have padded themselves with perks at our expense, and who have rigged the election system to avoid answering to the people." This was Ross Perot speaking, but it could just as well have been any one of a number of candidates, all of whom recycled the same charges and relied on the same alliterations.

The ground for an outsider institutional appeal, however, had been prepared by a decade of relentless "populist" attacks, from both the right and the left, on different parts of the political system. The right, believing that its positions generally enjoyed majority support in the country and that the left could succeed only by attaching itself to nonmajoritarian institutions, had partisan reasons to support populist attacks on bureaucracies, courts, and even legislatures. The left, ever mindful of being outflanked on questions of popular control, kept up attacks on wealth and on the "imperialism" of the presidency. Both sides engaged in a populist bidding war, which was often good politics but which left the "inside," even in its legitimate constitutional forms, undefended and unprotected.

This populist sentiment was "tapped into" by the general current of outsiderism in 1992, in ways that often dismayed those who had engaged in the bidding wars. In Duke, Brown, and finally Perot, outsiderism at times reached beyond normal institutional channels. If there were problems with the parties, why not just forget the parties altogether and run outside them? If there were blockages in Washington, why not just consult the public by electronic town meetings? If there were differences of opinion, why not set them aside and "just do it"? Institutionally, outsiderism takes place at the juncture between a legitimate quest to reform the political system and a species of attack on it that begins to depreciate representative political institutions as such. Outsiderism can thus manifest itself at one moment in reasonable populist argument for institutional change and in the next in an unreflective and intemperate "bashing" of constitutional forms.

It was in 1992 that country-court politics emerged full-blown on the American scene as a virtual faction inside each party and then as a virtual party of its own. One can locate three basic positions on this dimension: the outside, the middle (inside-outside), and the inside. Running with a strong appeal to the outside were presidential candidates David Duke, Jerry Brown, Pat Buchanan, Paul Tsongas (kindly, gently, and thoughtfully), and Ross Perot, whose independent candidacy garnered 19 percent of the popular vote. In congressional races, almost all of those who challenged incumbents relied on an outsider strategy. In addition, there were the proponents of the state initiatives for term limits for Congress. The insider party consisted of the anti-term limits position and, despite their best efforts to escape the label, the Washington-based members of the Democratic primary field (Senators Kerrey and Harkin), George Bush, and many of the less fortunate members of Congress. Indeed, the election year "opened" in November of 1991 with the stunning defeat in the Pennsylvania senatorial race of a highly touted insider, former Attorney General Richard Thornburgh, who had either the temerity or the naivete to run as an insider. He would be the last candidate to do so. Running a bit more to the middle on this dimension were Bill Clinton and some congressional incumbents who managed to separate themselves from the odium associated with Congress.

While the outside position was usually the one more coveted by candidates, this was not invariably the case. For as much as the great majority of the people wanted to punish the court in Washington, many Americans also sought the reassurance of knowing that their elected officials possessed adequate political skills and reliability to handle the offices for which they sought election. Thus, many Democratic voters during the primary were "wary of Jerry," preferring Bill Clinton at least partially because he was more of an insider. And while almost all candidates who were on the inside were fighting to get further out—this characterized Bush's strategy—there were also a few on the outside who were struggling to get in, at least partially. This was Ross Perot's strategy at the high point of his campaign in June, when he hired the noted strategists Ed Rollins and Hamilton Jordan and promised to choose a well-known (read slightly insider) vice-presidential candidate. (Ultimately, of course, Perot returned to a pure outside strategy in the fall, when he was content to run a campaign that had as its objective finishing a respectable third.)

Lest one get the wrong impression from this discussion, we are not arguing that the 1992 campaign was determined solely, or even primarily, by the country-court cleavage. The traditional dimension of politics—as we will discuss further on—was often at the heart of the campaign. Republicans had held the White House for twelve years, and a weak economy became a partisan issue. So did Democratic control of Congress. And Bill Clinton won his party's nomination and the presidency in no small part because he moved toward the center of the traditional philosophical spectrum.

The politics of 1992 thus were not characterized by an end to politics on the traditional dimension, but by an intermixture of traditional politics with the inside-outside division. This new situation transformed the plane geometry of traditional American politics into a new universe of solid geometry. Candidates who were at opposite ends of the traditional political spectrum (a Patrick Buchanan on the right and a Jerry Brown on the left) were on the same end on the inside-outside dimension, making many similar kinds of appeals. The same was true, if not of the appeals, then at any rate of the predicaments, of George Bush and Tom Harkin. Longtime partisan and ideological foes, these two politicians both suffered from their long association with court politics in Washington.

Virtually every major actor and even certain events in the 1992 elections can be placed on a grid based on these two dimensions. (See Table 1-1.) For the sake of simplicity, we have reduced the traditional dimension of the party-and-issue position to a single axis (left-center-right). The value of this grid does not lie in its "neatness" as a tool of modern social science, but in how it clarifies the way in which various actors often viewed their own situation.

Consider, for example, the effect of country-court politics on the strategies employed in congressional elections. First, challengers (who were to the outside, naturally, of incumbents), almost always took advantage of their position to run as outsiders. In campaign after campaign, there was a remarkable degree of "nationalization" of politics—on the country-court dimension. Second, Republicans sought to create a national image that would position them to the outside of Democrats. The plan was to "capture" the second dimension by depicting the national Democratic congressional party, which owned Congress, as the court party. Voters might then proceed to "clean House," enabling all Republicans (incumbents as well as challengers) to run as the outsiders. In the end, however, this

Table 1-1
The Rosetta Stone of American Politics: 1992

	OUTSIDE	MIDDLE (INSIDE-OUTSIDE)	INSIDE
LEFT	Jerry Brown Dem. congres- sional challengers		Tom Harkin Bob Kerrey Dem. congression- al incumbents
		Bill Clinton	
	Paul Tsongas		
CENTER	Ross Perot		
			George Bush
	GOP congressional challengers	GOP congres- sional incumbents	
RIGHT		Jack Kemp	
	Pat Buchanan		
	David Duke		

dimension largely escaped partisan control. Finally, women candidates—in a year the press dubbed "The Year of the Woman"—often made use of the gender issue in their campaigns as a mark of outsiderism. (Many women were also running as challengers.) Here, the court party was depicted as male-dominated Washington politics; and for some women candidates the symbolism of an all-male judiciary committee sitting in judgment of Anita Hill proved the point. As one female congressional candidate put it, "We're the ultimate outsiders. We're not corrupted by Washington politics."[5] Gendercentric voting (primarily women voting more for women candidates) reached a historic high point in congressional elections; and while this development clearly had causes of its own, it often ran parallel to and "tapped into" the court-country distinction.

The two dimensions depicted in Table 1-1 also help explain how strategists for both political parties sought to "script" their conventions in order to take account of the court-country cleavage. The aim of a well-run party convention today is to present a certain picture of the party and its candidate to the public. The convention is thus analogous to the campaign biography in the nineteenth century, and the conventions build to the all-important video biographies that take place just before the nominee's acceptance speech.

The scripts for the two conventions in 1992 were both prepared with the country-court distinction in mind. The Democrats attacked George Bush as an insider and hid their congressional leadership somewhere in the balconies of Madison Square Garden. The Republicans spent four days stressing the connections between the Democratic ticket and its congressional contingent, and George Bush made an effort, as valiant as it was vain, to put himself on the outside.

There are two further points to make about the positioning of the candidates on this second dimension. The first, noted earlier, is that a position on the outside was no guarantee of victory. Indeed, looking at the full presidential field in 1992, all of the pure outsiders lost, despite the fact that Tsongas and Brown won some primaries, Buchanan scored fairly well against a sitting president, and Ross Perot did extremely well as a third-party candidate. It would be incorrect, of course, to conclude that these outside candidates lost *because* they were outsiders. On the contrary, when one looks at who these candidates were, what liabilities they possessed, and what the strengths were of some of the other candidates (including being President of the United States!), outsiderism appears to be the factor that enabled them to get as far as they did. Nevertheless, when one examines these campaigns close up and considers how they might have succeeded, it becomes clear that there was a point at which the pure outsider position either became a liability or imposed a ceiling beyond which a candidate could not go. Going outside could take one only so far, and no further. The same proved to be true in many congressional races, although there were instances where a pure outsider campaign did succeed.

The second point is the more obvious one. Ultimately, the rhetorical advantage in 1992 lay more with the country party, and the campaign in many respects resolved itself to a question of who would best be able to take advantage of the other's insider vulnerabilities. The first to fold in the Democratic field were the insiders Kerrey and Harkin, and clearly one of the things that kept Richard Gephardt and Lloyd Bentsen from jumping into the race after the New Hampshire primary (both were on the verge of declaring) was their fear of the effect of their insider image. George Bush's strategists reportedly wanted Clinton as their opponent, which if true would only confirm how much they misunderstood the character of politics in 1992. Whatever Clinton's personal liabilities may have been, they could not compare in 1992 to those that would have attached to anyone forced to defend the court politics of the Democratic Congress. In the fall campaign Clinton distanced himself from court politics, which he labeled the "brain-dead politics in Washington," and, as a moderate outsider (flanked on the outside by Ross Perot), defeated the insider George Bush. The only way for the Republicans to have neutralized this advantage would have been to run a candidate from the same position on the second dimension, such as Jack Kemp. Many reasons can be advanced to explain President Bush's defeat, but Republicans must wonder if they might have won this election in a campaign fought on the first more traditional dimension alone.

Bill Clinton, it turns out, was the only major actor in the presidential contest in 1992 to be near to the center on both dimensions of American politics. He married centrism on the ideological plane to moderation on the inside-outside plane. This position almost squarely in the middle served him well in both his primary and general election campaigns, enabling him to tilt now to one side, now to another, as circumstances dictated. This was his slickest trick of all.

Having emphasized the two-dimensional schema as the key to understanding the 1992 campaign, we close the discussion of country-court politics with a major qualification. Outsider politics explains a great deal of what occurred in 1992, from the emergence of Ross Perot to the large influx of new members of Congress; and there is much in this mood that may affect the future course of American politics, from demands for campaign reform to the movement for congressional term limits. Yet we do not argue that outsiderism now constitutes a permanent feature of American politics. Its immediate future, of course, depends on political decisions and events which no one can now predict. But its staying power as a major political force is open to question, and we doubt whether outsiderism ever achieved anything approaching the strength many commentators assigned it at the time of the emergence of the "Perot phenomenon" in May and June. It was then, one may recall, that many were convinced that a revolution was taking place in American electoral politics that portended the imminent collapse of the traditional partisan dimension.

This assessment was doubtful, even at the time. Much of the outsider appeal lacked "substantiality," having been built up on vague symbolism and inflated by a communications system that favors new and outside appeals. Currents of opinion of this sort—popular "humors," to use an older term—generally lack the significance they are accorded by commentators and by the numerous experts who vie to supply explanations on demand for yesterday's opinion polls. Existing in a curious netherworld between being and nonbeing, these opinions are not as potent or real as they seem. They tend to crash, just as the Perot phenomenon crashed in late June and early July.

Yet, as this assessment speaks of a tendency, not a certainty, one is still left with the question of how the electoral process should be structured to respond to such currents of opinion. The prospect of growing outsiderism raises some of the most important issues of institutional theory. Should the object of the presidential selection process be to encourage these currents at the expense of the older divisions channeled in the parties, thereby allowing candidates to ride a new sentiment into the presidency? Should electoral institutions be altered, as Theodore Lowi and John Anderson proposed, to open the way to "new candidates like Ross Perot to run and to allow supporters of these candidates to vote their true beliefs"?[6] Or, as we prefer to ask, is the American presidential selection process already sufficiently open (or even unduly vulnerable) to currents of opinion and candidates who enter the process laterally? And should electoral institutions continue to serve the function of discouraging the "little arts of popularity" and deflecting "those brilliant appearances of genius and patriotism which, like transient meteors, sometimes mislead as well as dazzle"?[7]

THE CONVENTIONAL CHARACTER
OF THE 1992 ELECTION

Because of this new and confusing geometry of American politics in 1992, commentators throughout the year were virtually unanimous in echoing the view of Peter Jennings that 1992 was "the strangest election" they had witnessed. Chastened by erroneous predictions, many commentators despaired of ever getting an accurate fix on the campaign. Along with George Bush, originator of the "weird year" thesis, they seemed to think that the year itself possessed mysterious powers of its own that allowed it to defy all ordinary efforts at explanation. It was "voodoo politics."

Yet the moment the returns came in on November 3, there seemed to be relatively few mysteries to unravel, and it is hard to think of an election in recent times where there has been *less* agonizing over the meaning of the final results. If one confines the analysis to the traditional dimension and to the performance of the Republicans and Democrats, forgetting Ross Perot, the outcome does not appear to be especially controversial or difficult. Had the results only been known all along, everything would have been perfectly obvious.

In the presidential race, amidst all the early talk of Republican dominance, simple common sense should have demanded a qualification. As three leading electoral analysts noted the year before: "The Democrats will eventually enter an election with the Republican candidate unpopular, and with the economy weak."[8] George Bush was that man, and 1992 was that year. In the congressional elections, while it is unusual for a new president to experience an overall loss for his party in Congress, the nation had just gone through a process of redistricting that put Republicans in a far more favorable position in House contests than in 1990. The Democrats' loss of ten seats in the House—the Senate stayed the same—was thus no great shock, and, if anything, represented a major disappointment for the Republicans.

Not only were the election results not that mysterious, but (confining ourselves again to the performance of the two major parties) they were also devoid of any unusual or profound significance. By definition, of course, the defeat of George Bush in the 1992 election ended the Reagan-Bush era; but this was hardly the revolution some liked to proclaim. While there was clearly a vote for a different team, fresh faces, and new approaches, the election results per se provided no mandate for a dramatically new course of action. (The real significance of elections in any case is less in the returns and putative "mandates" than in the chance to exercise power and put into effect certain policies.)

It is difficult, for example, to read into the results evidence of any kind of partisan realignment. Not very much changed in this respect in 1992. After the election, as before the election, a bit more than a third of the electorate could be counted as (relatively) safe Republican voters in presidential elections, and a bit more than a third could be counted as (relatively) safe Democratic voters. The rest of the electorate consisted of a floating vote able to move with ease between the two parties (or even outside of them) depending on the prevailing candidates and circumstances. Indeed, so much did the election seem to hinge on the performance of the economy, that if the election had been held in December instead of November—after another month of evidence of a recovery—the outcome might well have been different. If there was no sign of a major partisan realignment, there was also no evidence of a radical ideological shift. Bill Clinton, as some of his intellectual supporters like to claim, may well approach issues in a way that transcends previous ideological categories; but the fact remains that for many voters what was important was Clinton's centrist or conservative views on a number of key issues. In contrast to Walter Mondale and Michael Dukakis, no one could stick Bill Clinton with the "L" word (liberal).

Confining the analysis to the traditional plane, therefore, the election of 1992 was neither "strange" nor "revolutionary." To call it banal might be to depreciate it unduly. Conventional seems just about right.

THE PRESIDENTIAL RACE

Popular explanations usually start from an unexamined assumption about what "should" happen and then proceed to ask why things do or do not turn out as expected. By common agreement, the "anticipated" result in 1992 was a victory by George Bush. What needed to be explained, therefore, was why George Bush lost.

This starting point might be defended on three grounds. First, George Bush was the incumbent, and there is a tendency in most explanations to privilege the status quo and ask why things deviate from it. Additionally, it is widely thought that incumbents so dominate the political scene that all elections are theirs to win or to lose.

Second, the Republican party was often said to be the majority party at the presidential level, the beneficiary of an electoral realignment in 1980. This fact was taken to "explain" the last three presidential victories, all Republican electoral landslides. This lofty, academic theory of voting behavior had a more down-to-earth parallel in the campaign consultants' theory of the electoral "lock." Under this view, Republicans had a solid base (or "lock") in enough key states to dominate the electoral college. From the election of Richard Nixon in 1968 to the election of George Bush in 1988, the Republicans had won 21 states, totaling 191 electoral votes, in each contest and another 14 states, totaling 151 electoral votes, in five of the six elections. This base of 342 electoral votes put the Republicans well over the 270 votes needed to win. Democrats, conversely, had won only the District of Columbia all six times, and Minnesota five of six, giving them a "base"—if one could call it that—of 13 electoral votes.

Finally, there was the general political expectation of political commentators and observers throughout 1991—the famed "conventional wisdom" of Washington. Only a year before the election the conventional wisdom had George Bush a certain winner, so much so that the only topic of discussion in presidential politics was who would be president—in 1996.

Yet, in light of the results of the 1992 election, perhaps the initial point of departure should be examined. Each of the three reasons just stated can be called into question—and, more to the point, could very easily have been called into question well before the election. First, while incumbent presidents do tend to win, it is rare for the same party to win four elections in a row. In itself such historical facts are meaningless, except to that curious sect that believes in the causal effect of numbers and cycles. But facts of this sort can lead us in search of actual causes. On this score, from the side of the public, there is undoubtedly something in the idea that a populace naturally grows a bit weary of the same faces in power and itches for change. ("Change" was Bill Clinton's central theme in 1992.) After a number of terms, potential supporters of the administration begin to forget or discount the shortcomings of the opposition party, the memory of whose faults is by now receding, and concentrate on the flaws of the incumbent. George Bush, after all, had run for national election three times in a row, and no candidate except FDR has run successfully in four consecutive national elections. The nation even required an eight-year respite from Richard Nixon between 1960 and 1968; and even then, Nixon felt obliged to return in 1968 as "the new Nixon." There was no new George Bush in 1992.

As for those in office, there is a tendency to grow complacent and to lose sight of the need to suppress internal disagreement for the larger objective of maintaining power. Power satisfies, and entrenched power satisfies absolutely. Administration officials cannot seem to resist reliving old feuds and settling petty scores. In the case of George Bush's administration, moreover, the President never fundamentally changed teams or directions, which left the same cliques inside the administration to fight with each other to the end.[9] Meanwhile, those who have been deprived of place grow hungrier and live in the hope that their own views may prevail.

Second, the theory of a Republican realignment at the presidential level was widely misunderstood, at least for those who bothered to examine it closely. Even on the surface, all this theory claimed was that the Republican party had gained adherents relative to the Democratic party (and perhaps held a slight advantage) among those voters having a decided partisan preference. But in the modern electorate—and on this count, the modern electorate differed considerably from the electorate of the previous era—there remained a large floating vote that could conceivably support either party's candidate. Hence in reality, the theory of realignment in the modern context was all along a "weak" theory, not a strong one. It stated a tendency that by the evidence itself was clearly too small to forecast the outcome of any election. At most, it was a starting point for political analysis.[10]

It is true, of course, that many of those who supported the case for a Republican realignment also produced arguments showing why the floating vote, for a number of reasons, could more easily be mobilized by the Republicans. But this argument was separate from— or should have been kept separate from—the question of realignment. The reasons why the floating vote was more easily mobilized by Republicans still left room for a change in their vote, depending on the circumstances and relative appeal of the candidates. What happened in 1992 was that the floating vote had more than sufficient reason to drift away from George Bush.

As for the electoral lock, when one examines it up close, it is far from being as secure as advertised. For it follows that if you win the election, you must have won the electoral college vote, and it is only natural that a party that wins a string of elections will tend to repeat a strong performance in the same states. Past periods of dominance by one party or the other also had produced "locks" of their own. By definition, then, if the Democrats were to win an election the lock would have to be broken, which was what happened in 1992. The lock all along was really a description of what had happened, not a prediction of what would happen.[11]

Third, while George Bush did enjoy unprecedentedly high approval rating in 1991, this measure has always been a lag rather than a lead indicator. An analysis of the pattern of Bush's approval scores shows that they tended to be boosted by successful foreign policy exploits. The first high point came after the Panama invasion, the second after the Gulf War. As the lustre of these exploits wore off, Bush's approval rating drifted downward, toward their more "natural" base. Bush's high-end support was a mile wide but an inch deep. Of course, everyone in Washington was aware of the great volatility in presidential support scores. But most believed—and who did not agree?—that the Gulf War was unique and that its effects would not quickly dissipate. This turned out to be at best only half true. George Bush forever succeeded in shedding his "wimp" image that dominated the early 1988 campaign, but he could not avoid being viewed as a vacillating domestic leader.

Perhaps, then, the question requiring explanation all along should not have been "Why did George Bush lose?" but rather "How could George Bush ever have won?" To persist in such a curious proposition, however, smacks of the classic intellectual vice of an undue fascination with paradox. Let us, therefore, stay with the commonsense view of the matter and ask why George Bush was not able to do what he was "supposed" to do. Indeed, to put the question in its starkest light, we can ask not only why George Bush lost, but why he received a smaller percentage of the popular vote than any incumbent president since 1912.

We start with a set of political factors in 1992 that were shaped by the record of the Bush's administration and by the general condition of the nation. These factors—the end of the Cold War, a weak economy, and a vacillating management of economic and indeed domestic affairs generally—constitute the deepest reasons for why George Bush lost.

First, the Cold War came to an end, and Soviet communism itself was rejected and destroyed from within. That so favorable a condition turned out to be harmful on balance to President Bush was a dismaying and frustrating paradox for Republicans. It was all the more frustrating because the "Reagan-Bush" administration did claim—and was actually accorded by the American people—much credit for this achievement. To be sure, Republicans in their rhetoric sometimes tried to take too much of the credit, and Democrats occasionally succeeded in chipping away at these excesses. But such skirmishes notwithstanding, few in the end challenged directly the Reagan-Bush record on this count, and there was almost no one to be found snickering at Ronald Reagan's "evil empire" statement. That once ridiculed view, as Reagan reminded everyone at the Republican convention, had now become entirely absorbed into the fashionable conventional wisdom.

The problem for Republicans was that the credit they received turned out to be incidental. The collapse of the Soviet empire removed the threat of communism, and eliminated national security and foreign policy generally as important electoral concerns in the 1992 election. These concerns had been Republican strong suits in recent elections and provided an important basis for attracting "Reagan Democrats" into the GOP's presidential coalition. Since 1968, the Republican party had been the party identified as stronger on defense and had benefited from the fears many Americans had about the world. (Democrats in the end conceded this point in their campaigns by stressing that the danger in electing Republicans was that their belligerence could lead to war.) The collapse of communism even served to depreciate the electoral significance of President Bush's finest hour in the Gulf War. If foreign affairs generally were unimportant, then Desert Storm—a widely acknowledged (though slightly tarnished) success—counted for little.

Many of the important effects of the end of the Cold War, however, did not show up in poll questions about foreign policy, but were disguised or concealed in other categories. And once again the nation's gain generally transferred into the Republicans' loss. Consider, for example, the impact of the new international situation on the internal coalitions of the two parties. The end of the Cold War increased tensions inside the Republican party, the component parts of which had been held together by common opposition to communist expansionism. Anyone who attended public rallies of the Republican party in the last decade would immediately have seen how anti-communism provided a sustaining, moral purpose to the party and helped to define and clarify for Republicans the meaning and importance of freedom. With the collapse of communism new tensions, largely centered on the social and cultural issues, came to the forefront, while older foreign policy divisions over free trade and isolationism found expression in the Buchanan campaign.

Not only had anti-communism been the salutary glue that helped hold the Republican coalition together, but it had also been a solvent corroding the Democratic coalition. If Democratic doves and critics of military spending dominated the party, a significant wing of the party still sought to break with this image and to leave behind the McGovern legacy. In this wing could be counted some of the members of the Democratic Leadership Council (DLC), which included such "responsible" Democrats as Senators Sam Nunn and Chuck Robb, as well as Bill Clinton. The problem that national security issues posed for Democrats was embodied in Michael Dukakis' ill-fated tank ride during the 1988 campaign. Dukakis jumped into the tank to attempt to show that the Democrats were breaking with their past, but the effect of the jaunt only served to reinforce in the public mind the idea of a party weak on defense.

The collapse of communism largely removed the security issue as a problem inside the Democratic coalition and paved the way for the exit of many "Reagan Democrats" from the GOP, a process that had already begun in 1988. Everyone, Republicans included, agreed on cutting military spending, and the whole issue simply did not play with the same interest or passion as before. Indeed, one of the bitter fruits of the "peace dividend" for Republicans was the huge unemployment in defense-related industries, especially in the key state of California. The situation was so bad in that state that the Bush campaign never even bothered to contest the election, a failure that contributed to the loss of a number of House contests for Republicans that were within striking distance. The decline of the security issue for Republicans also contributed to the decline of the Republican advantage among male voters. Men had been mobilized for Republicans in a significant degree on the basis of the security issue, and the wide support Bush enjoyed among the male population in 1988 literally collapsed in 1992. There was less of a gender gap in 1992, because the "men's vote" of the 1980s began to vanish.[12] The end of the Cold War marked the onset of a "feminization" of American politics. "Our stereotype," noted Congresswoman Pat Schroeder, "is finally in."[13]

Another effect of the ending of the Cold War was to diminish the usual advantage of incumbency. In a dangerous world, one of the benefits of incumbency is that people are apt to be less risk-prone and more inclined to support the person with experience in dealing with foreign leaders. George Bush was well suited to claim these advantages, and he did. Only they counted now for much less. Clinton's theme of change was consequently more acceptable. As one Bush official noted, "The end of the Cold War . . . makes the presidential race much more like a gubernatorial race—where people say get rid of the old guy, and take a chance."[14]

Many of the same points apply to the so-called "character issue," which operates independently of the question of incumbency. In many respects, the character issue over the years has implicitly been a foreign policy and national security issue. What one meant in assessing a person was not just good ethical conduct (a concern that often dominated the primaries), but the question of who possessed the steadiness as well as the toughness and shrewdness to lead a great nation in a dangerous world. The character issue focused on the questions "Who do you trust with his finger on the button?" and "Who do you think can stand up to the enemy?" (It was on this last point that Democrats of impeccable ethical character— Jimmy Carter in 1980, Walter Mondale, and Michael Dukakis—were nevertheless hurt by the character issue.) Bill Clinton, a person with little foreign policy experience and with draft problems, would thus seem to have been a "natural" for being undermined on this question. But, together with the fact that Clinton demonstrated an admirable toughness of character in the campaign, the security-related aspects of character counted less in a post-Cold War world.

Paradoxically, therefore, it was a sign of the weakness, not the strength, of the Republican campaign in 1992 that the aspect of character on which George Bush focused was Bill Clinton's displayed "pattern" in lacking "truthfulness." The purely ethical component of character, as distinct from toughness, had if anything been a theme

Democrats since 1968 have tried to use against Republicans, with little evident success. And George Bush on this score had pattern problems of his own, in the form of his broken "no new taxes" pledge and the old ghost of Iran-Contra.

Just as the character issue is not entirely distinct from foreign policy questions, so too is this the case with the so-called "cultural" or "social" question. This social question over the years has consisted of a cluster of disparate issues, including the death penalty, prayer in schools, abortion, and belief in traditional or family values. Whether these form an integral "package," tied together by a general support for or opposition to the liberal preference for personal self-expression, has long been a matter of dispute. Generally speaking, disaggregating the social question into unrelated issues has been a Democratic objective, keeping them loosely tied together a Republican objective. What strikes one is the extent to which the theme of patriotism—even, and perhaps especially, patriotism worn on the sleeve—was connected with the social question and essential to keeping it more or less as a package. Many who were mobilized to join the Republican presidential coalition, and who had doubts about one or two of the social issues, nevertheless remained in the traditional camp because of the power of the patriotic theme. This explains the importance of the flag, which was at the thematic center of the last three presidential elections. Its conspicuous absence in 1992, which was linked again to a changed international order, signaled the decline of on-the-sleeve patriotism as a major theme for the Republicans.

The 1992 election was the first election at "the end of history," the first election since the 1930s when the survival of the cause of democracy did not appear to be at stake. The great issues of security, war and peace, and totalitarian expansionism that had been at or near the top of the concerns in presidential politics for more than a half century had been replaced by more mundane preoccupations with the domestic economy and health care, in which Bill Clinton was able to transform virtually every question about foreign affairs into a question of competitiveness and job training. This new circumstance altered the character of political discourse, changing which arguments would work and which questions had to be answered. The result was mostly disadvantageous to Republicans and provided an opening or space in politics for something else—outsiderism and the Democrats. If Republican strategists were aware of these problems, as they clearly seemed to be, it is also true that they never succeeded in developing an effective strategy to deal with them.

The second reason why George Bush lost in 1992 was the condition of the American economy. From all indications in the polls, the economy—stupid!—was the dominant concern of the voters. About 60 percent of Americans listed the economy as the most important issue in deciding their votes (as opposed to 9 percent for foreign affairs). Administrations inevitably are held accountable in large measure for economic performance, and the nation's economic growth rate during the Bush years was anemic at best. Although the nation was not technically in recession at the time of the election, and interest rates and inflation were extremely low, the perception in the public was that the economy was bad and that prospects for improvement were poor. Furthermore, this recession and its aftermath, unlike the more serious recession a decade ago, cut more deeply into previously stable middle-class and white-collar jobs, leaving greater anxiety than the economic statistics suggested.

Third, while a weak economy would have hurt any president, George Bush was harmed even more by the public's judgment that he had failed in managing the economy, and indeed in managing domestic policy generally. Bush faced a dilemma after 1990 that he never managed to resolve. Having agreed to the 1990 budget agreement, breaking a solemn promise not to raise taxes, Bush thereafter could never decide whether he wished to embrace existing economic policy and claim credit for the performance of the economy or disassociate himself from the prevailing policies and denounce the performance of the economy (blaming it on the unwillingness of Democrats to pass an alternative program). In the end, as in so many other aspects of domestic policy, Bush split the difference or never adopted a very clear strategy.

Bush's problem in managing the economy was reflective of another and larger trait of his presidency and of his campaign. George Bush had an aversion to ideas, at least in the sense of a set of principles around which he organized his view of the world and conducted public policy. In some ways, perhaps, this uneasiness with ideas was a source of certain of his accomplishments. Unwedded to formulas and able to view each issue on its own terms, Bush could avoid some of the traps into which ideologues sometimes fall. Escaping the straightjacket of rigid ideas is what Bush meant when he continually referred to his own conduct of policy as being governed by "prudence," a word he used so often that it became for a time his trademark in political satires. In foreign policy, this flexibility often served him well. In conducting domestic policy, however, and in presenting a rationale to the American people in a campaign, the absence of anything resembling a "vision thing" proved a major liability. As a result, Bush failed to sustain (and sometimes positively damaged) the coalition that Reagan had left him.

Yet the argument that Bush lost because he had no ideas leaves one set of questions unanswered. Many commentators during the election, especially liberal commentators, argued that Bush would lose not because of the ideas he lacked, but because of the ideas he espoused. Bush, or so they said, was the equivalent of Reagan (or even Buchanan), and the Republican party was greatly damaged by tying itself to certain unpopular views, especially on cultural issues. Conservative commentators, by contrast, argued that it was the absence of any vision and the distance of Bush from conservative principles that helped produce his defeat. For conservatives it was not because he followed Reagan that he lost, but on the contrary because he distanced himself from Reagan. Of course *which* Reagan they were referring to depended on the types of conservative commentators in question. For some it was the traditional-values Reagan, to others the small-government Reagan, while to others still it was the supply-side Reagan.

Here, no doubt, lies the single most important unresolved question of the 1992 presidential campaign, and obviously one with important implications for Republican strategy in the future. The answer, however, probably cannot be found in the electoral data, and surely not in an analysis that proceeds on the basis of a simple dichotomy between ideas and no ideas. For if it is true that Bush suffered from a lack of vision, it surely does not follow that any so-called conservative vision he might have espoused would have worked to his advantage. Bush, Republicans point out, can be said to have lost because he did not hold his Republican base, as Republicans almost always have been able to do. Twenty-seven percent of Republican voters deserted Bush, as compared to only 23 percent of the Democrats deserting Clinton. Yet, complicating the picture, it was moderate, not conservative, Republicans who defected most.[15] Republicans will be left to ponder these questions.

These political reasons were the deepest causes of Bush's defeat. But there were other kinds of reasons, closer to the surface, that affected the results. One set applies to the way the Republicans conducted the campaign. The general view of those active in the Republican campaign was that Republican failures in this area, while undeniable and even glaring, were not sufficient to account for the Republican defeat. In a remarkable exculpatory mea culpa, a leading Bush strategist declared, "We've run a terrible campaign. But if we had run a perfect campaign, we'd still be in the same shape."[16] No one can be that certain.

First, Republicans over the past four years had allowed themselves to be placed in a position in which their foes could feel inoculated from Republican criticism. In all rhetorical wars, the most important battles are not those that are fought, but those that do not need to be fought. The latter reveal the more or less commonly accepted assumptions from which discourse begins. Of these assumptions, perhaps the most damaging to Republicans became the notion that Bush's 1988 campaign had been excessively negative and that his victory was somehow "illegitimate." Whatever the validity of this charge, the Republican party did not challenge the premise and thus allowed Willie Horton to become a shield behind which both Bill Clinton and Ross Perot sought to hide against any and all Republican attacks. Clinton and Perot did not always succeed, but the remarkable thing is that they could always plausibly try.

In the same vein, Republicans failed adequately to contest the assertion that the 1980s was the "decade of greed" and that this greed was a product of the Reagan-Bush presidency, not the Democratic Congress. This view became an article of faith to intellectuals, not to mention to various rock artists and to the cultural elite of Hollywood, never guilty of greed themselves. The failure to combat this curious idea probably stemmed in part from the fact that Bush himself, with his laudable ideas of duty and service, shared this view, at least in regard to the lax behavior of more than a few high officials in the Reagan administration. Yet, notwithstanding a fairly clean record of service for his own administration, Bush never challenged the greed theme or tried to turn it against his opponents.[17] Greed thus remained synonymous for many with the Reagan-Bush years, which gave the moral high ground in domestic politics to the critics of the administration.

Second, Republicans acted as if they did not want to win. While the Democrats rallied behind a flawed candidate, the Republicans did not. This was above all evident in the positions taken by the nation's mainline political commentators. Of course, commentators do not work for a party and are under no obligation to support any particular candidate. It is nonetheless a fact that the "Democratic" commentators ended up vigorously championing Clinton, while the "Republican" commentators subtly or openly sabotaged Bush. William Safire, widely considered the conservative columnist for the *New York Times*, endorsed Clinton; George Will, who occupies a similar station for the *Washington Post*, advocated a write-in vote for Jack

Kemp; and Kevin Phillips, frequent commentator for the *Los Angeles Times* and frequently described "conservative political analyst," supported Clinton.

Finally, the campaign itself was disorganized and ineffective. Of course there is always a tendency for commentators to exaggerate the skills of the winners and to label the losing team a bunch of—dare one say it?—bozos. But in this case, the evidence for this claim is more "objective," as it comes, so to speak, straight from the horse's mouth. In the spring and early summer the campaign was in disarray, so much so that those in charge of the campaign were actually anxious to step down at the last minute and turn over the reins to Jim Baker. Baker himself was reluctant to accept the position, and once there was reluctant to exert himself. He hardly ever met the press and went so far as to make evident that he never really was the campaign manager, a task he considered beneath the dignity of a former Secretary of State and world statesman. As the saying goes, this was no way to run a campaign.

There is a final reason for why George Bush lost that fits in neither of the previous two categories. It derived from the structure of the 1992 campaign itself. George Bush had the bad fortune of being in a race in which he faced two (or perhaps three) major opponents in the general election campaign, while Bill Clinton faced only one. The President was, as expected, attacked by the Democratic nominee, who represented the second great party in American politics. Bush was also attacked, however, by Ross Perot, who played—and at times was widely accorded—the role of disinterested referee, but who spent most of his free airtime and paid advertising decrying Bush's stewardship. Probably because he had no real strategy for victory in the fall, and because he so despised George Bush, Perot did not attack Bill Clinton until the very end of the campaign and even distanced himself from the comments of Admiral Stockdale about the importance of military service. If there was a single factor from the campaign itself that could have shaken everything up and altered the whole course of events, it was the opening of a second front by Perot against Bill Clinton.[18] It never really happened. Finally, in an old story for Republicans which is sad but frequently true, Bush was pummeled almost daily by a largely unfriendly mainline media. With all the other problems Bush faced, he could hardly afford to be beset by foes on three sides and allies on none.

Of course, even if George Bush lost the election, it remains worthy of mention that Bill Clinton won it. This in itself requires some explanation. For aside from not being George Bush, Bill Clinton possessed two important attributes that allowed him to take advantage of Bush's vulnerabilities. First, unlike Bush, Clinton was able successfully to wear the mantle of outsiderism—loosely. (Being flanked to the outside by Perot also allowed Clinton to appear when necessary as not too far outside.) Second, Clinton was sufficiently moderate on the ideological scale to deflect most charges of liberalism. He supported the Persian Gulf War (loosely), made a point of rejecting the "tax and spend" policies of the past, and had a stance on social issues, like the death penalty and welfare reform, that left little room for accusations of "soft" liberalism. He moved to the left only on certain issues, like abortion, where attacks on his liberalism rebounded in many areas to his favor. Thus the Republicans were left with mere shadows of the once-potent cultural issues, referring to Clinton's problems with the draft and the views of wife Hillary.

It would not be fair to suggest that Bill Clinton won solely because of what he was not—George Bush, an insider, and a liberal. But these were some of the most important reasons, and they were at the heart of his campaign all along. Nor is there anything in this strategy to be ashamed of. If not being elected a Democratic senator or representative in Washington was Bill Clinton's good fortune, his ability to escape the "liberal" label was clearly the product of years of work and organization in building up the DLC, of much hard thought, and—not the least—of great tactical skill in distancing himself from Jesse Jackson. Add to this an individual of formidable intelligence, great stamina, and an extraordinary ability to communicate and you get what you might have expected: a new president.

The Congressional Elections

Congressional elections are generally determined by a mixture of local and national issues, with local issues recently tending to dominate. In 1992, purely local issues did, as usual, play an important role; but in a striking way many of these were filtered through the dimension of outsiders versus insiders. Almost all challengers ran as outsiders, not only attacking Congress as an institution, but attacking incumbents for being part of it.

National partisan issues and ideology were expressed mostly in a dialogue about the state and management of the economy. By late summer, Democratic congressional candidates were trying to connect themselves to Bill Clinton, even as he was seeking to maintain a discreet distance from incumbents in his own party. Republican candidates first encouraged Bush to lead the attack against the

Democratic Congress; then, as Bush slipped in the polls, they sought to distance themselves from him, collectively and individually, to avoid partisan losses and win their own seats.

In the end, the results of the congressional elections showed the pull of outsiderism to be substantial, though far less than many predicted. The most important victory for outsiderism took place before the fall elections, in the form of 59 congressional retirements (52 in the House, seven in the Senate) and the defeat of 20 incumbents in primaries (19 in the House and one in the Senate). In the case of the House, both of these figures were postwar records. This preelection victory for outsiderism was the most significant factor in contributing to the large turnover in Congress of 122 new members, including a record number of women and minorities. A second victory for outsiderism occurred on election day. Term limitation initiatives passed in all 14 states where they were on the ballot, mostly by hefty margins. Finally, the rate of third-party voting in congressional elections increased dramatically in 1992 to a possible new high for modern politics. Although much of this vote went to candidates from previously established third parties rather than to candidates connected to Perot, it still was a clear reflection of an outsider sentiment.[19]

Nevertheless, the limits of outsiderism were clear in the fact that in the November elections 93 percent of the incumbents won, just about the modern average. Of course, this figure is slightly deceptive, as many of the weaker incumbents had already been weeded out in the retirements and primary campaigns. Moreover, many of the incumbents had managed only to eke out their victories, and the average margin of incumbent victory declined. Still, all things considered, incumbents did quite well; and they did especially well where they ran in something resembling their old districts before redistricting. The style of their campaigns shifted somewhat, with more incumbents than usual downplaying their incumbency. But this only indicates their resiliency. And particularly by the end of the campaign, incumbents in many races grew more confident in proclaiming some of the advantages of long service, while challengers saw the need to stress their experience. All in all, therefore, the results of 1992 may do little to allay those who seek larger average turnovers. If 1992 represented the zenith of outsiderism, rather than the onset of a growing force, turnover by 1994 may be back closer to usual.

A partisan dimension operated, at least beneath the surface.

Republicans who tried to turn the outsider dimension against Democrats and make it a partisan issue had only modest success, with two-thirds of the defeated House incumbents in November being Democrats. By traditional numerical standards, as noted, Republicans could claim a victory. Despite Clinton's election, Republicans gained ten seats in the House and lost none in the Senate. Still, there was a Democratic partisan trend as well. Because of redistricting and the outsider sentiment, Democratic seat losses paradoxically belied the existence of moderate Clinton coattails, which served to mitigate Democratic losses. There was at least some evidence that voters wanted to end gridlock, and saw unified Democratic control of government as the only viable alternative.

REAL HISTORY AND CAMPAIGN HISTORY:
SOME QUESTIONS FOR THE FUTURE

Every election raises a series of questions or deeper themes that go beyond the simple results of who won and who lost. So much analysis and "serious" commentary accompanies modern presidential campaigns that those who follow them closely are apt to begin to believe that the real issues of our time are—or at any rate ought to be—the most important issues of the campaign. In fact, however, this is more the exception than the rule. The intersection of real history and campaign history is sporadic and haphazard, and in this regard 1992 was probably a quite normal campaign. The unintended and unexamined consequences of the election seem more important than its intended and examined themes.

What security and foreign policy questions will eventually fill the vacuum left by the end of the Cold War? From the perspective of real history, perhaps the major question of our times is how America and the other nations of the free world will fare in groping their way to the "broad, sunlit uplands" that Churchill once promised as the reward for victory against totalitarianism. Yet the theme of foreign policy was virtually absent from the 1992 election campaign—by the deliberate design of the victorious candidate. It is unlikely, however, that it will remain so for his administration. The reconstruction of the post-Cold War world will almost certainly occupy a great deal of the attention of the new President and present a series of new concerns and issues for which the 1992 campaign provides hardly a clue.

Will gridlock end (or diminish) with the end of divided government? While it is probable that few Americans cast their ballots with
the explicit intention of ending divided government, that is what they
achieved (and may even have wanted). Although Bill Clinton did not
tie himself to congressional candidates from his party during the
campaign, as President he cannot easily disassociate himself from
them. Nor will he want to. Campaigning is one thing, governing another,
and no president can govern from the outside. Now that responsibility for governing lies clearly in the hands of one party, party spirit
and a greater tendency toward party voting across the board could
loom as more likely possibilities in the future.

What public philosophies are likely to dominate the nation's
parties? Public philosophies are given meaning more in action than
in words, and thus on this score the 1992 campaign poses more
questions than it provides answers. For the Democrats, it remains to
be seen how serious Bill Clinton is about moving the Democratic
party to the center and how he will fare against his party's left wing
and agglomeration of interest groups. For Republicans, the struggle
for the future meaning of conservatism among the divergent tendencies that claim the label—from supply-siders, to budget balancers,
to advocates of traditional and even Christian values—has only begun.

Finally, what is the future of outsiderism? Did it reach its peak
in 1992, or was 1992 only a plateau from which a future outsider
candidate will begin a steady ascent to the summit? If outsiderism
persists, will it take a new form, or will it be wed to the person of
Ross Perot? The rise of Ross Perot and the other manifestations of
outsiderism remind us of the volatility inherent in the candidate-
centered system of elections. Beyond this electoral volatility, however, outsiderism poses a more important and delicate challenge of
where and how to draw the line between a justifiable dissatisfaction
with the performance of the political system and an attack on rep-
resentational forms that threatens constitutional government itself.

NOTES

1. *Time*, July 27, 1992, p. 28.
2. David Hume, "Of The Parties of Great Britain," in Eugene Miller,
ed., *Essays* (Indianapolis: Liberty Classics, 1985). Hume's essay was first
published in 1741.

3. See, for example, Bernard Bailyn's, *The Ideological Origins of the American Revolution* (Cambridge, Mass.: Belknap Press, 1968).

4. Ross Perot, *United We Stand* (New York: Hyperion, 1992), p. 112.

5. Richard S. Dunham, "The Year of the Woman—Really," *Business Week,* October 26, 1922, p. 106. In a survey of the women elected to the Senate, Jeffrey Katz noted that "the new Democratic women senators had the appeal of being candidates outside the normal scope of power in Washington," *Congressional Quarterly Weekly Report,* November 7, 1992, p. 3559. Katz goes on to point out, as we note below, that pure outsiderism could also prove a liability. The victorious Democratic females were also veteran politicians.

6. Theodore Lowi, "Three-Party Politics: A Natural Order," *Campaign,* vol. 6, no. 8, August 1992, p. 46.

7. *The Federalist Papers,* numbers 68 and 64.

8. Paul Abramson, John Aldrich, and David Rohde, *Change and Continuity in the 1988 Election,* revised edition (Washington, D.C.: Congressional Quarterly Press, 1991), p. 301.

9. The replacement of Chief of Staff John Sununu by Samuel Skinner in December 1991 hardly affected policy and left the same major players in position.

10. This is the only reasonable conclusion to draw from the careful analysis of Paul Abramson, John Aldrich, and David Rohde in *Change and Continuity in the 1988 Election.*

11. Bill Clinton won nine of the 21 states that had voted Republican every year since 1968, and 11 of the 14 that Republicans had won five times out of six, accounting for 222 electoral votes.

12. Bush defeated Dukakis among men voters by a score of 57 percent to 41 percent, whereas the difference separating the two candidates among women voters was negligible (50 to 49). In 1992, Clinton beat Bush 41 to 38 among men and 46 to 37 among women. Thus Bush's share of the men's vote declined by 19 points from 1988 to 1992, while his share of the women's vote declined by only 12 points. These figures are from the exit polls used by the *New York Times*; the organizations conducting these polls have changed over the years. The poll results since 1976 may be found in the *New York Times,* November 5, 1992, p. B9.

13. Margaret Carlson, "It's Our Turn," *Time,* October 1, 1990, p. 16.

14. *Los Angeles Times,* September 19, 1992, p. A16.

15. According to the *New York Times* exit poll, Bush received 82 percent of the conservative Republican vote as compared to 63 percent of the moderate Republican vote. In itself, this larger margin among conservatives is not surprising; but it does at least pose questions about what kinds of conservative appeal might win back votes for the GOP.

16. *The Hotline,* October 15, 1992.

17.   The highly publicized involvement of one of Bush's sons, Neil, in the savings and loan morass undoubtedly played a role in placing the President on the defensive.

18.   The Clinton campaign lived in dread of this possibility. See the in-depth analysis of the campaign strategy by David Lauer, *Los Angeles Times*, November 5, 1992, p. A1.

19.   The figures for third-party voting in House elections are discussed in Chapter 5. See also John Hood, "The Third Way," *Reason*, February 1993, pp. 42-43.

CHAPTER TWO

The Republican
Nomination

When George Bush looked out at a joint session of Congress on March 6, 1991, just days after the end of the war with Iraq, he must have envisaged that his own path to reelection in 1992 would be as swift and sure as the allied sweep through Kuwait. Bush had led America to its first clear-cut military victory in a major war since World War II. In recognition of this feat, Americans rewarded him with an unprecedented 90 percent approval rating. While economic growth still lagged, the nation seemed to be emerging from a relatively short and mild recession. Furthermore, most of the Democrats considered to be frontline contenders had opposed the use of force in the Persian Gulf. The only question left for the Democrats seemed to be which Democrat would be offered up as fodder for the presidential election.

Less than a year later, however, Bush was reeling from a serious intra-party challenge from conservative commentator Patrick J. Buchanan. Buchanan ran as an outsider, forcing Bush not only to the right but as far to the outside as his temperament and record would permit. Contrary to any expectation he could have had the year before, Bush was compelled to leave the White House and campaign for his own renomination in the New Hampshire primary. The President was ultimately renominated without losing a primary, largely because Buchanan was never able to win the support of most conservatives and was perhaps too far to the outside to gain the confidence of the electorate. Bush's victory notwithstanding, both his campaign and his presidency were in an apparent state of disarray throughout the nominating season. Much of the key to under-

standing the Republican nomination race of 1992 lies in what occurred during the 11 months between Basra and Nashua.

THE BUSH PRESIDENCY

George Bush's unexpected troubles represented what some began
to see as a "Jimmy Carterization" of the Bush presidency, taking
place in a period that eerily recalled Carter's own travail during a
time of "national malaise." There were three major components of
this process: a pattern of indecision and policy reversals, inadequacy
in coping with economic troubles and anxieties, and major organizational confusion inside the campaign.

Indecision. Republican strategists hoped that decisive presidential
leadership in the seven months of the Persian Gulf crisis would dispel
any vestiges of the "wimp" image. The war almost certainly did provide
the President with an opportunity to seize the political initiative at
home. Indeed, the wimp image was vanquished; but it was replaced
with the equally dangerous phenomenon of high public expectations
of decisive domestic action. The administration quickly squandered
the opportunity. Rather than purely redefining George Bush, the war
served more as an aberration, a momentary deviation from a trend
that began in the summer of 1990 with the abandonment of the "no
new taxes" pledge. Bush's approval ratings had fallen precipitously
prior to the August 2 invasion of Kuwait by Iraq. His public standing
was resuscitated temporarily with the initiation of Operation Desert
Shield, but fell again by the midterm elections in November, which
occurred only days after the actual budget package (including major
tax increases) passed Congress. Indeed, Bush's approval ratings had
fallen from 76 percent in early September to 53 percent in mid-October.
Nothing less than the onset and successful completion of the war
itself sufficed to raise presidential approval to the 90 percent mark.
The administration had hoped that the budget deal would produce
(or at least coincide with) an economic turnaround by 1992 that would
overshadow the broken tax pledge. Instead, the recession deepened,
arguably at least in part as a result of the tax increase itself. Bush's
reversal on taxes was thus a continuing source of trouble, serving as
a political magnifying glass that focused and enlarged the effects of
subsequent reversals while simultaneously minimizing the credibility of new initiatives.
    From the end of the war to the end of the nominating season,

the Bush administration was engaged in a series of incidents characterized by temporizing and indecision at best and not infrequently by outright policy reversal. Within weeks, it was apparent that a premature cease-fire order by Bush had prevented U.S. forces from completing the task of dismantling Saddam Hussein's Republican Guard. After calling on the Iraqi people to overthrow Hussein, the administration refused to intervene on behalf of Kurdish and Shiite rebels who briefly threatened Saddam's regime. By the end of the year, Bush had come under increasing fire from domestic critics for having coddled Baghdad before the war.[1] The administration's indecision, both prewar and postwar, began to overshadow the war itself as the focus of public attention.

At the same time, Bush failed to capitalize on his popularity to push a domestic agenda. His speech to the joint session of Congress was designed not only to celebrate victory, but to focus the nation's enthusiasm (and his political capital) on a domestic program. Covering little new ground, the bifurcated speech moved from a stirring tribute to the American forces that liberated Kuwait to a litany of domestic proposals for education, energy, crime control, and transportation—a "hodgepodge" held together only by the fact that George Bush had proposed them all before. In short, Bush failed to present any sort of coherent conservative program. Aside from a $150 billion five-year transportation bill passed in late October, almost all of the proposals languished in Congress, a situation the administration seemed to accept. Bush's failure to launch a meaningful agenda marked the first in a series of three missed opportunities to seize the political initiative.

Another critical turning point was reached in the early fall. On October 25, the administration reversed its position and agreed, with a few amendments, to a civil rights bill it had long opposed as a "quota" bill. On the same day, it decided against an economic growth tax-cut package pushed by congressional conservatives. The reversal on the civil rights bill was widely seen as a full-scale retreat in the face of an attempt by congressional liberals and the elite media to link Bush and former KKK leader David Duke, who was at that time running for governor of Louisiana.[2] The rejection of the tax cut represented the second missed opportunity to regain the initiative. At this time, Republicans still led Democrats 45 to 39 in the polls on the question of which party was best able to handle the economy, and by a 4 to 1 margin respondents blamed Congress rather than the White House for economic troubles.[3]

Whether by design or by default, the administration failed to

act. The polls from that point forward revealed a steadily deterio-
rating situation for the administration. Conservatives within the
Republican party were particularly unhappy. They believed that
opposition to de facto quotas and support for low taxes were among
the relatively small number of issues in which good politics coincided with sound principle.

Shortly thereafter, the White House was thrown into turmoil
by the surprise victory of Democratic Senator Harris Wofford in Pennsylvania. Wofford defeated Bush confidant Richard Thornburgh, who
had served both as U.S. attorney general and Pennsylvania governor, and who had at one time led Wofford by 40 points in the polls.
Wofford ran as an outsider—despite his status as an appointed incumbent senator—against the "establishment" insider Thornburgh
on a platform of middle-class tax cuts, national health insurance,
and thinly veiled isolationism. Almost lost in the media concern with
the Pennsylvania race were substantial Republican successes in
Virginia, in Mississippi, and in New Jersey, where voters gave
Republicans a veto-proof legislative majority in reaction to Democratic Governor James Florio's tax increases. The administration
panicked and Bush canceled a long-planned trip to visit major U.S.
trading partners in Asia. When the Japanese leg of the trip was re-
scheduled weeks later, Bush brought with him the three major U.S.
automobile executives, who used the occasion to turn a goodwill
trip into an opportunity for Japan-bashing.

Economic news continued to worsen in late 1991, accentuated
by the announcement of 73,000 upcoming layoffs by General Mo-
tors. Meanwhile, the White House delayed any substantive response
until the State of the Union Address on January 28. This decision
was made on the advice of Richard Darman, director of the Office
of Management and Budget (OMB) and architect of the 1990 tax
compromise, and against the advice of an activist core of administration and congressional conservatives. The address, hyped by the
administration, received a modestly successful public response. Ultimately, however, it failed to establish a credible agenda, less because of the content of the proposals than because the administration, in what had by then become a pattern, almost immediately backed
away from some of its own recommendations and left the rest to
wither. Within days, the legislative package forwarded to Capitol
Hill had been stripped of all but seven provisions. A health care
reform proposal also promised by Bush was delivered late and left
to languish.

When the March 20 deadline that Bush set for congressional

action in his State of the Union Address came, and Congress had failed to act, Bush responded by criticizing Congress and proposing a list of spending rescissions. But there was nothing approaching a declaration of war. Having emphatically thrown down the gauntlet in January, he meekly picked it up again in March.

This pattern of indecision and reversal continued well into the primary season. Bush announced in March that he had made a mistake in agreeing to the tax increase in the 1990 budget agreement, but emphasized that he regretted it because he had paid too high a political price for it. After the April 29-30 riots in Los Angeles, he appeared alternately flustered and indifferent, finally proposing an urban aid program but allowing it to sit in Congress for months. At about the same time, the White House moved to recast Bush as the reform candidate, despite his 25-year Washington career and his instinctive attachment to the status quo.[4]

These incidents combined in the public mind to form a picture of an administration without direction and a president lacking in firm principles. This image was highlighted when Bush told David Frost in a televised interview in December of 1991 that he would "do anything" to get reelected, an unfortunate moment of candor his opponents never allowed him (or the voters) to forget. Even Bush's promises to be the "environmental president" and the "education president" were so extravagant and ultimately unattainable that they obscured his accomplishments and made them look like just another series of retreats.

Bush's proclivity to compromise even on issues he himself had previously put off-limits resulted in large part from his temperament and conception of governing, which clearly leaned away from ideology and toward practical accomplishment and workmanlike consensus-building. This temperament facilitated Bush's foreign policy successes, which relied on coalition-building among foreign leaders. But Bush almost certainly misapplied the lesson in domestic affairs, where success depends as much on educating and persuading the American people as on deal-making at the top where confrontation is sometimes as important as consensus-building. Furthermore, Bush almost certainly calculated that he could move to the left on issues like taxes, quotas, and the environment without losing his base on the right. Accordingly, one might speculate that George Bush, much as Lyndon Johnson, sought a grand consensus encompassing almost all of American society. A 70 percent approval rating was thus not capital to be expended as a means to an end, but was itself the end.[5]

As Johnson discovered, however, such a strategy jeopardizes the solidity of one's original coalition. As the *National Review* regularly lamented, "Every time they make the GOP tent bigger, more people want to leave."[6] Bush's pattern of indecision failed to convert the left, which gave him no credit for his compromises. It won him no respect among the American people at large, who expected more decisive leadership from its president than it now found in George Bush. And it lost him the support of conservatives, the backbone of the Republican party, who felt betrayed by Bush's policies. Bush had run as a conservative in 1988 and had capitalized on his close association with Ronald Reagan. Conservatives, while pleased by Bush's use of the veto to block numerous pieces of liberal legislation, became increasingly distressed by Bush's lack of clear policy direction. He seemed to be pursuing a course guided by compromise and equivocation, the very course, in the eyes of conservatives, guaranteed to deprive his party of the key issues it needed to win.

Democratic presidential candidates and most liberal columnists portrayed Bush's presidency as an extension of Ronald Reagan's administration.[7] By February 1992, most conservatives did not. To liberals, it was the "Reagan-Bush administration"; to conservatives, it was the Reagan administration and *then* the Bush administration. The three pillars of Reagan's economic strategy had been tax cuts, deregulation, and spending restraint. Bush raised taxes, allowed regulatory zeal to return to the levels of the Carter administration (before instituting a 90-day regulatory moratorium in 1992), and permitted domestic spending to increase at the fastest rate since the 1960s. "He has sold Ronald Reagan's inheritance," lamented Newt Gingrich after the 1990 budget deal, "for a potter's field." In foreign policy, while flirting briefly with a "new world order," Bush embraced a Kissingerian "realist" strategy that placed the United States on the side of "stability" rather than democracy on issues as wide-ranging as aid to the Iraqi revolution, relations with Red China, and support for the Soviet and Yugoslav central governments. Only on abortion did Bush hold firm, and many on both sides suspected that his firmness had its roots less in conviction than in politics.

Bush appeared a reactive president (some called him the "in-box president") who could deal magnificently with crises thrust at him, like the invasion of Kuwait or the Soviet coup in August 1991, and who could effectively wield the veto, but who could not formulate a positive program or draw political battle lines. His successes made his failures look all the more disappointing. He had, as he himself once said, a problem with "the vision thing."

The Economy. Closely tied to this record of vacillation and missed opportunities was a singular incapacity to deal with the nation's unsatisfactory economic performance. The administration had at first spent months denying that a recession was taking place, then prematurely declared the economy in recovery. By December 1991, the administration decided that something had to be done, but delayed action until the State of the Union Address. Modest growth in GNP in early 1992 fed hope that the worst was past, but it was accompanied by rising, not falling, unemployment and sluggish consumer confidence.

In a technical sense, Bush's claim that the economy was not as bad as people believed was accurate. Seven weeks after election day, economists announced that the recession had ended—in March 1991. Inflation was low, home mortgage rates were at their lowest levels in over two decades, and unemployment, even at its peak of 7.8 percent in June 1992, was well below the 10.8 percent mark reached at the trough of the last recession in October 1982. While many Americans were hurt by economic conditions in 1990-92, the greatest pain was regionally concentrated: over half of the nation's increase in unemployment came in the nation's two most important states, California and New York, which George Bush in the fall campaign would never even contest.

Americans' unease over the economy, however, was enormous. Perhaps the most crucial problem was that the recession touched more sectors of the economy than usual. For the first time, white-collar layoffs were a major part of increased unemployment. Also, in contrast to past recessions, more job losses resulted from permanent reductions in force rather than temporary layoffs. Whole sectors of the American economy that had never feared layoffs before now feared that their jobs would be permanently wiped out. And given the prevalence of employee health benefit packages and the skyrocketing cost of health care, unemployment would leave families one medical emergency away from financial ruin. These specific anxieties combined with broader concerns about the state of American competitiveness, the stagnation of real wages since 1973, and the federal budget deficit to create a "malaise" reminiscent of 1979-80. The fact that this malaise was at least partially grounded in contagious fear did not make it any less damaging to the President's fortunes.[8]

The recession and its aftermath of slow growth would have taken a toll on any president's popularity. But three factors aggravated

Bush's situation. First, there was no serious pro-growth program, and people were arguably more agitated by Bush's lack of action and his consistent denials that there was a problem than by the actual state of the economy. Second, Bush's patrician background made him an easy target of populist outsiders and complicated his efforts to appear sympathetic to the plight of working families. This problem was dramatized when news organizations reported that he had appeared dumbfounded by an electronic scanning device of the kind used in grocery stores for a decade. Finally, it was George Bush's economy. He had signed the tax increase, he had allowed the regulatory explosion, and not one of his numerous vetoes had been directed against overspending. He had chosen not to confront the Democratic Congress over economic policy, and hence could not disassociate himself from the nation's economic performance.

By the beginning of February, polls indicated that voters viewed the Democratic party as better able to handle the economy than Republicans by a margin of 49 to 38; two years before, Republicans had led 52 to 33.[9] This was perhaps the most important change in public opinion in 1992, and it marked an ominous sign for the Republicans. Since the beginning of the Reagan recovery, the issue of prosperity had belonged to them. It did so no longer.

Organization. Finally, the Carterization of George Bush manifested itself through organizational disarray in the White House that began with Wofford's victory in Pennsylvania. In December 1991, White House Chief of Staff John Sununu was replaced by Transportation Secretary Samuel Skinner. In February, Republican National Committee (RNC) Chairman Clayton Yeutter became a domestic policy adviser and was replaced by Bush loyalist Rich Bond. Six weeks after taking the reins, Skinner reshuffled the White House staff, bringing in half a dozen new senior aides, a maneuver critics within the administration privately called "rearranging chairs on the Titanic."[10] Within another six weeks, reports of extreme staff dissatisfaction with Skinner's regime (which, it was alleged, had produced "functional gridlock") surfaced on the front page of the *Washington Post*, along with rumors that Press Secretary Marlin Fitzwater had fled to the Bahamas out of disgust.[11]

The most serious problem, however, was in the direction of political affairs. No one had managed to fill the huge void left by the death of Lee Atwater in 1991.[12] Initially, with the appointment of Atwater to head the RNC, it seemed likely that Bush would run his reelection out of the RNC, thus placing the party apparatus at the center of presidential politics to a degree unseen for years. Atwater's death, as well as the unexpected Buchanan challenge (the RNC had to maintain a technical neutrality), prevented this plan from ever going into effect. Bush appointed longtime pollster Bob Teeter as campaign chairman, but he lacked the kind of "lean and hungry" attitude of an Atwater or, for that matter, a James Carville.

The weeks prior to the convention were spent in speculation that James Baker would leave the State Department and come to the rescue of the Bush campaign. A week before the opening of the convention in Houston, Baker replaced Skinner as chief of staff and—reluctantly—took the reins of the reelection effort. With him came top aides from the State Department. Even this change, however, failed to end the chaos within the White House and the campaign, which proved beyond the skills of Baker to overcome. Bush's campaign was widely seen as one of the worst run in recent memory, and Republicans were usually the first to proclaim this fact.

The same three problems that haunted Jimmy Carter in the final year of his presidency—an aura of indecisiveness, failure to come to grips with a bad economy, and a White House in disarray—also haunted George Bush. Yet the parallel between the two men is hardly perfect. Americans viewed George Bush more as a disappointment than a disaster. This disappointment was sufficient to ensure his defeat in 1992, but it is improbable that the Democrats will be able to run against George Bush for the next four elections.

THE NOMINATION BATTLE

There were at least four warning blips on George Bush's radar screen that he failed to heed as the primary season approached. First, his own standing in approval polls slipped noticeably, though still left him well over 50 percent. Second, substantial majorities (in some cases, upwards of 70 percent) began to tell pollsters that they believed the country to be on the wrong track. Third, while he continued to defeat named Democratic challengers in head-to-head polls, he began to lose when paired against an "unnamed" challenger. Finally, Louisiana State Representative and former KKK and Nazi party leader David Duke ran for the governorship of Louisiana against both Democratic and establishment Republican opposition on a platform of populist outsider outrage. Duke, who declared himself a Republican in 1989 one year after running for the Democratic presidential nomination, lost his bid for governor but threatened to challenge

Bush in the primaries or to run as an independent in November. (Less tangibly, commentators mulled the significance of an October storm that battered Bush's Kennebunkport vacation home on the same day he unofficially opened his campaign with a fundraiser in Houston.)

Duke announced his candidacy on December 4. The White House dismissed him as a less-than-credible messenger of protest. Within a week, Bush also faced a challenge from Patrick J. Buchanan, a television commentator and columnist who had served in communications positions with the Reagan and Nixon administrations. Buchanan espoused a no-holds-barred conservatism that he called a "conservatism of the heart." Buchanan adopted an anti-establishment populism that he associated with Ronald Reagan, but he departed significantly from Reaganism on issues such as immigration, free trade, and international engagement. Buchanan's position seemed more closely to resemble a pre-World War II conservatism. Buchanan was also accused of anti-Semitism and other prejudices as a result of controversial statements made as a commentator. He maintained that Bush's accommodation on the civil rights bill had been the final straw on the back of a camel already overburdened with betrayals of conservative principle.

While the White House debated the timing and content of anti-recession measures, Buchanan spent a month and a half in New Hampshire attacking "King George" for violating the tax pledge and doing nothing about an economic situation that was hitting New Hampshire harder than most states. Buchanan explicitly offered himself as a protest candidate, saying repeatedly, "Send a message." When Bush denied having ever signed the tax pledge in New Hampshire in 1988, Buchanan seized on this as further evidence of the President's lack of convictions. Bush, according to Buchanan, only "ran for president because he wanted to be president," then adding, "Well, he's been president."[13]

Bush did not appreciate the danger until quite late. He finally campaigned in New Hampshire with Arnold Schwartzeneggar, allowing the Terminator to attack Buchanan directly ("Hasta la vista, Buchanan!") while he himself remained "presidential." Other surrogates joined the attack on Buchanan, including such staunch conservatives as Vice President Dan Quayle, Jack Kemp, Newt Gingrich, and John Sununu. Bush's strategy in New Hampshire had two phases: the "I care" phase, in which he tried to identify and empathize with the state's plight, and the "I have a plan" phase, in which he emphasized his State of the Union proposals and tried to shift the blame for inaction to Congress.

In the end, Buchanan stunned the President by gaining 37 percent and holding Bush to 52 percent; the rest went to write-in candidates, including 7 percent for Democrat Paul Tsongas. (For individual primary results, see Table 2-1 on the following page.) Over half of the Republican electorate in New Hampshire disapproved of Bush's performance, and only one-third of Buchanan voters said they would vote for Bush in November. Buchanan's showing was the result of a somewhat inchoate protest. Over half of his supporters said they voted for him primarily as a protest and not because they thought he would make the best president, and he received almost equal levels of support among self-described conservatives, moderates, and liberals.[14] (This sort of diffuse protest vote is analogous to the Johnson-McCarthy race in 1968, in which three of five McCarthy voters claimed to have voted against Johnson because he was not prosecuting the war in Vietnam vigorously enough.)

It had required election-day proof of Buchanan's strength (or to be more precise, of Bush's weakness) to finally bring home to the White House the gravity of the situation. The Republican race now entered a second, more serious, phase. Buchanan remained on the attack, hoping for a breakthrough in a single state that would bring down the Bush edifice, but the Bush campaign responded more forcefully. Mirroring the governing difficulties of the administration, however, the campaign experienced numerous strategic fits and starts, and the President was consistently placed in the position of reacting to Buchanan's initiatives.

In the next set of primaries, Buchanan chose to concentrate his resources on the March 3 Georgia primary. He continued his general assault on Bush as wishy-washy, but shifted gears, emphasizing social and cultural issues rather than economic concerns. He attacked Bush's civil rights reversal and the funding by the National Endowment of the Arts of obscene "art." A Buchanan advertisement showed scenes of a controversial documentary about black homosexuals that had been partially produced with federal money. As a gesture to the upcoming round of Southern primaries, Buchanan laid flowers at the grave of his Confederate ancestors in Alabama. Bush struck back by attacking what he called Buchanan's "isolationism" on trade and the Persian Gulf. He also fired NEA chief John Frohnmeyer ("My first scalp," Buchanan said). In addition, the administration responded to the threat by arguing that Buchanan could not hope to win but only to damage the President, thereby risking a liberal Democratic victory in November.

The more hopeful in the administration harbored a belief that

Table 2-1
1992 Republican Primary Results, in percent

Place	Date	Bush	Buchanan	Duke	Others	Uncom
N.H.	2/18	53	37	--	10	--
S.Dak.	2/25	69	--	--	--	31
Colo.	3/3	68	30	--	2	--
Ga.	3/3	64	36	--	--	--
Md.	3/3	70	30	--	--	--
S.C.	3/7	67	26	7	*	--
Fla.	3/10	68	32	--	--	--
La.	3/10	62	27	9	2	--
Mass.	3/10	66	28	2	1	4
Miss.	3/10	72	17	11	*	--
Okla.	3/10	70	27	3	1	--
R.I.	3/10	63	32	2	*	3
Tenn.	3/10	73	22	3	--	2
Tex.	3/10	70	24	3	*	4
Ill.	3/17	76	23	--	1	--
Mich.	3/17	67	25	2	*	5
Conn.	3/24	67	22	2	--	9
P.R.	4/5	99	*	*	*	--
Kans.	4/7	62	15	2	5	17
Minn.	4/7	64	24	--	9	3
Wis.	4/7	76	16	3	4	2
Pa.	4/28	77	23	--	--	--
D.C.	5/5	82	18	--	--	--
Ind.	5/5	80	20	--	--	--
N.C.	5/5	71	20	--	--	10
Nebr.	5/12	81	14	2	4	--
W.Va.	5/12	81	15	--	5	--
Oreg.	5/19	67	19	2	12	--
Wash.	5/19	67	10	1	22	--
Ark.	5/26	83	12	--	--	5
Idaho	5/26	64	13	--	--	23
Ky.	5/26	75	--	--	--	25
Ala.	6/2	74	8	--	--	18
Calif.	6/2	74	26	--	--	--
Mont.	6/2	72	12	--	--	17
N.J.	6/2	78	15	--	8	--
N.Mex.	6/2	64	9	--	--	27
Ohio	6/2	83	17	--	--	--
N.Dak.	6/9	83	--	--	17	--

Source: Adapted from *Congressional Quarterly Guide to the 1992 Republican National Convention*, August 8, 1992, p. 63.

* = less than one percent.

New Hampshire had been the "worst case" because of its uniquely bad economic condition. But the Georgia results, in which Buchanan nearly matched his New Hampshire showing with 36 percent of the vote, made it abundantly clear that this was not the case. Buchanan also received 30 percent in Maryland and 30 percent in Colorado, where he hardly campaigned. In South Dakota, where Buchanan was not even on the ballot, Bush still lost 31 percent to an uncommitted slate. It seemed that there was a solid 30 percent anti-Bush vote virtually everywhere, regardless of economic conditions, key issues, and the degree of campaign effort expended. In this group of primaries, Buchanan again did nearly as well among moderates and liberals as among conservatives. Something beyond ideology was clearly at work. As in New Hampshire, large numbers of Republican voters said they would not vote for Bush in the fall (including eight of ten Buchanan voters in Maryland). Buchanan even went so far as to call on Bush to withdraw from the race.[15]

The next two weeks were hard-fought, with Buchanan concentrating on South Carolina (March 7), the Southern Super Tuesday primaries (March 10), and depressed Michigan (March 17). Duke also concentrated on South Carolina, Oklahoma, and his own Louisiana. Throughout this period Buchanan maintained the initiative. Attacks by Bush surrogates against Buchanan became much harsher. At the same time, however, the President retreated, calling the 1990 tax increase a "mistake" and seeking to "recast" his message with an attack on Congress.

Bush continued to overwhelm the challengers, winning every primary while losing about one-third of the vote. Duke did especially poorly, winning only 7 percent in his first primary in South Carolina, and exceeding 10 percent only once (in Mississippi, where he won 10.6 percent). When Bush beat Buchanan in Michigan, both campaigns acknowledged that the race was essentially over. The result had been speeded by the prevalence of winner-take-all rules in the Republican nominating process at either the state or the district level. Had proportional representation been the norm, Buchanan might have remained a presence for a longer time. Instead, while he did not withdraw from the race, he shifted his campaign to an attack on Democratic liberalism.

The nominating campaign entered its third and final stage, in which the main focus was no longer on Buchanan. Though it was still the primary season, Bush trained his guns largely on the Democratic Congress. Quayle exploited "wedge issues" like family values and the "cultural elite," and administration officials tried to stall

Ross Perot's rising appeal. Yet even with Buchanan effectively (though not officially) out of the picture, Republican primary voters continued to express dissatisfaction with Bush. From the beginning of May through the end of the primary season, votes for uncommitted delegates and write-ins for other candidates (including Ross Perot) blossomed. And in California, exit polls showed Perot as more popular than either Bush or the probable Democratic nominee Bill Clinton.[16] (For aggregate primary results, see Table 2-2.)

Table 2-2
The 1992 Republican Primary Results: A Summary

	Bush	Buchanan	Duke	Other/Uncom
Primaries on ballot	39	36	16	18 (uncom)
Total vote	73%	22%	1%	4%
East	73%	24%	0%	3%
South	69%	25%	2%	3%
Midwest	76%	19%	1%	4%
West	72%	24%	0%	4%
Winnowing stage (to 3/3)	65%	32%	0%	3%
Breakthrough stage (3/7–17)	70%	26%	2%	2%
Mop-up stage (3/24–6/9)	76%	19%	0%	5%

Source: Adapted from *Congressional Quarterly Guide to the 1992 Republican National Convention*, August 8, 1992, pp. 65, 67.

Having fended off a challenge from Buchanan, Bush decided to avoid going into "campaign mode" for as long as possible. The President remained even or slightly ahead in the polls, with his new principal rival being Perot, not Clinton. Clinton had slipped sufficiently that the Bush campaign team openly talked about the prospect of a two-man race, with Perot. However, everything soon turned upside down. When the June unemployment rate unexpectedly increased from 7.5 percent to 7.8 percent, and when Perot withdrew in July, Clinton immediately pulled ahead by a significant margin. Bush would never regain the lead.

In the final analysis, Buchanan had been simply outgunned. Bush had all of the advantages of incumbency, including the tacit support of the party establishment throughout the country. He had swept the primaries and had dominated the caucus states to an even greater degree, due to his party support and Buchanan's makeshift organization. Republican nominating rules permit greater influence on the process by party organizations than is possible in the Democratic party, which added to Bush's advantage. Indeed, the party successfully kept Buchanan off the ballot in New York, and he failed to file or filed late or incomplete delegate slates in South Dakota, Illinois, and Tennessee. Similarly, Duke was kept off the ballot in Florida and Georgia.[17] Bush retained the loyalty of the well-organized anti-abortion movement and many other dissatisfied conservatives who nonetheless found Buchanan unappealing; the President was also aided by women voters, who gave him a much wider margin of support than men. Buchanan and Duke were the very sort of harsh candidates that women voters traditionally shun.[18]

Additionally, Buchanan's defeat indicated the degree to which, even in a year of outsiders, it could be a disadvantage to be too far on the outside. The balance in the Republican party was held by the party's middle ground on the inside-outside dimension, which consisted of Reagan conservatives like Jack Kemp, William Bennett, and Dan Quayle. These conservatives maintained a distinct position between Bush and Buchanan, both ideologically and on the insider-outsider scale. Lacking a candidate of their own, they threw their decisive weight (with varying degrees of reluctance) behind Bush, ensuring him the party's nomination. An alliance between the inside and the inside-outside defeated the pure outside.

STRATEGIC DILEMMAS

Largely because of this complex balance within the party, the Bush nominating campaign faced numerous strategic dilemmas. The first was to assess the scope and intent of Buchanan's challenge. Buchanan's main motive was clear: to punish Bush for his perceived surrender of conservative principles by denying him renomination and, failing that, to extract as many concessions as possible. There were, however, at least two complicating factors that Bush had to consider: Buchanan was seeking to recast the image of conservatism itself, and his voters ranged the ideological spectrum, making it difficult to calculate how best to appease them.

The size of Buchanan's vote surprised the administration, leaving only the question of whether the protest could be contained at the 30 percent level. By mid-March, that had been answered in the affirmative. The questions Bush strategists then faced were how to beat Buchanan without alienating his conservative supporters, how to pacify conservatives without accentuating the public impression of Bush as rudderless, and how to campaign effectively without losing the presidential aura.

The best way to beat Buchanan would clearly have been to ignore his candidacy and allow his weakness to sink him. But the President's own weakness made this strategy impossible. His campaign therefore adopted an approach of attacking Buchanan directly, while at the same time seeking to woo away his ideological supporters. They would, after all, have to serve as a large part of Bush's ideological base in November.

Bush continued to seek conservative support on all fronts. He sought out Ronald Reagan for a photo opportunity (which was marred when Reagan was reported to have told friends that Bush "doesn't seem to stand for anything").[19] Bush sacked the head of NEA, John Frohnmeyer, apologized for the tax hike, and pushed a balanced budget amendment proposal that fell only a handful of votes short of two-thirds in the House. In addition, the administration granted Wisconsin a waiver to pursue major welfare reform and promulgated rules that gave practical effect to a 1989 Supreme Court decision (*Communications Workers of America v. Beck*) banning the use of union fees for political purposes. The President even changed plans and went to a fundamentalist Baptist church instead of an "establishment" Presbyterian church in Atlanta the Sunday before the Georgia primary.

Although the concerns of Bush's conservative base had to be assuaged, Bush now ran the risk of reinforcing the general public's image of a president without firm convictions. His admission that the tax increase had been a mistake produced jokes that he was now guilty of a "flip-flop-flip."[20] Bill Clinton, who supported the Beck decision, derided Bush's sudden decision to enforce it, saying, "Even when he does things that have some merit, they are obviously political calculations."[21]

The strategy of attacking Buchanan went through several phases, starting first with the use of surrogates to direct television attack ads coupled with milder criticism from the chief executive himself. This still left the question of how best to handle the substance of the attacks. New RNC Chairman Rich Bond actually accused Buchanan of "flirting with fascism," leading Buchanan to demand Bond's ouster as a condition for support of the ticket. Commentators also pointed out that attacks on Buchanan's use of social issues could have the effect of depriving Bush of those issues in the fall.

The decision to preserve Bush's presidential aura by directing his criticisms more at Congress than Buchanan was probably the best approach under the circumstances. Bush could not attack Buchanan directly without tarnishing his presidential image and without making reconciliation more difficult. But with voter disdain for insiders running strong, Bush could hardly rest his case on the mere fact of being president. Meanwhile, Congress was at its lowest popularity in decades, providing Bush with a tempting "inside" target. Hence Bush's attempt to present himself as a "reform" candidate in contrast to a corrupt and deadlocked legislative branch.

The plan to run against Congress was in truth the only viable strategy. In the end, George Bush was running not against Pat Buchanan but against himself. No attack on Buchanan could change Bush's negatives. But the anti-Congress campaign, while sensibly conceived, was poorly executed, largely because the President himself did not fully believe in it. Prior to the March 20 deadline, Gingrich, representing the views of a large Republican congressional faction, presented the White House with a memo urging forceful action, including an executive order to index capital gains taxes. For Gingrich, the problem was "vision driven." But rather than press Congress too hard, Bush chose instead the "minimalist" option.

THE INTRA-CONSERVATIVE BATTLE

It was a curious feature of the 1992 primary campaign that its most important effect did not involve George Bush. The campaign provoked a major battle over the nature and character of the conservative movement that will undoubtedly have consequences that reach far beyond the 1992 campaign. Buchanan sought a redefinition of the conservative movement along prewar lines that supported trade protectionism, heavy restrictions on immigration, and foreign policy isolationism. This version stood in contrast to the modern variant, associated by many with Ronald Reagan, that embraced free trade, international engagement on behalf of American principles, dynamic growth-oriented economic strategies, and an emphasis on inclusive coalition-building. This Reagan conservatism (as we shall call it) was represented by individuals such as Jack Kemp and Dan Quayle in the administration; Newt Gingrich, Vin Weber, Phil Gramm, and the "Conservative Opportunity Society" in Congress; and Pete DuPont and William Bennett outside of government. William F. Buckley's *National Review* and the Washington-based Heritage Foundation might also be considered in this camp, though their role was more ambiguous.[22]

In some respects, the Bush-Buchanan race mirrored the Dewey-Taft race of 1948, with Bush as Dewey (a moderate, pragmatic Republican) and Buchanan as Taft. But in the philosophical battle Bush and his coterie, which included Jim Baker and Richard Darman, were irrelevant. The real struggle of ideas was waged beneath the surface between Buchanan and the Reagan conservatives. The Reagan conservatives held the political balance, as Bush himself could hardly run as a Deweyite and win. Reagan conservatives joined Buchanan in their disdain for the "establishment" character of the Bush administration, and they were no less outraged at Bush's retreat on taxes and some of the social issues. But they faced a difficult choice. Buchanan offered an alternative that they found no more palatable than Bush's revisionism. Moreover, Buchanan's alternative posed a threat to their position in the party and to their understanding of conservatism. As one Republican congressman put it, the question was "whether it was more important to save the Republican party from George Bush or the conservative movement from Pat Buchanan."[23] Most chose to support Bush, although there were tactical disagreements about how long to leave him on the hook before publicly endorsing him.

For Reagan conservatives in the administration and in Congress, support for Bush was immediate, no doubt because their fate seemed to depend on Bush retaining his office. Thus Quayle, Kemp, and Gingrich became key surrogate speakers for Bush from New Hampshire on. William Bennett also joined in. Others were not so fast. The *National Review*, which had long criticized the administration's meandering, came out three weeks before the New Hampshire primary with an unflattering cover story entitled "The Goofy Politics of George Bush." The magazine refused to endorse Buchanan, however, citing the danger of splitting the Republican party, significant policy differences, and Buchanan's inexperience and brush with anti-Semitism. It nevertheless urged a "tactical vote" for Buchanan in

New Hampshire and gave him a positive cover story before calling on him to withdraw.[24] Bush's concessions to conservatives on taxes and the NEA undoubtedly solidified some of his conservative support, but they also increased the temptation of at least a few conservatives to withhold their support in hopes of more of the same.

The "pragmatists" surrounding Bush no doubt viewed Reagan conservatives in tactical terms as tools to be used in Bush's effort to gain and hold power. Bush campaign spokesperson Victoria Clarke caused quite a stir when she remarked after Ronald Reagan's speech at the Republican convention, "Now we've got that conservative crap out of the way." For their part, Reagan conservatives by 1992 probably viewed the Bush campaign as a tactical weapon to beat down the Buchanan heresy and a Bush second term as a holding device until 1996. Reagan conservatives who backed Bush did so with a minimum of enthusiasm; indeed, at a meeting of conservatives the week after New Hampshire, the "unspoken question" was whether the movement might not be best served by Buchanan losing in the spring and Bush losing in the fall.[25] More importantly, Reagan conservatives began to regret that one of their own had not made the effort instead of Buchanan. The New Hampshire primary showed what no one before had suspected: George Bush was beatable.[26]

The skirmishes between the two conservative camps were the first round of a battle over the direction of the conservative movement that would be renewed with greater intensity after November. Buchanan gained a certain amount of respect by being the only conservative willing to take on George Bush. He also gained valuable lists of contributors and volunteers on which to build in the future. Nevertheless, at the end of the primary season, the upper hand appeared to belong to the Kemp-Quayle-Bennett wing. They had, after all, won despite the handicap of defending Bush. Furthermore, the Los Angeles riots, while not helping the Bush administration, served to highlight Kemp as a brand of conservative who was offering solutions to inner-city decay. Polls taken at the convention in Houston indicated that Kemp was the favorite of 51 percent of the delegates for the nomination in 1996. Four years in politics, however, is a veritable eternity.

WHAT HAPPENED TO DAVID DUKE?

In October 1991, the political world was seized with apprehension at the prospect that David Duke might win the Louisiana governor's runoff election and use the office as a springboard for a primary challenge to George Bush or an independent candidacy. He had already disposed of incumbent Governor Buddy Roemer in the first-round election, despite the best efforts of the state and national Republican parties. Duke ran an outsider and populist campaign attacking welfare, affirmative action, and the "establishment," but as always his platform was suspected of providing a facade behind which lurked unrepentant racial hatred.

Prior to the runoff election, Duke assured reporters that "President Bush doesn't have anything to fear from me," which turned out to be true. But it would not be for a lack of trying. Although Duke lost the Louisiana runoff to Edwin Edwards, he had in effect used the state election to launch his national campaign. Duke announced his candidacy on December 4. On April 17, 1992, he withdrew from the race after winning no primaries, no caucuses, and no delegates.

It seems clear that what happened to David Duke was, in short, Pat Buchanan. Buchanan overwhelmed Duke as a legitimate protest candidate, offering most of the same criticisms of Bush but absent the KKK and Nazi baggage. Duke attacked Bush on taxes and quotas; Buchanan attacked Bush on taxes and quotas, with far greater resources and credibility at his disposal. Buchanan captured the protest banner immediately by contesting New Hampshire, which Duke (probably correctly) deemed not to be fertile territory for himself. In South Carolina, Duke's chosen "breakthrough" state, he looked "insubstantial, frail, and uncertain" in comparison to Buchanan, and received only 7 percent, essentially finishing his campaign as it began.[27] For his part, Buchanan raided Duke's base by emphasizing his issues, making symbolic gestures like the visit to the Confederate cemetery, and declining to denounce Duke by name. When voters were offered a choice of who could send the same message, all but the most angry ditched Duke, even in the South. In his own Louisiana, he failed to reach 10 percent of the vote, and he finished third even among those who had voted for him for governor only months before.[28] In the end, Duke's significance lay in being the first (and most extreme) of the year's long string of outsiders, a harbinger of things to come.

BUCHANAN'S CHALLENGE IN HISTORICAL PERSPECTIVE

Pat Buchanan's challenge bears comparison with other challenges to sitting presidents in this century. There are three important factors to consider in such a comparison: the effects of the nominating process, the circumstances surrounding the challenge, and the strength of the challenge.

Buchanan's campaign confirms that a strong performance in early primaries is the key to any kind of meaningful challenge, which is consistent with the records of challengers ever since Theodore Roosevelt in 1912. Buchanan parlayed a closer-than-expected finish in New Hampshire into publicity and credibility that served him for weeks. Buchanan did best in primaries rather than caucuses.

In terms of circumstances, there are two kinds of challenges: those responding to specific crises and those based on general ideological dissatisfaction. In the first category, one can place the challenge of Estes Kefauver in 1952, which was driven by Harry Truman's faltering popularity as a result of the Korean War and corruption in the administration; and the challenge by Eugene McCarthy in 1968, which focused on the Vietnam War.

By contrast, Buchanan's effort falls into the second category, coming closest to Edward Kennedy's campaign against Jimmy Carter in 1980, John Ashbrook's campaign against Richard Nixon in 1972, and Teddy Roosevelt's bid to unseat William Howard Taft in 1912. In each case, the challenger attacked the incumbent president not for mismanaging a particular crisis, but for abandoning the broader philosophical underpinnings of the party; in each case the president was deemed insufficiently "pure." Taft, in the eyes of Roosevelt and the progressives, had "sold out" on tariffs, antitrust, and reform in general; Nixon had embraced wage and price guidelines, signed arms control treaties with the Soviets, and gone soft on Red China; and Carter had strayed from the liberal spending agenda, going so far as to make cuts in food stamps and other social programs. Reagan's challenge to Ford in 1976 can also be placed in this second category—a broad philosophical assault—but it contained the complication of being aimed at an "incumbent" who, because he had not been elected either president or vice president, lacked the usual legitimacy of his position.

Compared to the strength and impact of other challenges to incumbents, Buchanan's campaign falls on the lower end of the scale. At the upper end lies Roosevelt, who narrowly lost but split the GOP sufficiently to deprive Taft of reelection; Kefauver and McCarthy, who also lost but drove Truman and Johnson from the race; and Reagan, who came within a handful of votes of prevailing in Kansas City. But Buchanan's challenge was much stronger than Ashbrook's. The closest parallel is probably with Kennedy's challenge in 1980. In terms of voting strength and credibility as a major candidate, Kennedy was stronger than Buchanan, but Buchanan had greater success in pulling his intended target in his direction. Neither Kennedy nor Buchanan could be brushed off like Ashbrook, but neither did well enough to leave the convention's choice in doubt.

An interesting question is why Buchanan, running as a conservative like Reagan and Ashbrook before him, and facing a "pragmatist" not philosophically unlike Nixon and Ford, did so much better than Ashbrook and so much worse than Reagan. In 1972, Ashbrook was less well known than Buchanan and faced less favorable circumstances. While Nixon had aroused the wrath of many conservatives, that wrath had not been joined to deep discontent in the broader electorate. Furthermore, although Nixon may have strayed from the path, he at least seemed to know where he was going. Conversely, Ford suffered from the aforementioned problem of being only a quasi-incumbent, and he faced a challenge of a formidable two-time governor from the most populous state in the union. In 1992 Buchanan had the support of only a small part of the conservative movement, while Reagan in 1976 was the movement's undisputed political leader.

Finally, did George Bush benefit or was he hurt by the Buchanan challenge? Conventional wisdom holds that such challenges are always harmful. Historically, no president whose challenger won or finished a close second in New Hampshire has gone on to reelection. The reasons seem obvious. The president is subjected to a pincer movement between challenger and opposition party; in this case, Buchanan and the Democrats echoed each other's claims that Bush was out of touch with ordinary Americans and lacked direction. Presidents facing challenges also face the dilemma of having to defeat their challenger without alienating him and his supporters. The 1992 battle pitting Buchanan's cries of "King George" against presidential surrogates' accusations of "fascism" was not one likely to make reconciliation easy.

Nevertheless, the conventional wisdom cannot be swallowed whole. Buchanan's challenge perhaps served to awaken the White House to the extent of national and party discontent. Buchanan may also have forced the Bush campaign to gear up organizationally and better define its message. Indeed, Buchanan himself claimed credit for such a result, saying in mid-April that "George Bush is a far better candidate in April than he was in December, January, or February. I think I've helped him to sharpen the differences and disagreements" with the Democrats.[29]

In any case, Pat Buchanan did not create George Bush's problems, he merely exposed them. The administration's failure to respond to these signs of trouble cannot be laid at the feet of Buchanan. And unlike Roosevelt in 1912, McCarthy in 1968, Kennedy in 1980, and arguably Reagan in 1976, Buchanan wholeheartedly endorsed the winner at the party's convention—for some moderates, no doubt, too wholeheartedly. There were no scenes of a Ted Kennedy spurning Jimmy Carter's hand on the platform.

THE CONVENTION

At the end of the primary season, the President's popularity was in "free-fall," his program stalled, and his administration in disarray. Reports of higher unemployment indicated that the strong economic recovery on which Bush pinned all of his hopes was not in the offing. The President's trip to Panama, meant to be a victorious salute, was marred by anti-American protests. Bush came under serious fire when he decided not to attend the environmental summit in Brazil; he then changed his mind, but faced a public relations debacle when he refused to sign the Biodiversity Treaty.

The political and policy problems that led to the Buchanan challenge were far from resolved. Bush had inherited from Ronald Reagan a coalition based on the appeal of an active agenda of limited government, dynamic capitalism, tempered social conservatism, and the promotion of democracy. This coalition would have been difficult enough to maintain in the new circumstances at the end of the Cold War, but Bush's presidency had succeeded over four years in weakening each component that held it together. The Buchanan and Perot campaigns were reflections of that fact. As *The New Republic* commented, George Bush had "done to conservatism what no liberal opponent could have done: he has destroyed it from within."[30]

In the weeks immediately preceding the convention, Bush's political standing rapidly deteriorated, as he slipped further and further behind a resurging Bill Clinton. Rumors abounded that Vice President Dan Quayle might be dropped from the ticket. But then the inevitable question arose: should Bush himself step aside? A mini-campaign to this effect was waged by some conservatives, with Bill Bennett and George Will testing the waters.[31] But it was too late—at least by the standards by which modern party conventions operate. Not that it has ever been easy at this stage to deny a sitting president renomination. But conventions in the past have on several occasions gotten rid of incumbents after a first term.[32] The point is that today even a serious discussion of this possibility seems inconceivable. The logic of the reformed system today binds delegates to their candidate so tightly that they cannot escape, even when the interests of the party might demand it. This inflexibility casts doubt on one of the central claims of party reformers of the 1970s: that the selection of delegates prior to the calendar year of the convention locked the race into place so early that changed circumstances could not affect the contest. The opposite, in fact, may be more true. It is the selecting and binding of delegates during the election year that makes conventions unable to respond to changed circumstances.

The Republican convention did, however, continue the process of reassimilating dissenters on the right. A conservative platform was drafted similar to those adopted in 1980, 1984, and 1988. Conservative proposals such as tax cuts and school vouchers, which had long been submerged in the administration, were given prominent attention. And Bush himself sought not only to reestablish his credibility with the American people at large but to secure his base by acknowledging that he regretted the 1990 tax increase. Bush also temporarily adopted the strategy of frontal assault on Congress that he had so long resisted, and the fight he displayed convinced those who had doubts that he was determined to win. By the end of the Republican convention, Bush had cut Clinton's lead to high single or low double digits.

Nevertheless, new schisms were opened at the convention as a result of the party's embrace of the "family values" issue and its continuing anti-abortion stand. Bush's presidency may have veered so far to the left that the Bush campaign overcompensated by veering too far to the right at the convention. Despite the improving poll numbers, the convention produced disaffection among some moderate Republicans and Republican-leaning independents, who were particularly susceptible to Bill Clinton's appeals. Whatever initial disenchantment moderates may have felt was surely reinforced by the caricature of the convention repeated almost daily in the mainline media for the remainder of the campaign.[33] Taking everything into account, however, George Bush at the convention seemed to have made at least some progress toward reunifying his party and shaking the lethargy that had plagued the administration for months. Bush's next task was to show that the improvement had come in time and that his new vigor might later translate into an energetic second term.

NOTES

1.   See for example Stephen J. Hedges and Brian Duffy, "Special Report: Iraqgate," *U.S. News & World Report*, May 18, 1992, pp. 42-51; Stephen

S. Rosenfeld, "Thin Cheers for an Unfinished War," *Washington Post*, February 28, 1992, p. A23.

2. See Pamela Fessler, with Joan Biskupic and Phil Kuntz, "Rights Bill Rises From the Ashes of Senate's Thomas Fight," *CQ Weekly Report*, October 26, 1991, pp. 3124-3126.

3. William Schneider, "What Keeps Bush High in the Polls?," *National Journal*, October 12, 1991, p. 2522.

4. David S. Broder, "Bush Seeking Mantle of 'Reform' Candidate," *Washington Post*, April 3, 1992, p. A1.

5. On LBJ, see Michael Barone, *Our Country: The Shaping of America from Roosevelt to Reagan* (New York: Free Press, 1990), pp. 409-10.

6. *National Review*, August 31, 1992, p. 8.

7. See Richard Cohen, "The Wages of Servility," *Washington Post*, February 28, 1992, p. A23; Michael Kinsley, "Reagan's Heir," *Washington Post*, March 5, 1992, p. A21.

8. The importance of the nation's mood, in addition to objective economic reality, was underscored by the failure in 1992 of the venerable Fair model of election predictions. Economist Ray Fair has predicted presidential elections as far back as 1912 with stunning accuracy on the basis of a calculation incorporating the inflation rate and rate of GNP growth. In 1992, Fair announced that George Bush would win with 57 percent of the vote. Of course, it is an open question whether the model failed because it did not take adequate account of intangible factors like national mood or whether it simply failed to identify the proper tangible factors, for instance the unemployment rate. Nevertheless, 1992 was the first failure of the model in almost a century.

9. Ann Devroy and Richard Morin, "Democratic Governors, Bush Tangle on Budget," *Washington Post*, February 4, 1992, p. A1.

10 Ann Devroy, "Skinner Shuffles Personnel," *Washington Post*, February 28, 1992, p. A1.

11. Ann Devroy, "White House Said to Be in Gridlock," *Washington Post*, April 4, 1992, p. A1; see also Rowland Evans and Robert Novak, "Cheney to the Rescue?," *Washington Post*, April 8, 1992, p. A23.

12. See Jack Anderson and Michael Binstein, "Quayle Off the Leash," *Washington Post*, March 8, 1992, p. C7; also Anderson and Binstein, "Waiting for the New Atwater," *Washington Post*, June 28, 1992, p. C7.

13. "Bush Appeals to Voters For a Strong Victory," *Washington Post*, February 11, 1992, p. A8.

14. E.J. Dionne, Jr., "GOP Challenger Exceeds Projections," *Washington Post*, February 19, 1992, p. A1.

15. See Richard Tapscott and Richard Morin, "It's Bush, Tsongas, and Malaise in Maryland," *Washington Post*, March 4, 1992, p. A1; E.J. Dionne, Jr. and John E. Yang, "GOP Discontent Apparent," *Washington Post*, March 4, 1992, p. A1.

16. E.J. Dionne, Jr., "Bush, Clinton, and Yeakel Win Pennsylvania Primary," *Washington Post*, April 29, 1992, p. A1; James A. Barnes, "Exit Polls: The 'Big Mo' Is With Perot," *National Journal*, June 6, 1992, p. 1368.

17. Ballot access in some states, such as Florida and Georgia, is determined by "party-controlled presidential candidate selection committees," with no alternative petition route. Rhodes Cook, "Candidate Field Shapes Up As Primaries Approach," *CQ Weekly Report*, January 4, 1992, p. 28.

18. E.J. Dionne, Jr., "Democratic Primaries Draw 53% Female Vote," *Washington Post*, March 8, 1992, p. A18.

19. Lou Cannon, "Bush Supporters Fear He Will Lose California," *Washington Post*, February 25, 1992, p. A1.

20. "Flip, Flop . . . Flip?," *Washington Post*, March 5, 1992, p. A20.

21. Nat Hentoff, "Bush and Clinton: 'Friends' of the Rank and File," *Washington Post*, May 2, 1992, p. A27.

22. It must be noted that Pat Buchanan also claimed to be the true heir of Ronald Reagan. Given the much closer proximity of Kemp, Bennett, Gingrich et al. to Reagan's positions on trade, international engagement, and a number of other issues, Buchanan's claim seems difficult to defend.

23. "Could Be the Start of Something Big," *U.S. News & World Report*, March 2, 1992, p. 42.

24. See "Fortune Favors the Brave," *National Review*, December 16, 1991, pp. 14-16; William F. Buckley, "In Search of Anti-Semitism," *National Review*, December 30, 1991, pp. 31-40; John O'Sullivan, "The Goofy Politics of George Bush," *National Review*, February 3, 1992, pp. 26-33; "Four More Years?," *National Review*, February 17, 1992, pp. 12-14; Tom Bethell, "The Case For Buchanan," *National Review*, March 2, 1992, pp. 34-38.

25. Rowland Evans and Robert Novak, "Thunder on the Right," *Washington Post*, February 26, 1992, p. A17.

26. David S. Broder, "Winners and Losers," *Washington Post*, February 20, 1992, p. A25.

27. See Thomas B. Edsall, "Duke Losing Leverage With Whites," *Washington Post*, March 7, 1992, p. A10.

28. E.J. Dionne, Jr. and Ann Devroy, "Buchanan Urged to Quit," *Washington Post*, March 11, 1992, p. A1.

29. E.J. Dionne, Jr., "Buchanan Returns, Looks to California," *Washington Post*, April 15, 1992, p. A1.

30. George F. Will, "My Write-In Vote," *Washington Post*, November 1, 1992, p. C7.

31. See George Will's column, *Washington Post*, July 29, 1992, p. A23.

32. Illustrious nineteenth-century presidents in this group included Millard Fillmore, Franklin Pierce, Andrew Johnson, and Chester Arthur.

33. See Brent Bozell, "Annoy the Media, Elect Bush," *Wall Street Journal*, November 2, 1992.

CHAPTER THREE

The Democratic Nomination

For almost a year after the war with Iraq, most Democrats seemed to be asking not so much which one of their possible candidates could beat Bush as who would be foolish enough to try. Yet by the time Bill Clinton delivered his acceptance speech before his party's convention at Madison Square Garden on July 16, 1992, he was pulling ahead of President Bush by 20 points in the polls. In the audience that night, each of at least a half-dozen other Democrats must have been thinking that, but for his own timidity, he could just as easily be standing before the nation, poised for a mighty upset.

Bill Clinton was the most conservative nominee of the Democratic party since at least 1976. His nomination represented the first victory for the Democratic Leadership Council (DLC), a group within the Democratic party that Clinton helped to found and which aimed to push the party back to the center. The DLC had made a concerted effort to capture the nomination in 1988, when it helped arrange the "Super Tuesday" Southern regional primary and backed Senator Al Gore of Tennessee for the nomination. Gore's failure in 1988 brought redoubled effort and greater focus by the DLC, while another Democratic defeat in November brought greater willingness by liberal Democrats to experiment with moderation. Bill Clinton's nomination in July, and then his victory in November, signified a major philosophic shift within the Democratic party, although its full nature and durability remain uncertain.

At the same time, Clinton won the nomination at least partially because he was well positioned on the inside-outside axis. He lacked the insider liabilities of his Washington-based opponents. Yet he could gain the support of the politicians and interest groups on the inside of the Democratic party because his tempered "outsiderism" was much less threatening to them than the genuine article found in Paul Tsongas and (especially) Jerry Brown.

Bill Clinton's nomination, though won by much determination, hard work, and skill, was also very much a product of good fortune. By the end of the primary season, observers were calling Clinton the Come-Back Kid, and he himself boasted of his ability to be able "to take a punch." But the truth is that when he was on the ropes in the primary season, there was really no one else in the ring able to deliver a knockout blow. For all intents and purposes Bill Clinton ran for the Democratic nomination in a race against himself. That he was able to win, with all his liabilities, was no small achievement.

THE DEMOCRATIC FIELD

The 1992 Democratic nominating race was shaped above all by the simple matter of who chose to run and who did not. From 1988 on, there was a field of prominent Democratic politicians who were widely mentioned as potential candidates in 1992. Bill Clinton was probably toward the bottom of this "first tier" of potential candidates. Ultimately, he would be the only one of them to actually run. This group of Democrats included:

• Bill Bradley, former basketball star and senior senator from New Jersey. Bradley, who with Jack Kemp had spearheaded tax reform in 1986, had long been considered a thoughtful, articulate, and pragmatic liberal. He, like Kemp, was deeply interested in issues, to the extent of gaining a reputation for being excessively cerebral. Bradley was seriously hurt in November 1990, however, when he barely won reelection against a little-known Republican challenger whom he outspent 13 to 1.

• Mario Cuomo, three-term governor of New York and champion of the liberal cause. Cuomo had gained the affection of Democratic activists in 1984 when he delivered the keynote address at the Democratic national convention in San Francisco. Because of his rhetorical skills, his substantial political base (New York possessing more delegates to the Democratic convention than any state but California), and his organizational and fundraising strengths (aided by his close association with organized labor), Cuomo was considered perhaps the heaviest of the heavyweights. But Cuomo too had suffered some embarrassment in 1990 when he received only 53 percent in his reelection bid against two lightly regarded opponents.

• Jesse Jackson, a candidate in the two previous elections under the banner of the left-wing "Rainbow Coalition." Jackson had behind him the organizational strength of this movement, which incorporated civil rights, feminist, environmental, homosexual, and anti-military pressure groups. He could be expected to dominate the loyalties of black voters, who make up a large and increasing share of the Democratic primary electorate. In 1988, Jackson had won 95 percent of the black vote.

• Richard Gephardt, winner of the Iowa caucuses in 1988 and beneficiary of substantial labor support for his protectionist views. In 1989, Gephardt had become House Majority Leader, and he clearly had the support of a substantial majority of congressional Democrats, many of whom would become superdelegates.

• Al Gore, the great hope of the moderate Democrats four years before and the only congressional contender to support the Gulf War. In 1988, Gore had done well on Super Tuesday before wilting in the crucial New York primary after aligning himself with controversial New York Mayor Ed Koch. Gore would probably be the first choice of the majority of the DLC wing of the Democratic party.

• Lloyd Bentsen, Michael Dukakis' running mate in 1988 and self-proclaimed "friend of John Kennedy" in the vice-presidential debate with Dan Quayle. Bentsen had run an abortive campaign for president in 1976, had substantial fundraising potential as chairman of the Senate Finance Committee, and had impressed numerous Democrats during the 1988 campaign. As a Texan, he could be presumed to begin with a solid anchor in the South.

• Jay Rockefeller, West Virginia senator and a leading advocate for health care and children's issues. Rockefeller had a famous name, though it could work against him as well as for him. Coming from a small and poor state, Rockefeller lacked a substantial political base.

• Bill Clinton himself. Clinton was a founding member and one-time chairman of the DLC and, like Gore, could lay claim to the moderate Democratic mantle. He clearly possessed strong coalition-building capabilities, in the manner of Jimmy Carter. But, like Rockefeller, his political base was fairly small, and his stock among Democratic activists was not nearly as high as most of his first-tier competitors. Clinton had hurt himself badly with an overly long keynote address at the 1988 convention, to the extent that some commentators had declared his presidential aspirations dead.

With President Bush's popularity towering above them, all but

one of the first-tier contenders found excuses not to run. Bradley
was the first to withdraw. Gephardt followed in July. Gore and
Rockefeller declined to run in August. Finally—after much teasing
on both of their parts—Jackson bowed out in November and Cuomo
in December. Cuomo in particular dragged out the process for months,
making himself a tempting target for numerous editorial cartoons
picturing the New York governor as a political Hamlet. As a result
of these withdrawals and delays, the nominating campaign—already
running well behind the pace of recent years—was slowed further.
Citizens in Iowa and New Hampshire, accustomed to seeing the
candidates walking their streets throughout the year before the election, were surprised at the relative paucity of campaigning until the
end of 1991.

As the first-tier candidates gradually melted away, Clinton alone
among them decided to make a challenge, officially announcing in
October 1991. Clinton, in fact, hesitated to run because of an important political problem back home: in seeking a sixth term for governor of Arkansas in 1990, he had made a pledge to his constituents
to finish out his term and not seek the presidency. He had to find an
acceptable way to escape that pledge. In making his decision to enter
the race, Clinton may also have considered himself in a no-lose
situation. He and his closest advisers had already come to the conclusion that George Bush had serious weaknesses that could be
exploited. And even if he lost, he could position himself for 1996,
when circumstances would presumably be more propitious.

With all of the first-tier candidates except Clinton abandoning
the race, another group came to the fore. Paul Tsongas, former
Massachusetts senator, had announced well before anyone else,
entering the race in April 1991 when George Bush's approval ratings were still in the 80 percent range. Tsongas had served one term
in the Senate, choosing not to run for reelection in 1984 in order to
receive cancer treatment. Tsongas vowed to change what he called
the Democratic party's anti-business posture. Initially viewed as more
than a long-shot, Tsongas was not taken seriously until January of
1992.

Senators Tom Harkin of Iowa and Bob Kerrey of Nebraska threw
their hats into the ring in September, as did Virginia's first black
governor, L. Douglas Wilder. Harkin, a self-described New Dealer,
claimed to be the only "real Democrat" in the race and made a strong
bid for labor support. Kerrey was a Vietnam Congressional Medal
of Honor winner who was solidly liberal but who could claim to
offset his opposition to the war with Iraq with his own war record.
Wilder had been in office less than two years after winning election

with 50.1 percent of the vote, but hoped to challenge Jesse Jackson for the loyalties of black voters while wooing moderates with his fiscal conservatism. Wilder dropped back out of the campaign on January 8, at 2 percent in the polls. Finally, former California Governor Jerry Brown, who had run for president in 1976 and 1980 before being driven from office by the Mediterranean fruit fly (a crop pest infestation that many Californians believed was mishandled by the governor), decided to run again as an outsider.[1] Although the outsiders Tsongas and Brown were in the end the only ones seriously to challenge Clinton, most observers believed the insiders Harkin and Kerrey to be the more formidable candidates. As two well-known journalists commented, the Democratic candidates "sound like the short list for vice presidential nominees."[2]

Instead of being positioned at the bottom of a strong field, Clinton thus found himself at the top of a weak field. Clinton was helped by the premature surrender of the first tier, as he clearly appeared as one of the most "presidential" of the remaining candidates. He also stood to gain particularly from Gore's and Jackson's withdrawals, which opened the possibility of decisive wins in the South on Super Tuesday. In this respect, Clinton was also well positioned to take advantage of Wilder's withdrawal.[3]

Clinton was, however, presented with a strategic dilemma as well. He had to perform up to the expectations engendered by his newfound front-running status, and he no longer faced a well-known liberal such as Cuomo against whom he could position himself as the moderate alternative. Indeed, at the beginning of 1992, he found himself outflanked on the right (at least on economic policy) by a surging Tsongas campaign. Additionally, aside from the left-right spectrum, Clinton unexpectedly faced two opponents—Tsongas and Brown—whose unconventional campaigns threatened to make Clinton look by contrast like a conventional status quo politician. Having planned to run from the outside, Clinton was outflanked by two more plausible outsiders. Both of these difficulties—the scrutiny attending front-running status and his positioning within the field—combined to nearly derail the Clinton campaign at the outset. Yet he was ultimately able to survive the scrutiny and turn his position problem to his own advantage.

THE NOMINATION CAMPAIGN

Traditionally, the campaign season begins with two crucial dates: the Iowa caucuses and the New Hampshire primary. In 1992 Iowa was discounted because a favorite son, Senator Tom Harkin, was running. Accordingly, no candidate but Kerrey from neighboring Nebraska chose to challenge him. When Harkin won with 76 percent of the vote, it provided him with little benefit. (For individual primary and caucus results, see Table 3-1.)

Table 3-1
1992 Democratic Primary and Caucus Results, in percent

Place	Date	C	T	B	H	K	O	U
Iowa	2/10	3	4	2	76	3	1	12
N.H.	**2/18**	25	33	8	10	11	13	--
Maine	2/23	15	29	30	5	3	2	16
S.Dak.	**2/25**	19	10	4	25	40	2	--
Colo.	**3/3**	27	26	29	2	12	2	2
Ga.	**3/3**	57	24	8	2	5	--	4
Md.	**3/3**	34	41	8	6	5	1	6
Idaho	3/3	11	28	5	30	8	1	17
Minn.	3/3	10	19	8	27	8	4	24
Utah	3/3	18	33	28	4	11	3	2
Wash.	3/3	13	32	19	8	3	2	23
Amer. Samoa	3/3	4	--	--	--	9	--	87
N.Dak.	3/5–19	46	10	8	7	1	2	26
S.C.	**3/7**	63	18	6	7	1	3	3
Ariz.	3/7	29	34	28	8	--	--	1
Wyo.	3/7	29	12	23	14	--	*	22
DA **	3/7/9	27	37	12	7	--	18	--
Nev.	3/8	27	20	34	--	--	--	19
Fla.	**3/10**	51	35	12	1	1	--	--
La.	**3/10**	70	11	7	1	1	11	--
Mass.	**3/10**	11	66	15	1	1	6	2
Miss.	**3/10**	73	8	10	1	1	1	6
Okla.	**3/10**	71	--	17	3	3	12	--
R.I.	**3/10**	21	53	19	1	1	4	1
Tenn.	**3/10**	67	19	8	1	1	*	4
Tex.	**3/10**	66	19	8	1	1	5	--
Del.	3/10	21	30	20	--	--	--	30
Hawaii	3/10	52	14	14	13	*	--	8
Mo.	3/10	45	10	6	--	--	--	39
Tex.	3/10	Results not available						

		C	T	B	H	K	O	U
Ill.	**3/17**	52	26	15	2	1	1	5
Mich.	**3/17**	51	17	26	1	1	1	5
Conn.	**3/24**	36	20	37	1	1	3	3
V.I.	3/28	40	--	4	--	--	--	56
Vt.	3/31	17	9	47	--	--	2	25
Alaska	4/2	31	1	33	--	--	1	35
P.R.	**4/5**	96	*	2	*	1	1	*
Kans.	**4/7**	51	15	13	1	1	5	14
Minn.	**4/7**	31	21	31	2	1	9	6
N.Y.	**4/7**	41	29	26	1	1	2	--
Wis.	**4/7**	37	22	35	1	*	3	2
Va.	4/11,13	52	--	12	--	--	--	36
Pa.	**4/28**	57	13	26	2	2	2	--
Guam	5/3	49	--	20	--	--	--	31
D.C.	**5/5**	74	10	7	--	--	--	9
Ind.	**5/5**	63	12	22	--	3	--	--
N.C.	**5/5**	64	8	10	1	1	--	15
Nebr.	**5/12**	45	7	21	3	--	7	16
W.Va.	**5/12**	74	7	12	1	1	5	--
Oreg.	**5/19**	45	11	31	--	--	13	--
Wash.	**5/19**	42	13	23	1	1	20	--
Ark.	**5/26**	68	--	11	--	--	3	18
Idaho	**5/26**	49	--	17	--	--	5	29
Ky.	**5/26**	56	5	8	2	1	--	28
Ala.	**6/2**	68	--	7	--	--	5	20
Calif.	**6/2**	48	8	40	--	1	4	--
Mont.	**6/2**	47	11	19	--	--	--	24
N.J.	**6/2**	59	11	20	--	--	3	7
N.Mex.	**6/2**	53	6	17	2	--	3	19
Ohio	**6/2**	61	11	19	2	2	5	--
N.Dak.	**6/9**	13	--	--	--	--	87	--

Source: Adapted from *Congressional Quarterly Guide to the 1992 Democratic National Convention,* July 4, 1992, p. 69.

C=Clinton; T=Tsongas (suspended campaign 3/19); B=Brown; H=Harkin (withdrew 3/9); K=Kerrey (withdrew 3/5); O=others; U=uncommitted.

Boldface=primary.
Non-bold=caucus.
*=less than 0.05 percent.
**=Democrats abroad.
All fractions are rounded; some lines may equal more than 100 percent.

At the beginning of 1992, Clinton held a sizable lead in New Hampshire, fueled by favorable media coverage touting him as the front-runner.[4] Within a matter of weeks, however, Clinton saw his lead turn into a nearly fatal deficit. There were at least two major reasons for this reversal. First, Paul Tsongas, operating from his base in neighboring Massachusetts, proved adept at addressing the economic concerns that dominated the debate in New Hampshire. His 85-page "Call to Economic Arms" and his promise that "I am not Santa Claus" seemed to many to be refreshing bursts of frankness in a year when voters were uncommonly dissatisfied with politics as usual. He became the intellectual's outsider candidate of the 1992 campaign, a modern-day Adlai Stevenson.

Second, Clinton was left reeling from a series of scandalous disclosures. A former Arkansas state employee claimed that Clinton had carried on several affairs while governor. A week later, another former state employee, Gennifer Flowers, publicly alleged that she had maintained a twelve-year affair with Clinton. Her allegations were first published in the tabloid *The Star*, which paid her for the story. Flowers then produced audiotapes of phone conversations with Clinton that allegedly proved her charges. Shortly after, the first questions arose about Clinton's draft avoidance during the Vietnam War. These revelations threatened the heart of Clinton's strategy, which depended on convincing liberal Democrats that he possessed superior electability. As his standing in the polls plummeted, Democratic party insiders prepared to find a new candidate in the belief that Clinton was in the process of self-destructing and that Tsongas' success was a fluke. At the top of the list were Gephardt, Bentsen, and Cuomo, for whom a write-in campaign was being conducted in New Hampshire.[5]

Clinton's campaign revived somewhat in the last week before the New Hampshire primary. Clinton was able to mitigate the damage of the Flowers charges. He and his wife, Hillary, appeared together on *60 Minutes*, where he flatly denied having had an affair with Flowers, while implicitly admitting extramarital relations with other women. Clinton was somehow able to avoid the fate of Gary Hart, who was depicted as insensitive to women—perhaps because Flowers was perceived by many as being a mere opportunist. No leaders of women's groups indignantly attacked Clinton for his extramarital liaisons, alleged or conceded. He salvaged his campaign by attacking the press and lashing out against "the politics of division and distraction and destruction," sensing—as it turned out correctly—that the American public had had its fill of voyeurism.

He bypassed the news media with two half-hour televised talks and with the direct distribution of 20,000 free videotapes to voters. Clinton campaign surveys later indicated that as many as one-half of undecided voters who watched the videotapes ultimately voted for him.[6]

Tsongas held on to win the New Hampshire primary, finishing with 33 percent to Clinton's 25 percent. But Clinton's closer-than-expected finish was enough for him to claim (or for the press to give him) a moral victory. The greatest loser in the New Hampshire primary was someone whose name never appeared on the ballot. Mario Cuomo, who had received up to 20 percent in some preelection polls, gained only 3 percent of the real vote from write-ins. This poor showing finally ended the campaign that never was. Gephardt, who had made preliminary preparations for entering the race, also backed off when Clinton climbed to 25 percent from the 20 percent range where he had been hovering.[7]

Democratic leaders remained skeptical of Clinton, but faced no less a problem in Tsongas, whom many considered equally unelectable and more philosophically suspect to boot. Tsongas had challenged the party by stating that if he were elected president he would veto the congressional Democrats' middle-class tax cut. Tsongas had also been caught remarking to a voter in New Hampshire who had called on him to "save us from Bush" that "First, I have to save you from the Democratic party."[8] In the final analysis nearly everyone seemed dissatisfied: Three of ten New Hampshire Democratic primary voters claimed that they would prefer to vote for some other candidate than those in the race.[9]

Such a candidate was increasingly unlikely to come from outside the existing field, since Clinton had at least survived New Hampshire and since filing deadlines for future contests were rapidly passing. Within the field, Harkin and Kerrey engaged in what seemed then to be a crucial struggle for third place in New Hampshire, with Kerrey coming out slightly ahead (12 percent to 10 percent). But the closeness of this contest and the distance of both candidates from Clinton's second-place showing seriously reduced the benefit of the third position. Although Kerrey went on to win the South Dakota primary in a duel mostly with Harkin, his theme of universal health care never really caught on as a defining campaign issue. In desperation he decided to go negative and turned his focus on Clinton's character. In Georgia Kerrey charged that Clinton would "be opened up like a soft peanut in November." The attack failed.

Harkin won the Minnesota caucuses with the help of fellow left-wing Democratic Senator Paul Wellstone, but gained little in

terms of exposure or momentum. Harkin never seemed able to convince the electorate that he was "the only real Democrat" in the race.
Or perhaps he did, which was why he lost. In any case, both Kerrey
and Harkin were out by March 9, Kerrey after failing to win any
primaries on March 3 and Harkin after being crushed by Clinton in
South Carolina despite having targeted the state's large black electorate. Jerry Brown, who had finished with 9 percent in New Hampshire and whose campaign was still considered as more symbolic
than serious, stayed in.

Super Tuesday and Beyond

Thus by the time of Super Tuesday on March 10, the campaign
had resolved itself to a virtual two-man race between Clinton and
Tsongas, with party regulars and voters alike not fully comfortable
with either man. Each candidate had strength in half of the necessary Democratic coalition: Tsongas among liberal intellectuals and
white, upscale suburban voters, and Clinton among blue-collar workers
and blacks.[10] Clinton focused his campaign on middle-class tax cuts.
Tsongas emphasized deficit reduction and business incentives, labeling his chief rival a "pander bear."

Tsongas held his own in the March 3 grouping of primaries,
winning Maryland and finishing in nearly a dead heat for second
with Clinton in Colorado, which Brown actually won. Clinton won
Georgia big, and finished second elsewhere. Once the primaries headed
South, however, the bottom dropped from Tsongas' appeal. If he
was the favorite in Cambridge, no one much cared for him in Tu-
pelo. On Super Tuesday, Clinton won six Southern states, including
Texas and Florida, by enormous margins, while Tsongas won Dela-
ware and his own Massachusetts.

Clinton delivered the knockout blow to Tsongas when the race
moved to the industrial Midwest on March 17. Illinois and Michigan
gave Clinton substantial victories. While Tsongas might have done
well in upcoming primaries in Wisconsin and New York, he surpris-
ingly decided to "suspend" his campaign, citing fundraising difficulties and an enormous delegate deficit. It now appeared that Clinton
had the nomination sewed up.

Clinton's ability to overpower Tsongas can be attributed to three
main factors. First, electoral geography clearly played to Clinton's
advantage after New Hampshire. Just as George Bush had considered the South his "fire wall" in the 1988 primaries, Clinton had the
good fortune of facing Tsongas on his home turf when he needed

most to regain his momentum. The demographic base of Clinton's support—blacks and lower-income working-class whites—was most strongly centered in the South and industrial Midwest. Second, Clinton enjoyed the advantage of superior reserves of funding and organization. Tsongas had expended his resources in trying to gain a breakthrough in New Hampshire, but once the breakthrough occurred he had insufficient resources to exploit it.[11]

Finally, Clinton had succeeded in adding the liberal interest groups to his coalition. This process had already started in New Hampshire, and it accelerated when it became clear that the choice had narrowed to Clinton and Tsongas.[12] Tsongas clearly had placed Clinton in an uncomfortable position. The aim of DLC rhetoric had always been to seize the intellectual high ground by standing in principled opposition to the party's "interest-group liberalism." Yet Tsongas took that ground instead, making Clinton appear more and more like another Walter Mondale, an image that stuck long after Tsongas had left the scene. Even the sympathetic *Washington Monthly* later lamented that Clinton sounded "more like another concubine than the man who's come to close down the harem."[13] Forced for a time to play the insider and interest-group liberal, Clinton turned Tsongas' attacks to his advantage and sewed up support with some of the party's traditional constituency groups.

Yet only five days after gaining his hard-won position as the presumptive Democratic nominee, Clinton was faced with a challenge that threw the race into an unexpected third stage. Jerry Brown, who had earlier won the Colorado primary and the Maine caucuses but had remained overshadowed by the Clinton-Tsongas matchup, upset Clinton in the Connecticut primary. Brown harassed Clinton for another month, during which time more revelations about Clinton's draft avoidance surfaced. Clinton also confessed to having tried marijuana as a student at Oxford while denying that he had inhaled. It was not clear what harmed him more—the confession or the denial. Brown, as the latest outsider in a year of outsiders, also attacked Clinton for being a special-interest candidate. The former California governor proposed to replace the current income tax system with a flat tax, and refused to take contributions over $100, relying instead on a much publicized 1-800 number. He also had increasing success at winning union votes, beginning with an appeal to auto workers concerned about the two front-runners' pro-free trade position.

Despite Clinton's huge delegate lead, the upcoming New York and Wisconsin primaries took on the appearance of "make or break" contests for Clinton.[14] Clinton was savaged by the New York tabloids, Brown appeared stronger than anyone had previously imagined, and Tsongas entertained the possibility of reentering the race depending on his New York showing (he was still on the ballot). Brown at this point made an enormous blunder, announcing in New York that he would make Jesse Jackson his running mate if nominated. This decision hurt Brown badly with Jewish voters in New York City. As in New Hampshire, Clinton attacked the media for its rough treatment of his character and then soundly defeated Brown in a statewide two-man debate. When the votes were counted in New York, Clinton had won by a landslide. Brown had accomplished the impossible of finishing third in a two-man race, behind Tsongas. Yet Tsongas too had finished far behind Clinton. Simultaneously, Clinton won a narrow victory in Wisconsin, where Brown had led for a time in the polls.

Table 3-2

The 1992 Democratic Primary Results: A Summary

	C	T	B	H	K	Other/Uncom
Primaries on ballot	39	35	39	30	30	25 (uncom)
Total vote	52%	18%	20%	1.5%	1.5%	7%
East	42%	29%	20%			9%
South	63%	15%	10%			12%
Midwest	51%	18%	21%			10%
West	46%	9%	36%			9%
Winnowing stage (to 3/3)	38%	31%	11%			20%
Breakthrough stage (3/7–17)	53%	27%	13%			7%
Mop-up stage (3/24–6/9)	53%	11%	25%			11%

Source: Adapted from *Congressional Quarterly Guide to the 1992 Democratic National Convention*, July 4, 1992, pp. 71-72.

C=Clinton; T=Tsongas; B=Brown; H=Harkin; K=Kerrey; Uncom=uncommitted.

Clinton's New York and Wisconsin victories ended Brown's threat and eliminated any possibility that Tsongas might reenter the race. The danger, in any event, had never been that Brown would win the nomination (he was too far behind and too much despised by the superdelegates), but that he could deny it to Clinton. For a short time speculation had again revived that a new candidate would enter to take advantage of Clinton's low standing in the polls.[15] Brown remained in the race through the convention, refusing to endorse Clinton, but after the Pennsylvania primary on April 28 he was largely ignored.

Preparing for the Nomination

Bill Clinton reached the end of the primary campaign with the nomination in hand—indeed, with a higher share of the delegates than any Democratic nominee since Lyndon Johnson in 1964—but literally staggering to the finish line. Just as important, he was stuck in third place at around 20 percent in national polls, trailing both Bush and Perot. If ever there had been a purely Pyrrhic victory in a nomination contest, it looked to be Clinton's win in 1992.

Clinton's victory was a confirmation of the importance of momentum in primary contests, but only in a qualified sense. He was the only candidate of either party in recent memory to win the nomination without having won either Iowa or New Hampshire, and his defeat in New Hampshire came at the end of a long slide in which he had lost a substantial lead. He steadied himself by winning Georgia on March 3, however, and gained insurmountable momentum by sweeping the South on Super Tuesday. The delegate lead he accumulated at that time, as well as the favorable press coverage he received, were sufficient to shut off financial support for his rivals and permit him to continue winning through the upper Midwest. In this respect, Clinton's campaign strikingly resembles that of Walter Mondale, who lost the momentum early but regained it with the help of superior financial and organizational reserves and a fortuitous primary schedule.

Clinton's victory was more a testament to his sheer personal determination and the manifest weakness of his opponents than to his own strength as a candidate. He had suffered from a seemingly unending string of charges: marital infidelity and draft avoidance in February, questionable land deals in early March, Hillary's law firm's business with the state in mid-March, improper ties with the Arkansas chicken industry and the awarding of a $30 million state bond contract to a major campaign contributor in late March, marijuana use at the very end of March, and more draft revelations in early April. It is difficult to imagine that Bill Clinton could have survived another strong Democrat, such as Al Gore, similarly placed inside the party. Even after New Hampshire, 40 percent of the Democrats who voted for Clinton in Maryland said they wanted a new candidate; by Connecticut, 58 percent of all Democratic voters wanted a new candidate; in New York on April 4, with a meager 25 percent turnout, two-thirds wanted a new candidate.[16]

Not until Pennsylvania at the end of April did Clinton improve substantially in polling questions about his honesty and integrity, perhaps because Brown's attacks were no longer at the center of attention. But even then primary turnout remained extremely low.[17] In the final round of primaries, only 29 percent of Clinton's voters strongly favored his candidacy in California, 34 percent in New Jersey, and 25 percent in Ohio.[18]

Furthermore, Democratic primary turnout had fallen precipitously nationwide; and even in the South, the impressiveness of Clinton's victories was diminished by the accelerating flight of white voters to the Republican primaries. Two-thirds of Democratic primary states experienced reduced turnout, including four states (Mississippi, Tennessee, Louisiana, and New York) where turnout declined 35 to 50 percent.[19] And as his stock fell, the stock of Ross Perot rose, to the extent that Clinton was nearly eclipsed by Perot from the middle of April until July. Indeed, Perot did better than Clinton in exit polls of Democratic voters in numerous states, including a 47 to 34 margin in Ohio.[20] In short, the primaries were full of ominous signs that Clinton may have won the nomination but could not win the presidency. While the Clinton campaign had originally planned to begin attacking Bush after Pennsylvania, it found itself struggling to stay in the news and ultimately took an approach of trying to rehabilitate Clinton's battered image while letting Perot take the lead in Bush-bashing.

There were three key events in this process of rehabilitation: Clinton's celebrated attack on the rap singer Sister Souljah, the release of his economic plan, and a meeting with big-city mayors in mid-June. In a speech to Jesse Jackson's Rainbow Coalition, Clinton shocked his host by chastising the Rainbow Coalition for honoring Sister Souljah, who had recently been quoted as remarking about the Los Angeles riots that "if black people kill black people every day, why not have a week and kill white people?" The incident, which was clearly contrived by the Clinton campaign for the purposes of distancing Clinton from Jackson, was the source of newspaper columns and radio talk shows for days, mostly approving Clinton's stand. Numerous black officials, including Mississippi Congressman and future Secretary of Agriculture Mike Espy, rose to Clinton's defense.[21] Not only did Clinton succeed in following the DLC formula of distancing himself from the cultural left, but he also succeeded in exposing the weakness of Jackson as a black leader.

Next, Clinton released a detailed economic plan, the key feature of which was a $220 billion proposal for new domestic spending, covered by a curtailing of the tax cut that had been the centerpiece of his campaign in the spring and the main point of contention between himself and Tsongas. This reversal was noted by the press, but generally in a manner very different from the treatment afforded Bush's tax reversal: Clinton, by these largely approving accounts, was displaying tactical flexibility and political skill in adapting to a changed environment.[22]

Finally, the mayors had called for $35 billion in new federal aid to the cities. Clinton called their $35 billion and raised them another $15 billion, eliciting enthusiastic responses, at least from the Democratic mayors, who had earlier flirted with Ross Perot. In a less substantive vein, the refurbishment of Clinton's image was aided by a saxophone performance on the Arsenio Hall show and an appearance on MTV. Clinton was making headway now among the young and the college students, who later would provide him with strong support in the general election. As the Democratic national convention approached, Clinton had steadily climbed in the polls while allowing Bush and Perot to savage each other. On the eve of the convention, he had pulled to a virtual three-way tie. Indeed, it seems probable that Perot's meteoric rise had served to take public scrutiny away from Clinton and enabled him to reintroduce himself at the Democratic convention.

THE VICE-PRESIDENTIAL SELECTION

The process by which Clinton chose Senator Albert Gore to be his running mate was unique in recent campaign history, as was the nature of the choice itself. Procedurally, Clinton appointed a three-member vice-presidential selection team to provide him with recommendations. The team was headed by longtime Democratic insider Warren Christopher and included civil rights leader Vernon Jordan and former Vermont Governor Madeleine Kunin. While the media ultimately discerned the main contenders for the position, the process itself was kept largely secret. Throughout the vice-presidential selection process, Clinton and his campaign refused to confirm who was being considered or even how many were on "the list." All interviews with contenders were conducted in secret.

There were at least two benefits to this process. First, it allowed the selection of a vice-presidential candidate to be conducted out of the glare of circus-like publicity and posturing that had characterized and hampered other selections, such as Walter Mondale's choice of Geraldine Ferraro. At the same time it allowed considerable input by party insiders like Christopher, thus strengthening the impression that the decision (or at least the field) was based on a sober consideration of credentials. The process also produced increasing suspense, thus creating a drama that focused intense attention on the decision.

The content of the choice also deviated from conventional wisdom and practice. Although the Clinton campaign refused to confirm speculation, it seems probable that along with Gore the field consisted of Clinton's primary rival Kerrey; Senator Harris Wofford of Pennsylvania, whose upset win over Richard Thornburgh in November had first alerted Democrats to George Bush's potential vulnerability; Senator Jay Rockefeller of West Virginia; and Representative Lee Hamilton of Indiana. Other names anonymously floated but less seriously considered were Senator Bob Graham of Florida, Governor Ann Richards of Texas, and even Mario Cuomo. Finally, Clinton aides took pains to leave open the possibility of a "surprise" choice.

In many respects, the choice of Gore represented an unconventional gamble. Gore was of the same generation as Clinton, was also a Baptist, and was from the same geographical and philosophical wing of the party. In the traditional sense of the term, no concern was given to the imperative of "ticket balancing." Any of the other possibilities on the shortlist could have provided more geographical balance than Gore. The same is true of ideology. And greater generational diversity could have been achieved with either Wofford or Hamilton. Both Wofford and Hamilton (the latter a far stronger contender) were apparently disqualified because of their support for the Supreme Court's *Casey* decision in early July which upheld *Roe v. Wade* but permitted moderate restrictions on abortion.

In other respects, however, the choice of Gore was not a rejection of ticket balancing but a redefinition of it, for Gore did complement Clinton in ways that were arguably more important than the traditional criteria. He had served in Vietnam, at least partially helping to make up for Clinton's avoidance of military service; he had served in the Senate and taken a great interest in arms control and other foreign policy issues, thus shoring up a weak spot in Clinton's experience and providing a little help on the "inside"; he was, despite a reputation for moderation, clearly in the left wing of the Democratic party on environmental issues, which were considered a Clinton vulnerability; and his wife Tipper's family orientation could provide a contrast to Hillary Clinton's feminist image. At the same time, the basic similarity of generation and ideology would permit the team to present a coherent message, and the all-Southern ticket could pose a serious threat to the Republican's Southern electoral base.

The decision, once made, was widely acclaimed. To David Broder, for example, the choice of Gore was "absolutely right."[23] Only Jesse Jackson seemed to complain, saying, "It takes two wings to fly and here you have two of the same wing."[24] The choice of Gore clearly added to Clinton's momentum going into the convention. Looking back, Clinton's advisers would say after November 3 that "no decision was more important" to the success of the campaign than the selection of Albert Gore.[25]

It could prove important for the future as well. By selecting a running mate with similar views, Clinton has possibly laid the groundwork for a continuity of Democratic party policy for four terms. In this sense, Clinton avoided the error committed by Ronald Reagan when Reagan named as his heir-apparent a man who was temperamentally and philosophically incapable of carrying on the Reagan revolution. In modifying the old rules, Clinton opened up new possibilities for future nominees.

THE DEMOCRATIC CONVENTION

As the opening for the fall campaign, the Democratic gathering in Madison Square Garden was probably the most successful convention since 1976. It was also the most tightly controlled. There were few challenges to the nominee, and almost all of the speakers (Jerry Brown excepted) strongly endorsed the ticket. Jesse Jackson was given his usual spot in prime time, but on the nominee's terms, in contrast to the previous two conventions. The Democratic party largely succeeded in its goal of appearing more moderate, and Perot's withdrawal coupled with Clinton's acceptance speech propelled the Arkansas Governor into a 20-point lead virtually overnight.

Clinton's acceptance speech, only slightly shorter than his infamous 1988 keynote address, emphasized the theme of "change" and relied on the basic philosophy of the Democratic Leadership

Council. The centerpiece was his call for a "new covenant" mixing opportunity and responsibility:

> The choice we offer is not conservative or liberal; in many ways it is not even Republican or Democrat. It is different. It is new. And it will work.

Clinton attacked George Bush as being an insider lacking in vision. Appealing directly to the Perot voters who had just been cut adrift, Clinton offered himself as the true heir and nominee of the outside party, making a populist argument that government had been "hijacked by privileged, private interests."

There were, however, a few loose ends. On the left, Jerry Brown refused to withdraw from the race or to endorse Clinton. He was accordingly prevented from speaking in prime time. Many of Brown's delegates persisted in voting for him and protested the steamrolling of a "moderate" platform through the convention. On the right, pro-life Democrats like Pennsylvania Governor Robert Casey were equally upset at what they perceived to be an extremist pro-choice plank. Casey was denied an opportunity to speak at all. The Democrats at times also had difficulty reconciling the tensions within the party on the inside-outside axis. Brown clung to his pure position to the outside of Clinton. Meanwhile, Clinton sought to remain well to the outside of his party's congressional power brokers, an objective that was delicately achieved by downplaying their role throughout the convention.

While some questions still remained about Clinton's ability to hold his party together going into the fall, the convention had shown the party to be fairly united—especially by past standards. This was certainly the image presented by the mainline media. By the end of the convention, Clinton had gained enormous momentum, fueled in part by the fortuitous withdrawal of Ross Perot. It was a remarkable recovery. Clinton had (barely) survived a grueling primary campaign, and he had just revived himself from a position where many thought he would be the first Democratic candidate in the history of the party to finish third in a general election. He was now poised for a serious run for the presidency itself.

THE IDEOLOGICAL STRUGGLE

The nomination of Clinton and Gore marked a new turn in a long-lasting ideological battle within the Democratic party. Since the 1972 nomination of George McGovern, Democratic presidential politics have largely been controlled by "new politics" liberalism, consisting of activist economic policy, cultural permissiveness, and foreign policy isolationism. Jimmy Carter partially overcame and partially accommodated the change, but liberal dominance reasserted itself in the 1980s.

Moderate Southern and suburban Democratic officeholders gradually coalesced to present an alternative to this liberal dominance. This process went through three major stages. In the early 1980s, Louisiana Representative Gillis Long began informal discussions with sympathetic colleagues who hoped to moderate the Democratic party's image. Most Southern Democrats, however, hoped to weather the storm simply by distancing themselves from the national party.

The second stage began after the 1984 Reagan landslide, which pulled down moderate Democrats in Kentucky and North Carolina and coincided with the end of Democratic dominance in voter identification among white Southerners. At this point, a simple strategy of distancing themselves from the national ticket seemed impossible. In February of 1985, moderate to conservative Democrats including Senators Sam Nunn of Georgia and Lawton Chiles of Florida, Governor Charles Robb of Virginia, Long's top aide Al From, Clinton himself, and others launched the Democratic Leadership Council, with the purpose of enlisting Democratic elected officials in a campaign to moderate the party's image. For the next four years, the DLC grew substantially. Its strength, however, came from two different and partially opposed camps. The first group, which was the driving force behind the DLC, thought the public perception of Democratic extremism was correct, and that the solution lay in substantive policy shifts. The second group believed that the public perception of the party's extremism was unjustified and hence could be solved by introducing a new rhetoric while retaining the old substance. At this point, the DLC was in large part a forum for elected officials without any grassroots organizational structure.

Finally, yet another liberal defeat in 1988 energized the DLC to make a more active and focused effort to save the party from what Al From called "liberal fundamentalism." Now the plan was to build the organizational and intellectual infrastructure necessary to take over the party. The DLC, for instance, established in June 1989 a think tank called the Progressive Policy Institute to help fashion a more cogent philosophy. It also worked to create a stronger membership network among grassroots activists and leaders. In 1990, DLC state chapters were first established, and by 1992 organizations could be found in 26 states. The May 1991 DLC meeting in Cleveland was in large measure a "declaration of war" on the party's left; Jesse Jackson was denied an invitation to speak, in contrast to the more inclusive tenor of past DLC meetings.

Ideologically, the DLC (with the help of the Progressive Policy Institute) fine-tuned its message, maintaining that old left-right distinctions were no longer relevant and calling for a "third way" between new-politics liberalism and Republican conservatism. This "third way" embraced an activist government but also included an emphasis on economic growth, strategies for "debureaucratizing" government (not unlike the "New Paradigm" suggested by White House aide James Pinkerton but largely ignored in Bush policy), law and order, free trade, American assertiveness abroad, and promotion of civic responsibility.[26]

The DLC was clearly swimming upstream for most of its existence. It consistently provoked a combination of derision and outrage from the more doctrinaire portions of the Democratic coalition, which accused it of trying to create a second Republican party. Among the most vocal of its critics was Jesse Jackson, whose Rainbow Coalition was an explicit organizational attempt to drive the party further leftward. In 1984 and even more so in 1988, Jackson had driven fear into the hearts of party leaders and fellow presidential candidates and had managed to anchor the party on the left. In 1988, Jackson vastly outpolled Gore, his key DLC rival in the 1988 field, besting him even in the South.

Jackson's absence from the 1992 race, and Clinton's position as the only (though probably weakest) of the potential first-tier candidates, significantly altered the ideological character of the race. Even party activists on the left, weary of suffering defeat after defeat, were finally persuaded of the importance of electability. Hence, in the nominating campaign itself, signs abounded of the left's declining influence in the party.

In New Hampshire, the two most conservative candidates of the Democratic field (Tsongas and Clinton) vied for first place and received a combined 58 percent of the vote. Within two weeks, Kerrey, who had run his campaign on a call for national health insurance, was gone. A week later, Harkin too was gone. One of his supporters lamented, "I don't know what to make of this. Here is the most progressive candidate running in what is supposed to be the progressive party, but he can't win."[27] Once Tsongas (who Bush campaign chairman Bob Teeter said was "running very much like a Republican") left the campaign, only Brown could challenge Clinton.[28] Brown did so from Clinton's left, but failed. The DLC victory appeared complete when Clinton challenged Jackson directly in the Sister Souljah incident and chose Gore as his running mate, ignoring an earlier ultimatum by Jackson, who had said in April, "If I am rejected this time, I am prepared to react." Jackson went so far as to refuse to rule out supporting Perot, but his threats were to no avail.

While it is largely true that the Democratic party had shifted to the right, it is necessary to qualify this simple picture. Clinton and Tsongas may have both been on the right of the Democratic party in a broad sense, but Clinton clearly acted to flank Tsongas on the left. A large part of his success can be attributed to his ability to adapt to this unexpected situation by convincing party activists and officials that he was closer to them than was Tsongas. One key group lured in this manner were black voters, who were cut free when Jackson decided not to run. Clinton won by building a coalition of blacks, labor (despite its misgivings), and moderate whites. In June, Clinton faced a decision of whether to veer even further left in expectation of a three-man race (the so-called "40 percent solution") or to expect a two-man race and reconcentrate on the center. Only then did Clinton choose the latter course and halt his leftward slide.[29]

The nature of Clinton's winning coalition casts some doubt on the depth of the DLC "triumph," since a large and perhaps decisive portion of his support came from voters who had only been interested in changing the Democratic party's image but not its substance. And Clinton himself, though he served as DLC chairman in the early 1990s, was eclectic in his approach. On one hand, he offered the DLC formula of civic responsibility, economic growth, middle-class tax relief, welfare reform, and support for the death penalty. On the other hand, he espoused a litany of very un-DLC-like causes from abortion on demand to a 50 percent defense cut to an economic recovery program vaguely resembling the Works Progress Administration (WPA).

Thus, there are two alternative analyses of the outcome of the ideological struggle within the Democratic party. Either little had changed from before, because Clinton won running as the most viable liberal candidate. Or much had changed, if the most viable "liberal" candidate in 1992 was a former chair of the DLC. In either case, it is clear that in style if not substance the center of gravity in the Democratic party has shifted to the right.

DEMOCRATIC PARTY RULES

Just as the Democratic party has been riven by ideological divisions since 1968, it has also been divided by quadrennial conflicts over party nominating rules. Beginning with the McGovern-Fraser Commission report, which first went into effect in 1972, the Democrats have been locked in a battle over the degree to which their nominating process should be plebiscitary and participatory or deliberative and subject to continued influence by party regulars. After the perceived excesses of "democratic" reforms from 1972 through 1980, party leaders took several steps to try to restore some of their previous power and to promote more moderate nomination outcomes. Their efforts were opposed by Jesse Jackson, who sought to continue and even expand the McGovern-Fraser reforms. The resulting nominating system of 1992 was thus a curious mixture of reform and anti-reform elements.

There are several important features of the 1992 nominating system that generated comment as the election approached. Perhaps the most significant was the reinstitution of universal proportional representation, which many analysts predicted might lead to a deadlock that would have to be resolved either by the superdelegates or at the convention. Jackson had forced proportional representation on the party prior to the 1988 convention, and some speculated in late 1991 that in a race with fairly evenly matched regional candidates, no one would be able to garner a majority.[30] Clinton confounded these predictions by wrapping up the race well before the convention.

The law of candidate momentum overrode the mechanical effects of proportional representation, just as it had done in 1976. Even when the delegate totals separating the candidates were not very large, those winning primaries gained a great advantage. Defeated candidates saw their ratings fall and their sources of funding dry up; faced with the futility of their situation, they dropped out. For a genuine deadlock to develop, it would have been necessary to have candidates of roughly equal strength and appeal, especially in the regions that hold primaries near the beginning of the nominating season. (A candidate with strong regional appeal, such as Bill Clinton, whose region comes early in the race could gain a decisive advantage over his rivals.) Furthermore, the field in 1992 was clearly not equal, underscoring the importance of Clinton's status as the only first-tier candidate in the race. Had Cuomo, Bradley, and Jackson run, deadlock under proportional representation would have been more likely.

In another respect, however, proportional representation actually reduced the prospects of deadlock. Once Tsongas and Brown fell behind, the lack of winner-take-all primaries seriously reduced their capacity to catch up. Had California or New York been based on some form of plurality rules, a comeback would have been more plausible. Instead, Tsongas withdrew and Brown faded into irrelevance.

State requirements for filing delegate slates for primaries and caucuses also reduced the prospects of a late entrant, and hence of deadlock. These requirements are also a component of the post-1968 reformed system, since they reflect the entire candidate-centered logic of the system. Yet far from making the process more open and responsive to changing circumstances, they help—inadvertently to be sure—to lock in political calculations from an earlier period. At Clinton's first point of weakness in February, potential latecomers like Gephardt and Bentsen were discouraged by the fact that filing deadlines had already passed for contests accounting for almost 60 percent of the delegates. At the second point of Clinton's weakness in April, filing deadlines again provided a disincentive to enter, this time magnified by Clinton's delegate lead. In the pre-1972 nominating system, with its easier filing procedures, a tradition of write-in campaigns, substantial delegate discretion, and plurality primaries, a late entry was more feasible.

While proportional representation and candidate-centered contests promoted the goals of the reform ethos, the two "supers"—superdelegates and Super Tuesday—worked in the opposite direction. At the recommendation of a party commission following the 1980 race (the Hunt Commission), the 1984 Democratic nominating process included for the first time the selection of "superdelegates," or ex officio delegates drawn from Congress and state and local party leaders. The purpose of this change was to reinject the official party into the nominating process from which it had been largely expelled by the McGovern-Fraser reforms.

In 1984 superdelegates drew mixed reviews. They were instrumental in saving the nomination of Walter Mondale from Gary Hart, but most superdelegates pledged their votes very early in the campaign and thus were in no position to engage in deliberation or bargaining at a critical point. At the insistence of Jackson and Hart, the 1988 congressional superdelegates were chosen later in the election year. The vast majority of the 1988 superdelegates supported Michael Dukakis. Jackson again demanded changes and extracted an agreement from Dukakis before the convention to reduce the number of superdelegates in the future. But this agreement was quietly reversed by the Democratic National Committee in 1989, and the number of superdelegates actually grew from 648 in 1988 to 766 in 1992, more than one-third of the total needed for nomination.

In 1992, the superdelegates ultimately supported Clinton by a wide margin, but unlike 1984 most of them waited a long time before committing. Many were active in the behind-the-scenes efforts to convince Gephardt to run in February and Bentsen in April. When the choice resolved itself first to one between Tsongas and Clinton and then to one between Brown and Clinton, Clinton was the obvious choice, although many superdelegates remained skeptical about his electability.[31] They began to come to the conclusion that Clinton would be the nominee after the New York and Wisconsin primaries in early April. In this decision they were prodded by Democratic National Committee Chairman Ron Brown, who argued that it was necessary to close ranks behind Clinton. Nevertheless, as late as mid-May, superdelegates were divided fifty-fifty between Clinton and uncommitted.[32]

Super Tuesday worked more unambiguously to Clinton's advantage. "Super Tuesday" was a label coined in 1984 to refer to a primary day in early March on which several states, many of them Southern, held their primaries. After the 1984 election, the newly formed DLC made a concerted effort to add more Southern states to Super Tuesday, hoping that the event could help propel a Southern moderate to the nomination. This plan backfired in 1988. Albert Gore did well on Super Tuesday, but Jesse Jackson did even better. And Michael Dukakis held his own by winning Florida, Texas, Maryland, and four other Northern and Western states. There were other problems as well. So many states had jumped on the bandwagon of Super Tuesday (16 primaries and six caucuses) that the candidates had no choice but to ignore some of the states. As a result, several states withdrew from Super Tuesday in 1992, and the number of contests fell back to eight primaries and four caucuses, slightly more than in 1984.

Super Tuesday in 1992 nevertheless worked precisely as its founders had hoped. Clinton revived his sagging campaign and won a large number of delegates in decisive victories across the South. Six Southern states held primaries on Super Tuesday, in contrast to 14 in 1988. Clinton won them all. He was also aided by wins in Georgia, which had moved its primary up a week at the last moment, and South Carolina, which voted the Saturday before Super Tuesday. The concept of a Southern regional primary held early in the nominating process thus proved basically a sound one from the perspective of Southern moderates, but only in modified form—with few enough contests that a moderate candidate can focus on them all, and only if black votes are not concentrated behind a left-wing candidate like Jesse Jackson. Since the Jackson phenomenon may be not be duplicated, the DLC can reasonably hope that its success in 1992 was no accident.

Finally, the compression of the campaign calendar in 1992 worked to Clinton's benefit. In 1976, 50 days separated the Iowa caucuses from the first substantial set of primaries after New Hampshire. By 1992 that figure had fallen to 21 days, and the actual window was even shorter because of Iowa's unimportance. This compression could theoretically have meant an extra boost for the winner of New Hampshire, but it seemed instead to put an increased premium on the depth of campaign resources, which Clinton had and Tsongas did not. In 1976, for example, Jimmy Carter was able to use the break after winning in Iowa to catch his breath, raise money, and reinforce his organization.[33] In 1992, the interval between New Hampshire and Super Tuesday was too brief for Tsongas to take full advantage of his victory.

Clinton's election in November saved the Democratic party—regrettably, perhaps—from a major struggle over its rules. There was a period during the primary season when many Democratic politicians were prepared to revamp the nomination system and undo many of the reforms of the 1970s. Appalled at the spectacle of the campaign and worried by Clinton's simultaneous weakness and continuing ascent, some party leaders publicly called for a restoration of deliberative conventions as the mechanism for party nominations.[34] Former Virginia Governor Gerald Baliles, for instance, argued that campaigns conducted under the current rules are "exercises in personal promotion at the expense of party building and cohesion. . . . Simplistic debate over symbols and personalities leaves little room for the true business and for leadership. On the Democratic side, [the system] has too often left us with a nominee who cannot win."[35] Since the debate within the party has derived as much from unsatisfactory electoral returns as from deep-seated principles, these voices have now been stilled.

THE ROLE OF THE MEDIA

The news media was the force that nearly destroyed Bill Clinton's candidacy, but it proved in the end to be the instrument of his salvation. The media was at the center of the turmoil over Bill Clinton's past, conveying the series of charges that shook the campaign from the early days. The major media reluctantly covered Gennifer Flowers' accusation of her affair with Bill Clinton after the story had been broken by the tabloid press. Clearly uncomfortable with this kind of story, the major media abruptly dropped it after the New Hampshire primary without ever ascertaining the veracity of Flowers' charges (or Clinton's denial) or seriously examining the question of her state employment. Draft avoidance kept recurring as an issue in no small part because the media did not investigate the question thoroughly enough the first time. Other scandalous accusations flitted across the pages, including the matter of marijuana use and charges by other women of Clinton's marital infidelity.

Apart from the scandals, the Clinton campaign did not always appear to be subjected to the level of scrutiny that one might expect from an adversarial press. Even sympathetic members of the press noted the media's apparent haste to declare Tsongas dead and Clinton triumphant.[36] Clinton's reversal in June on the middle-class tax cut that was the centerpiece of his spring campaign was scarcely criticized. The favorable coverage of the Democratic convention a month later, in contrast to the harsh scrutiny the Republican convention received in August, became a frequent topic of Republican complaint. The unity of the Democratic party and splits in the Republican ranks became consistent media themes, even though Pat Buchanan endorsed his party's victor in a way that Brown never did, and even though the Democratic platform drew far more dissenting votes than the Republican platform. In contrast to the Republican convention, where divisions on abortion were prominently featured, there were few attempts to discover and give airtime to dissenting pro-life Democrats. When Pennsylvania Governor Bob Casey gave a news conference at the Democratic convention, he received no major network coverage and only one paragraph in the *New York Times*.

Clinton's survival and recovery in the race were thus aided in no small part by the mild scrutiny he received from the press once all the accusations were duly reported. His "escape" was a result of a number of factors. Consciously or unconsciously, the media may have decided to forgo intense coverage of personal attacks as a result of a backlash against the destruction of Gary Hart in 1987. Clinton may thus have enjoyed the good fortune of having been preceded by Hart. Public response may also have played a role in leading the media to redirect its energies. The public's reaction in New Hampshire to the first revelations was a combination of negative reaction against Clinton (he did, after all, drop precipitously in the polls) but equal or greater anger against the media for turning the campaign into a soap opera. Clinton audiences in the Granite State literally shouted down journalists' questions about marital infidelity. The scandals that preoccupied journalists and frightened Democratic operatives seemed to carry much less weight in public opinion at large. It was a case of the public moderating the media.

Above all, perhaps, the elite print and broadcast media genuinely liked and admired Bill Clinton. If, as some hold, the major journalists today should play a deliberate role in "screening candidates" for the public, then it appears that the press wanted to help Bill Clinton. Helping, of course, does not mean a dereliction of the basic responsibility of covering the stories. But it does refer to the tone of coverage and how much emphasis is placed on certain things. The press's collective judgment of Bill Clinton—as distinct, say, from their assessment of Ross Perot—was very favorable. He was probably their favorite presidential candidate since Robert Kennedy in 1968. It was not exactly Camelot, but almost. As Richard Cohen of the *Washington Post* wrote:

> The late Bernard Malamud wrote a wonderful novel about a supremely gifted baseball player: "The Natural." In politics, Clinton is that sort of talent. There is not a pitch he cannot hit, no question he cannot answer. He's a political polymath who seems to have the facts and the data at his fingertips and—an instant later—the solution. It seems he can talk on any subject. Political reporters, who see a lot of clods, are in awe of Clinton. It is this admiration, this keen appreciation of his abilities, that may have saved him in the Terrible Days when he was accused of cheating on his wife. The establishment press cast a reproving eye on any who would trash this Golden Boy. He had to be allowed to prove himself.[37]

The journalists' love of Bill Clinton was not always requited. Though well treated by the press, except by the tabloids in New York, he seldom passed up an opportunity to attack the media and play the role of victim when the news itself was bad. In New Hampshire, he sensed the public's negative reaction to the media's coverage of his personal life, and he sought to deflect personal criticisms by attacking the sensationalism of the media. Moreover, Clinton's campaign pioneered techniques that would be perfected by Ross Perot of going around the major journalists and news media and relying instead on appearances on talk shows and entertainment programs.

Does the treatment the media gave Bill Clinton spell an end to the kind of "feeding frenzies" in which the media retains the power to drive candidates from the race on the basis of personal revelations? Or was the confluence of factors that caused the media ultimately to ease up on Clinton particular to this candidate? Paradoxically, although almost all of the revelations were reported, a precedent for some restraint on the part of the media may have been established. It remains to be seen, however, whether others will ever enjoy the same good fortune as the "Golden Boy" in 1992.

CONCLUSION

Bill Clinton's victory in the Democratic nominating campaign hinged on several factors: his position as the only first-tier candidate in the field; the willingness of many liberal Democrats to accept at least a cosmetic move to the center for the sake of electability; the benefits deriving from electoral geography and chronology; his own determination and political skill; and last, but not least, a certain amount of protection from the news media.

The battle between the "centrists" and the hard left within the Democratic party was won by the center, but this only shifted the battleground between these different tendencies in the party into the White House. Similarly, the battle between the inside and the outside was won by the middle. The Washington insiders (Bob Kerrey and Tom Harkin) were quickly driven from the race, forcing Clinton, against his expectations and his preference, to deal with a challenge not from his inside but from his outside. Ever resourceful, Clinton turned this situation to his advantage by swooping up the allegiance of the major interest groups in the Democratic party.

Clinton was near the middle on both the major dimensions that defined American politics in 1992. He was closer to the ideological center than any Democratic candidate except Tsongas, and had the good fortune in the general presidential campaign to be flanked by a candidate to his outside (Ross Perot) and one to his inside (George Bush). As Bill Clinton's victory proved, the center is often the best place to be in American politics.

NOTES

1. For a discussion of the Democratic situation in 1991 and the evolving Democratic field of contenders, see Myron A. Levine, *Presidential Campaigns and Elections* (Itasca, Ill.: Peacock Publishers, 1992), chapter 1.

2.　Jack W. Germond and Jules Witcover, *National Journal*, September 7, 1991, p. 2168.

3.　See Rhodes Cook, "Wilder's Exit From Race Leaves Question About Black Vote," *CQ Weekly Report*, January 11, 1992, p. 66.

4.　See Jack W. Germond and Jules Witcover, "Clinton is Riding a Strong Message," *National Journal*, November 30, 1991, p. 2934.

5.　Dan Balz and David S. Broder, "Democrats Talk of New Candidates," *Washington Post*, February 14, 1992, p. A1; Rowland Evans and Robert Novak, "Illinois and Clinton...," *Washington Post*, February 7, 1992, p. A25.

6.　David Maraniss, "'Liberated After New Hampshire Pressure, Clinton Plots Southern Strategy," *Washington Post*, February 20, 1992, p. A14.

7.　See Evans and Novak, "After New Hampshire: Two Deluded Parties," *Washington Post*, February 21, 1992, p. A19; Lally Weymouth, "Waiting in the Wings," *Washington Post*, March 1, 1992, p. C1.

8.　See David S. Broder, "Favorite Makes the Faithful Uneasy," *Washington Post*, February 16, 1992, p. A1.

9.　Dan Balz, "Kerrey and Harkin Fight for 3rd Place," *Washington Post*, February 19, 1992, p. A1.

10.　See Thomas Edsall, "Each Front-Runner Holds Half the Winning Hand," *Washington Post*, March 5, 1992, p. A1.

11.　See Dan Balz, "Next 16 Days to Test Candidates' Strategy," *Washington Post*, February 23, 1992, p. A14. Clinton had raised $1.6 million in January; Tsongas $321,000. Also David S. Broder, "Tsongas Forced to Play Organizational Catch-Up," *Washington Post*, March 8, 1992, p. A19; Charles R. Babcock, "Clinton Faced Cash Crunch Before N.Y. Primary," *Washington Post*, May 1, 1992, p. A10.

12.　See Rowland Evans and Robert Novak, "The Democrats' Dilemma In New Hampshire," *Washington Post*, February 10, 1992, p. A11.

13.　Chris Mitchell, "Gang of Three," *The Washington Monthly*, September 1992, p. 26.

14.　See Rhodes Cook, "New York Gives Brown Chance to Solidify Challenger Role," *CQ Weekly Report*, April 4, 1992, pp. 895-900.

15.　See Richard E. Cohen, "Keeping Their Distance," *National Journal*, April 11, 1992, p. 865; David Van Drehle, "Cuomo Tempers Clinton Prediction," *Washington Post*, March 26, 1992, p. A24.

16.　Richard Tapscott and Richard Morin, "It's Bush, Tsongas, and Malaise in Maryland," *Washington Post*, March 4, 1992, p. A1; "Connecticut Presidential Exit Poll," *Washington Post*, March 26, 1992, p. A24; E.J. Dionne, Jr. and Thomas B. Edsall, "Clinton Leads N.Y.; Tsongas, Brown Vie for Second," *Washington Post*, April 8, 1992, p. A1.

17.　E.J. Dionne, Jr., "Bush, Clinton and Yeakel Win Pennsylvania Primary," *Washington Post*, April 29, 1992, p. A1.

18.　James A. Barnes, "Exit Polls: The 'Big Mo' Is With Perot," *National Journal*, June 6, 1992, p. 1368.

19.   Thomas B. Edsall, "Southern Primaries Reveal Contradictions for Democrats," *Washington Post*, March 12, 1992, p. A14; Dan Balz, "Voter Turnout in '92 Primaries Down Almost 12%, Study Finds," *Washington Post*, April 14, 1992, p. A6; "Democrats' Dilemma: Falling Turnout," *CQ Weekly Report*, May 16, 1992, p. 1376.

20.   James A. Barnes, "Exit Polls: The 'Big Mo' Is With Perot," *National Journal*, June 6, 1992, p. 1368.

21.   David S. Broder and Thomas B. Edsall, "Clinton Finds Biracial Support for Criticism of Rap-Singer," *Washington Post*, June 16, 1992, p. A7.

22.   See Jack W. Germond and Jules Witcover, "Clinton Finally Takes the Offensive," *National Journal*, June 27, 1992, p. 1539; Dan Balz, "End Attained, Clinton Mutes Talk of Middle-Class Tax Cut," *Washington Post*, June 23, 1992, p. A12.

23.   David S. Broder, "A Tougher Race for Clinton," *Washington Post*, July 19, 1992, p. C7; also David S. Broder, "The Gore Choice," *Washington Post*, July 10, 1992, p. A21.

24.   Jack Anderson and Michael Binstein, "Sourness in the Jackson Camp," *Washington Post*, July 12, 1992, p. C7.

25.   Edward Walsh, "Clinton Victory Founded on Discipline, Energy, GOP Miscues," *Washington Post*, November 5, 1992, p. A31.

26.   Much of the foregoing discussion is drawn from Jon F. Hale, "'New Politics' Liberals and 'DLC' Centrists: Factionalism in the Democratic Party, 1968-1992," paper delivered at the annual meeting of the American Political Science Association, Chicago, September 3-6, 1992.

27.   Thomas B. Edsall, "Harkin Is Expected To Quit Race Today," *Washington Post*, March 9, 1992, p. A1.

28.   Dan Balz, "Democrats Jockey For Advantage in New Hampshire," *Washington Post*, February 17, 1992, p. A1.

29.   Rowland Evans and Robert Novak, "Tempest in the Ranks," *Washington Post*, June 17, 1992, p. A25.

30.   See Anthony Corrado, "Party Rules Reform and Candidate Nomination Strategies: Consequences for the 1990s," paper presented at the annual meeting of the American Political Science Association, Washington, D.C., August 29-September 1, 1991.

31.   See Richard E. Cohen, "Keeping Their Distance," *National Journal*, April 11, 1992, p. 865; Dan Balz and David S. Broder, "From Hill, View of Clinton Partly Sunny," *Washington Post*, March 12, 1992, p. A1.

32.   Dan Balz and E.J. Dionne, Jr., "Clinton Hopes Victories Convince 'Superdelegates,'" *Washington Post*, April 9, 1992, p. A1; "Delegate Hunt," *National Journal*, June 13, 1992, p. 1419.

33.   See David Shribman, "New Rules for '92 Democratic Primary Mean Chance of Early Nominee Amid Faster Pace," *Wall Street Journal*, January 2, 1992, p. 34.

34.   See Walter F. Mondale, "Primaries Are No Test of Character," *New York Times*, February 26, 1992, p. A21 ; Gerald L. Baliles, "'A Better Way to Pick a President' (Cont'd)", *Washington Post*, April 19, 1992, p. C7.

35.   Gerald L. Baliles, "'A Better Way to Pick a President' (Cont'd)," *Washington Post*, April 19, 1992, p. C7.

36.   See Charles Peters, "The Media's Rush to Annointment," *Washington Post*, March 15, 1992, p. C5.

37.   Richard Cohen, "A 'Natural' but . . .", *Washington Post*, February 18, 1992, p. A17.

CHAPTER FOUR

The Strange Career
of Ross Perot

No aspect of the 1992 presidential campaign received more attention or generated more commentary than what became known as "the Perot phenomenon." This occurrence, event, or happening— one is at a loss to know exactly what word to employ—was invariably described in the most momentous, even ominous, of terms. For political scientist Theodore Lowi, Perot's candidacy signified "the large-scale radicalization of the political mainstream—a phenomenon unprecedented in this century." For historian Alan Brinkley, it was a harbinger of a "passage to a new political order—a beginning of a fundamental realignment of American politics." For political columnist George Will, it offered our first glimpse into the "watery Caesarism [that] the 21st century has up its nasty sleeve."[1]

One must be clear, however, about just what this alleged "phenomenon" refers to. For there was not one but *two* Perot campaigns in 1992: a spring campaign, which began with Perot's indication of availability in February and lasted until his withdrawal in July, and a fall campaign, which dated from Perot's eleventh-hour reentrance into the race on October 1. These two campaigns had completely different meanings. In the spring campaign, Perot was regarded as a major candidate who could win the presidency or at a minimum capture a large number of states. Most commentators spoke of a three-person race, and spokesmen for the Clinton and especially the Bush campaigns thought Perot a serious enough threat to attack him directly. A Senate committee commenced hearings in June to prepare a constitutional amendment for the electoral college in the hopes of making a change before the election and averting a potential crisis.

Recall that the reason Perot gave for pulling out in July, deemed at the time plausible if not believable, was that his campaign might prove "disruptive" to the country by throwing the election into the House of Representatives.

By contrast, in the fall campaign Perot was never anything more than a third-party candidate, no matter how impressive his 19 percent final showing proved to be. Few thought that Perot had a chance to win the presidency or to finish ahead of either of the major candidates, let alone claim a significant share of electoral votes. The only question seemed to be which of the two major candidates Perot's campaign would hurt the most. Perot himself at this point may have been running more to regain personal respectability and keep his movement alive than to win. Although Bush and Clinton for tactical reasons accorded Perot all of the privileges of a major contender, including a place on the podium of the presidential debates, neither candidate regarded Perot as a genuine rival or paid him the ultimate compliment of seriously attacking his programs. In the end, Perot was given a free ride.

Of course the two campaigns of Ross Perot are related, since it was Ross Perot, or some version of him, who ran in both. If there was a "Perot phenomenon," however, it must refer to the first campaign, when Perot was said to be reshaping the American political landscape, and not to the second. But was there a Perot phenomenon that was anywhere near as momentous as many claimed? Or was Perot's "real" strength closer all along to his November total (or perhaps, considering his free ride in October, slightly less)?

Even if one accepts the lower estimate, Perot's 19 percent share of the popular vote—the best showing of a third-party candidate since Teddy Roosevelt in 1912—provides sufficient grounds for maintaining that he represents an important force in American politics. The durability of that support, however, is difficult to assess. Unlike important previous non-major party candidates, Perot is not identified with a particular ideological position to the left or right of the major parties. Nor does he enjoy any particular regional base—if this still counts in American politics. His movement, best described as a revolt of the radical middle, found its support in an outsider appeal that emphasized that government had lost touch with the people, rendering it incapable of confronting long-term national problems such as the national debt. Whether this force will be kept alive and whether Perot will lead it depends on political circumstances and on the success or failure of the Clinton presidency.

THE ANNOUNCEMENT

You all did see that on the Lupercal I thrice presented him a kingly
crown, which he did thrice refuse. . . . Did this in Caesar seem
ambitious?—Marc Anthony, *Julius Caesar*, Act III scene 2

Ross Perot's candidacy is quite unlike anything else in modern
electoral politics. As a story, at least, it surely is unprecedented,
beginning with its curious opening scene. On February 20, 1992—
just after George Bush had been humiliated in New Hampshire by
Pat Buchanan, and Bill Clinton, suffering from numerous attacks on
his character, finished second to Paul Tsongas—citizen Ross Perot
appeared for an interview on CNN's *Larry King Live* talk show. Early
in the program, King asked Perot if he planned to run for president
in 1992. Perot said no. A minute later, King posed the question a
second time. Again Perot declined, adding, perhaps prophetically, "I
would not be temperamentally fit for it." Undaunted, King went for
another try. Perot would not thrice refuse, at least not completely:
"If voters in all 50 states put me on the ballot—not 48 or 49 states,
but all 50—I will agree to run." Perot would assume the burden of
becoming the people's "servant" and attending to matters of state.
Or, as he later put it, "if the volunteers say 'Ross, it's a dirty job but
you've got to do it,' I belong to them."[2]
   Was this announcement the spontaneous reaction of someone
with no ambition to be president, as Perot himself would always
thereafter insist? Or was it, as many would later suggest, an elabo-
rately choreographed piece of political theater, in which kingmaker
Larry King (who later boasted "I was his New Hampshire") unwit-
tingly played Marc Anthony to Perot's Julius Caesar?[3]
   A comparison of Perot to Caesar, however entertaining, is unlikely
to shed much light on this campaign. After all, we know Julius Caesar,
and Ross Perot is no Julius Caesar—at any rate not yet. Had Perot
been elected president, there might be reason to pore over the tran-
scripts of *Larry King Live* or *Donahue* in search of minute clues
about his inner psychological disposition. For now, however, we can
forgo such research and focus on the successive icons of Ross Perot
that flitted across the screen of American politics from February through
November. It is in these pictures that the most interesting elements
of the Perot campaign may be discovered.

THE MANY FACES OF ROSS PEROT

Americans over a nine-month period came to know at least five
Ross Perots. Each Perot was the product of pieces of assembled

biographical information ("spun" by different sources), of the public's direct responses to Perot's innumerable television appearances, and of the commentators' need to present a persona who could appear to account for the dramatically changing estimates of his campaign.

Table 4-1
Poll Ratings: Perot versus Bush and Clinton

	% Perot	% Bush	% Clinton
April 9	21	40	25
May 14	33	28	24
June 4	39	31	25
July 9	26	26	28
Oct. 1	8	35	51
Oct. 12	12	33	48
Oct. 20	15	32	45
Oct. 28	16	38	41

Source: Time/CNN (April 9, May 14, and July 9) and USA Today/CNN/ Gallup (June 4, Oct. 1, Oct. 12, Oct. 20, and Oct. 28).

Note: Undecided not shown.

Meet first, then, Ross Perot I, who was the Ross Perot that Ross Perot wanted to present. This persona was built on the foundation of Perot's version of his involvement in the 1992 campaign. With few analysts initially taking a Perot candidacy seriously, there was no rush to challenge his account. Commentators depicted Perot as a sincere, if somewhat peculiar, figure—an American original, genuinely troubled by America's economic decline and the inability of the political system to respond to it.

This view fit into a more elaborate version of Ross Perot that already was latent in the public mind and that Perot's aides assiduously began to cultivate. The image had Perot as one-part Horatio Alger— a classic self-made man who prevailed over circumstance to create a business empire—and one-part Cincinnatus—a super patriot willing to sacrifice all for his countrymen, including pursuing the fate of America's forgotten Vietnam War POWs and MIAs. Of all of Perot's exploits, there was one that stood out for capturing his true grit: the rescue mission Perot planned and directed to save two of his employees from an Iranian jail in 1979, at the height of the Ayatollah's reign. The story of this rescue, told in the 1984 book *On Wings of Eagles* and later in a made-for-TV movie, demonstrated Perot's loyalty and his action-oriented style of patriotism. Perot showed American resolve at just the moment when the Iranian revolutionary leaders were humiliating the United States government and its President. Ross Perot's foreign policy succeeded where the United States government's had failed. Here was evidence that Perot could "just do it," whereas the politicians could not. While they just talked, he acted. He was Nike-man.

Ross Perot II was fashioned by professional commentators to offer an explanation for the meteoric rise of the Perot candidacy. Embarrassed that they had missed the real "story" (and had swallowed too much of the Perot myth), commentators scrambled to make amends. Ross Perot I, it was now argued, was a carefully crafted image that Perot had created to conceal his ambitions. The real Perot had been planning things all along and had seized on just the right strategy to catapult himself to the top. He was a shrewd mastermind who knew only too well how to manipulate the system, the media included.

It is interesting to pause a moment and reflect on the vast industry in the modern media that meets the supposed demand to have every major event "explained." These efforts have the character of beginning from an anticipated result and then working back from it to build what seems like a plausible account of its causes. As the anticipated results changes—in this case from the Perot candidacy as a nonevent to "a phenomenon unprecedented in this century"—so too must the explanation. The prevailing causes are quickly discarded and the machinery of analysis is cranked up to produce entirely new ones. Few things, it appears, contribute more to the current distortion of reality than the insatiable demand to explain it.

Perot II began with a different interpretation of what had occurred that fateful February night on *Larry King Live*. Looking back on that announcement in the light of the campaign's success, analysts now saw in it a stroke of political genius, too artful by far to have been a mere accident. It is well understood that under the current presidential selection system the candidates are compelled to solicit public support with an unseemly persistence and to reveal—or have revealed for them—virtually every facet of their personal lives. This position of supplication, pursued in an exposed posture, had former candidate Walter Mondale worried enough to warn in February that the process was destroying all the candidates: "Everyone involved is cheapened—the candidates, the reporters, and the voters."[4] What, then, could be a more skillful ploy than to place oneself in a position of setting the conditions under which one "agrees" to run, proffering a candidacy without quite becoming a candidate? Perot, for a brief moment, recaptured that precious aura of reluctance of a bygone era, when the office would seek the person, not the person the office.

Ross Perot, moreover, seemed to succeed in this gambit where others had failed. One thinks, for example, of Governor Mario Cuomo, who for the past two elections had dallied with the American public, trying to win an "invitation" to run. But Cuomo kept coming square up against the reality that a draft under the modern nominating system is a near impossibility. His tantalizing offers, which early on earned him respectful comparisons to Hamlet, ended by becoming objects of mild ridicule.

Perot would bypass parties and nominations. He would accept only a real draft—a draft that came from the people and that expressed the general will outside of, and even against, the parties. For unlike John Anderson (or even Teddy Roosevelt), Perot was not a "sore loser" who, having just been denied his party's nomination, was begging for a second chance. Nor was he, like Henry Wallace or George Wallace, identified with a particular ideological point of view. He could claim to represent all of us and to be our "servant." As political columnist William Rasberry noted, Perot "will deign to be our president—not because he needs the job but because we need him; . . . he'll allow people to choose him."[5] The sheer effrontery of his humility proved the brilliance of Perot's strategy.

But this was the least part of the genius of Perot II. In a nation where people harbor deep suspicions about the use of private wealth to win office, a candidacy by one of America's wealthiest citizens would seem to offer the perfect target for the charge of trying to buy the presidency. After all, it had been just twelve years since John Connally, another conspicuously rich Texan (albeit a mere millionaire), was driven from a presidential nomination race after spending $11 million and winning exactly one delegate.[6] In contrast, Ross Perot—a veritable billionaire—was poised to invert the whole situation. His promise to spend up to $100 million for a "world-class campaign" was presented as a gesture of sacrifice, the least a mighty servant could do for his humble master.

Finally, as analysts zeroed in on the campaign, they began to wonder whether the whole operation, from the names on computer lists to the amazing outpouring of support by the volunteers, was all quite as innocent or spontaneous as Perot had made out. As in a fantastic *Mission Impossible* plot, where everything falls miraculously into place the moment the signal is given, many believed that Perot had been laying a foundation for a campaign for some time.

Perot II, though not an image of Ross Perot's own creation, in all probability contributed to the campaign's momentum. For whatever it may have cost Perot in sincerity, it added in shrewdness, and in politics it is better to be thought shrewd than sincere. (Perot himself, on reentering the race in October, rather clumsily conceded this point, when he defended a rigged telephone "poll" that was supposed to demonstrate whether "the people" wanted him to come back in. This poll, as it turned out, would record only positive responses. Replying to a suitably scandalized Katie Couric, Perot said, "I'm a businessman. I'm not going to pay for the phone call of some fellow who says 'Don't do it.'"[7])

Ross Perot III, who emerged in May, was the dark side or reverse image of Perot I—the Darth Vader to the earlier Obie Wan Konobie. Perot III was not just ambitious and shrewd, but dangerous, personally and politically. He was authoritarian, paranoid, megalomaniacal and hypocritical—in a word, less than "temperamentally suited" to be president.

Perot III, Perot charged, was invented as a plot by the Republican party to destroy his candidacy: "Most of this stuff is not originated in the press. . . . The party in power has this interesting network of contacts, feeds, leaks, and the press people's incomes really depend on their contacts, keeping their access."[8] To defend their own honor from Perot's charges of being Bush lackeys, many in the press were forced, albeit with considerable reluctance, to exonerate the Republican party. In fact, Perot III was mostly the creation of journalists in the major media, with Republicans playing only a minor role. And once the story got going, the Bush campaign desisted from further attacks on Perot, preferring, in the kind of macho phrases in which young presidential aides revel, "to stand back and watch him bleed."[9]

A bit late in getting started, major journalists began in April and May to provide an in-depth biographical sketch of Perot's life, scrutinizing some of the points that the commissioned biographies ignored or glossed over. On the personal side, they found Perot to have a strange fascination for the militaristic—a streak that showed up in his curious attachment to the Boy Scouts and in the rigidity with which he managed his own company (including strict dress codes). Perot possessed a streak of paranoia, as revealed in his penchant for employing private investigators to check out employees or political enemies, and a susceptibility to conspiracy theories, as shown in his unwillingness to accept any reasonable proof on some MIA questions. *Time* magazine referred to Perot as a "confirmed conspiracy theorist" with "a seeming ability to convince himself of the truth of whatever he wants to believe."[10]

Perot III was also hypocritical in his "outsider" appeal. He had pulled many a political string in his time, using all the standard insider tactics to win sweetheart deals. Not only had his original company been built largely on government contracts for computerizing Medicare and Medicaid records, but Perot had also made campaign contributions to various congressmen in an effort to save himself $15 million on a tax break on the construction of the Ft. Worth Airport.

The political implications of Perot III were—to say the least—worrisome. No matter whether Perot was sincere or merely a shrewd imposter (or some mixture of the two), he was dangerous—above all in his dismissal for or disregard of the regular processes of government and constitutional forms. David Broder described him as a "man with a strange mixture of naive, idealistic, cynical and conspiratorial ideas in his head."[11] According to political scientist Harvey Mansfield, "Perot is an unprincipled businessman of the kind Adam Smith warned against. . . . His claimed concern for the country is sincere but unguided as well as unrestrained."[12]

Ross Perot IV emerged when the campaign began collapsing all around him in early July. Suddenly, Perot no longer resembled that "great Colossus who bestrode Rome." He was now cutting a far more modest figure as a "paranoid little ferret," in a not very flattering description by humorist Dave Barry. Perot IV added to the negative view of Perot III the old idea of Perot I that Perot was an amateur, only amateurism now was no longer quaint and positive, but pathetic or threatening. Having been frightened and even bullied by amateurism and outsiderism—monsters they had helped to create—establishment journalists were now circling the wagons against the new foe. In the kind of "tough" images modern journalists love to invoke (often to buffer themselves from charges that they are soft liberals), Perot was pronounced to be "not ready for the big leagues." His amateurism now worked to "explain" not only the failure of the campaign, but also his inability to hang tough and suffer the rigors that the big boys and real players accepted as part of the game.

Only Perot's friends were prepared to see in this fall something that merited understanding, if not compassion. Professional commentators were not so generous. Operating here was also a motive as simple as it is old: revenge. Ross Perot had taken delight in attacking and belittling the "insider" and establishment world of

Washington, with its perks, its "conventional thinking," its "handlers," and its "cosmeticians." Journalists might have applauded this kind of attack, except that Perot had lumped them together with the politicians. Perot's rhetorical assaults, moreover, were laced with "masculine" imagery. He presented himself as the "tough" and manly figure who could deal with the situation, while the insiders (the press included) were weak, ineffective, and sissylike. Perot boasted of his ability to stand tall and of his fortitude in the face of threats from terrorists. If the campaign was getting "rough," as he conceded it was in June, it was nothing to him. Presidential politics was merely "Mickey Mouse tossed salad."[13]

The journalists' courage having been challenged, it is no wonder that their response to his withdrawal was to reply in kind. Two headlines in the popular press tell the story: WHAT A WIMP (*The New York Post*) and CAN-DO CANDIDATE COULDN'T (*The New York Daily News*). The mainstream press was only slightly less restrained. The *Newsweek* cover was entitled simply: QUITTER; a *Washington Post* headline read: "Texan Couldn't Stomach Prospect of Politics."[14] And Tom Brokaw's "take" (as they say) was: "Perot, who promised his followers that he would stand and fight, decided to cut and run."

Stories describing why Perot pulled out focused on his personal weaknesses. *Time* had him wilting under the fire of negative campaigning and whining, "When is this going to be any fun again?"[15] He reportedly "lost heart" after finally analyzing what might actually be required to control the deficit and was unable to "take the heat in the kitchen." Perot himself, in his "postgame" interview on *Larry King Live*, seemed to give the overheated kitchen thesis some credence: "Brutal, brutal, brutal, . . . we've created a system that is so intrusive and brutal and so unrelated to getting the facts straight."[16]

Then, too, there was the sorry plight of the volunteers. Television news treated them a bit like a Greek chorus, ushering them onto the stage at just the right moment to rage and wail at the distant protagonist, who was now depicted as a callous figure on high who played with the lives and fortunes of the common people. Their response to the withdrawal was one of stunned disbelief, followed by feelings of grief or betrayal. As one volunteer commented, "He made fools out of us volunteers, using us for his own ends."[17]

Ross Perot V—the final Perot of the campaign—was born about a week after his reentrance into the race in October and thus some eight months after being conceived on *Larry King Live*, a television first. Though a month premature, Perot V arrived in the nick of time.

This Perot was a product of the public's direct reaction to his person as presented through television interviews, through lengthy half-hour television ads, and especially through the debates. Perot V revived many of the positive qualities of Perot I, although what stood out now was not the mock militarism, but the element of a straight-talking, commonsensical American who cut through the politicians' jargon and disdained the privileges of the political establishment. Just after the Republican convention in August, first President Bush and then Bill Clinton vied—absurdly, when one thinks about it—to cast themselves in the image of Harry Truman. The one who would come closest to claiming Truman's mantle was none other than Ross Perot.

The launching of Ross Perot V was a rescue mission as daring and successful as the one Perot directed for his employees in Iran twelve years earlier. Perot V saved Ross Perot from the obloquy, disgrace, and humiliation of Perot IV. It is difficult to conceive how a person so accomplished and so devoted to his country as Ross Perot could have endured living the rest of his days with the thought that his final public image was that of the nasty and pitiful figure who had exited the stage of American politics in July.

The birth of Perot V did not correspond exactly with Perot's reentrance into the race. For the first week, Perot's campaign met with a reaction that served to reinforce Perot IV. Pollsters reported that Perot had fallen in public estimation, and that the unfavorable reactions (66 percent) were "almost as bad as you would expect from an extremist like David Duke or some politician in the midst of a major political scandal."[18] Perot's new campaign was initially presented by the media as a caricature of the original one. As most commentators saw it, the scam was now up: If you hadn't detected it in the first campaign, Perot was foolish enough to play everything over again, just to make sure you caught on. Was Ross Perot, for example, really listening to the Republican and Democratic party delegations when they crawled to him in Dallas in late September to present their budget plans? Of course not, and everyone could now plainly see that this was only a pretext for capturing national attention. Was Perot's decision to reenter really to be decided by "the people" in those telephone polls? Of course not. It was evident that Perot had already made up his mind, and in any case many of "the people" were paid volunteers. Was Perot really the people's "servant"? The claim brought contemptuous laughter from reporters covering his initial press conference. (Perot would later refine and Americanize this theme, claiming, "I'm Ross, you're the boss.")

So evident had this sham become that most commentators

concluded that the campaign could be safely ignored. But this initial, negative image quickly underwent an amazing transformation. If Bill Clinton could successfully reintroduce himself to the American public in July, after being hidden in May and June in the shadow of Ross Perot, perhaps Ross Perot could do the same in October, after being hidden in August and September by Bill Clinton. Perot could get that "second look" and prove that he was the plain-speaking Texas businessman and outsider he originally claimed to be. (Reintroducing oneself seemed to be a subtext to the 1992 campaign. Bill Clinton did it; Dan Quayle did it; Ross Perot did it. Only George Bush, it seemed, was stuck with himself for the whole campaign.)

Perot's successful reintroduction was assisted by his having a forum—the presidential debates—in which he could appear as an equal with the other two candidates and by the tactical situation of the campaign, which dictated that neither of the two other candidates should initially attack him. The Bush team hoped Perot might somehow shake up the dynamic of a campaign that had remained frozen since Labor Day, while Governor Clinton, comfortably ahead in the polls, dared not risk opening up a second front of opposition to his candidacy.

But if Perot was given a free ride, he proved adept enough to take it. He scored very well in the debates, winning, in the judgment of the American people, the first and third encounters. After the first debate, his resurgence may have been temporarily slowed by Admiral Stockdale's performance in the vice-presidential debate, which wanted in credibility. Still, Stockdale's opening line, "Who am I? Why am I here?," which one observer saw as a blatant appeal to the existentialist vote, will probably remain the most memorable line of the campaign.[19] Perot came back to perform effectively in the final debate, and the refurbishment of his image continued with Perot's talk show appearances and his revolutionary half-hour paid commercials which, contrary to all expectations, were watched in record numbers.

Perot V dominated the last weeks of the campaign, with the exception of one particularly damaging reversion to Perot III, when Perot revealed that the real reason he had left the campaign in July was because of fears that the Republican party, in a *Godfather*-type scenario, planned to disrupt his daughter's marriage. Apart from having no proof of this charge, it undercut Perot's "public-spirited" reason for withdrawing and revived the early summer's charges of paranoia.

Perot V saved more, of course, than his personal reputation.

He also revived a possible future political option for Ross Perot and salvaged something of the Perot movement. Having won a large share of the vote, Perot could now press a claim to be consulted in public dialogue, especially on matters relating to the deficit and (perhaps) campaign and ethics reform. After all, Jesse Jackson with far less political backing emerged from the 1984 and 1988 campaigns as a nonelected spokesman whose views the media often felt obliged to take into account. Of course, Ross Perot's standing inside the media establishment is quite different. But Perot enjoys close ties with the deficit-conscious wing of the Republican party led by Robert Dole and is a logical ally of the bipartisan deficit-reduction movement led by former Senators Rudman and Tsongas.

THE PEROT PHENOMENON: FACT OR FICTION?

We owe a debt to the historian Daniel Boorstin for calling attention to the interesting distinction between a "pseudo" event and a "real" event. By a pseudo event, Boorstin had in mind an event that does not occur within the realm of what, in common understanding, is the concrete world in which things happen. For example, a poll is a pseudo event (nothing real has happened), whereas an election is a real event (someone has actually won or lost an office).[20]

Many today would no doubt object to the absolutist quality of Boorstin's distinction, as it assigns phenomena either to the shadowy realm of nonbeing inside the cave or to the bright realm of reality (or "being") outside of it. Today this kind of distinction seems too rigid. We live in an age in which the line between these two realms is constantly crossed and blurred—in which, for example, high diplomacy is often conducted on television interviews. Still, the idea behind the distinction remains compelling, and it may be helpful to speak of a hierarchy of events that ranges from the less tangible ("pseudo") to the more tangible ("real").

The future historian who surveys the 1992 election will certainly find many tangible signs of Ross Perot's existence: his formation of an impressive organization of volunteers; his name on all of the ballots; his appearance in the national debates with both major candidates; and his vote total. These were all tangible occurrences, clear signs of something real and fairly important.

But to come to grips with the Perot *phenomenon* itself (meaning his campaign in the spring), it is not primarily these tangible signs the historian will have to weigh, but a set of intangible ones.

With the exception of the volunteers, all of the other signs of the phenomenon were "pseudo" events. Indeed, the Perot phenomenon itself, in its entirety, was a massive pseudo event. For in one sense it never really "happened." During the whole period of Perot's first candidacy, up to and including the moment when he withdrew in July, Perot was never actually a declared candidate. Nor was this fact incidental to his success. People enjoyed the luxury of "choosing" an alternative that was not being offered.

The first and most conspicuous of the intangible signs of the Perot phenomenon was the way Perot eventually was treated by others in the political elite. By late spring, both observers and politicians were speaking routinely of a three-person race in 1992. President Bush declared it to be so. So did Governor Clinton. And so did Jesse Jackson, who was seriously dallying with a Perot alliance as late as July. The keynote speaker at the Democratic convention in New York, Governor Zell Miller of Georgia, characterized the upcoming campaign as one with "an aristocrat, an autocrat, and a Democrat."

In fact, to say that Perot was viewed as part of a three-way race is probably an understatement. By late June, many considered it a *two*-way race—between Ross Perot and George Bush. One commentator advised Bush in July to "engage Clinton to keep him in the race; the Democrat has disappeared, and that's bad news for Bush."[21] Abe Rosenthal of the *New York Times* professed himself to be happy Perot was running, because it "made the campaign a two-way race again."[22] The final proof of Perot's stature in the eyes of the other candidates occurred when he suddenly withdrew from the race. Both Bush and Clinton rushed to issue sycophantic statements that virtually accorded Perot the status of "world-class" statesman.

A second indicator of the Perot phenomenon was the scope of news coverage Perot received during the spring and early summer. Researchers will no doubt eventually count the column inches devoted to his campaign, but first impressions surely cannot err in pronouncing the Perot phenomenon one of the great media boomlets of our time. Just flip back, for example, through the major news magazines of the period, and you will see Perot's face on the cover of *Newsweek, Time, U.S. News & World Report, Business Week, Fortune,* not to mention major foreign newsweeklies such as *L'Express, The Economist,* and *Der Spiegel.* Newspaper and television coverage of Perot was also massive. Twice, in fact, Perot managed to upstage the Democratic nominee in events that, by all rights, should have belonged to him. After clinching enough delegates in the last day of the primaries to win his party's nomination, Bill Clinton awoke the next day to headlines that Ross Perot had finished first in that day's exit polls. And the day after Clinton delivered his nomination acceptance speech, the top news story was that Ross Perot had withdrawn from the race.

This brings us to the final and most important of the intangible signs that marked the Perot phenomenon: his "showing" in the polls. It was this showing that was at the source of so much of the media coverage and that helped sustain the elite's conviction that 1992 was a three-person race. Perot's rise in the polls from February to late June was as spectacular as it was unexpected. From a mere blip on the screen in February, Perot's score kept climbing to his extraordinary media-declared exit poll victory in the California primary in June. His first-place "finish" in the polls marked an event that pollster Patrick Caddell called "unprecedented in the history of polling." This "fact"—or pseudo fact—was duly recorded and celebrated with all the solemnity of a world-historical event, like Caesar's crossing the Rubicon.

BEING AND PEROT: THE METAPHYSICS OF THE PEROT PHENOMENON

It was largely on the basis of these three intangible indicators that the conclusion was reached that a full-scale "revolution" had occurred in American electoral politics. So much rests on the polls and their significance that no assessment of the scope of the Perot phenomenon can begin without addressing, at least briefly, the meaning of these polls.

To dismiss the polls as mere "pseudo" phenomena would not do justice to them, as they purportedly tell us about something that has tangibility: the state of public opinion. And certainly the extensive activity by thousands of volunteers was a genuine sign of some kind of movement. But as almost all pollsters will attest, the "reality" of opinion at certain moments, when the public is undecided or is seized momentarily by one humor or another, is itself hardly very substantial. Opinions widely believed to be firm and real may suddenly vanish into thin air.

The analysis of the unreality of certain opinions can be taken a step further. Under some circumstances, the polls and the news commentary about them help to drive "opinion" as much as "opinion" drives the polls. Thus in the case of Ross Perot, the intense coverage and daily discussion of the phenomenon may have helped create it. The high (or low) point of this process was the earlier-noted priority in coverage given by the major media to their exit polls, rather than the real event of the primary election results.

This line of speculation poses another question, as important and as metaphysical as that of the "reality" of certain opinions. That question is whether an opinion manufactured in the sense just noted can begin to acquire reality by virtue of its being said to exist. In other words, in the case at hand, could the manufacturing of a "Perot phenomenon" in the media actually have created a real "Perot phenomenon" at the polls?

Here there are two schools of thought. One is that a manufactured opinion or pseudo event, by virtue of its being artificial, is destined to flounder when it meets the test of reality. It will crash, showing itself to be as insubstantial as the thin air out of which it was created. Under this view, criticism of the media for promoting these "opinions," while perhaps well deserved, is not in the end very important. Polls and news-driven opinions are mere phantoms that may temporarily divert us. The most these manufactured opinions "do" is sustain the now well-established industry of interpreting opinion, as well as the start-up industry of criticizing the interpreting of opinion.

A second school of thought contends that it is possible for manufactured opinion to become real—to cross the metaphysical line from nonbeing to being—or at any rate to remain in effect long enough to affect reality. Polls and media-driven opinions thus constitute a genuine problem, as they may impinge on or displace other processes of opinion formation, such as discussion, political rhetoric, assessments of interest, and even elections. Pollocracy—a system in which poll-driven opinions acquire substantial influence over electoral and political processes—looms as a great danger. Earl Shorris gave this idea one of its clearest expressions in 1978: "For the sake of the illusion of power the press has inflated the importance of the polls to such a degree that the political nature of the nation may be permanently changed and the ability of government to exercise its constitutional function permanently damaged."[23]

There is merit in the views of both schools of thought. Pseudo opinions do indeed tend to show their unsubstantiality, and this is part of what eventually happened to the Perot phenomenon. And yet, this kind of collapse is not inevitable, and everyone can think of instances when manufactured opinions have succeeded in carrying the day. It is the seriousness, if not necessarily the frequency, of this possibility that warrants its consideration as a major problem for political and electoral institutions. An important aim of the electoral process traditionally has been to arrange the presidential selection process so as to deter—or, at any rate, avoid succumbing to the worst effects of—pollocracy and its close cousin, political demagoguery. The Perot phenomenon raises these concerns anew.

THE IMMACULATE EXPLANATION

The claim on behalf of the "unprecedented" scope of the Perot movement did not end with the mere identification and description of the Perot phenomenon, for that phenomenon had to be explained. In the modern science of political explanation it is a virtual law that a momentous occurrence must be the result of a deep cause. And so it was said to be. The Perot phenomenon flowed ultimately from a major institutional change. A chorus of commentators declared, "The two-party system is dying."

By accepting too readily the existence of the Perot phenomenon, one is thus locked into finding a major cause. Where the alleged cause is more important than the effect, the usually harmless journalistic-academic industry of explaining has its dangers. It is no small thing today to begin thinking in terms of the "death" of the two-party system, for that conclusion could very easily have an impact on proposals for major reforms.

Our view of the scope of the Perot phenomenon is far more limited. Of course something important was happening during the spring campaign, of which Perot's strong showing in the fall offers an indication. But the "phenomenon" was greatly exaggerated by pollsters, journalists, and academics, often for reasons of professional bias or ideological interest. So while we shall examine the causes of the Perot movement, we shall be skeptical of claims of an imminent collapse of the parties as the generally recognized institutions for screening presidential aspirants.

There is, of course, no lack of evidence today showing that the two major parties are weaker than they once were and that they structure the opinions and voting behavior of fewer voters. Nor does anyone dispute that the transformation of the nominating process, along with the character of the modern media, have led voters to believe that "one should vote for the candidate, not the party."[24] But these responses were all given in a context in which the "candidate" was either a Democrat or a Republican, and it is only by inference that the candidate-centered focus of our politics can be said to have progressed already to a point where an independent begins on a near-equal footing with the candidates of the major parties. What evidence can be marshaled, then, in behalf of the inference that parties are dying as the presumptive agents of nomination? The answer some offer is Perot's showing in the polls from May through July, which is hardly a very compelling case.

There is an alternative interpretation of what the 1992 election shows us about the continuing pull of partisan attachment and about how it operates. Consider what actually occurred in late June and early July. Perot began a rapid slide in the polls. This slide, which precipitated his withdrawal, coincided with the Democrats' completion of their selection process, the healing of some of the party's wounds, and the partial rehabilitation of their nominee. As this process occurred, as the party in Ross Perot's words became "revitalized," a large number of voters began to return to the party fold. If a party with a candidate who at that moment was still considered to be extremely weak can, merely by the act of coming together and sounding the party tocsin, drive down a large portion of an independent's following, then the pull of the political party hardly seems negligible. There is every reason, moreover, to think that the same thing would have taken place the next month at the Republican convention, when Republicans began to rally around George Bush. Just as Perot lost a part of his Democratic following in July, so he would have lost a part of his Republican base in August.

All this is another indication that there may never have been "a Perot phenomenon" in a real sense. It began to fade as soon as it encountered the force of party attachment.

Let us not overstate the case, however. The attachment to parties is not what it once was—a fact that undoubtedly opens up certain opportunities for independent candidacies. There are more independent voters in the electorate than there were years ago, and independents were more inclined than the rest of the electorate to indicate support for Perot in the spring and to vote for him in the fall. (Thirty percent of declared independents gave Perot their vote as compared to half that amount for partisan identifiers.) But these facts are still very far from supporting hasty conclusions about the death of parties as the normal, presumptive screening mechanisms for presidential selection. The tether of party attachment may be looser than it once was, voters may drift further away from their moorings, and more effort may be needed to reel them back in. But for now at least, most voters are still bound in some way to the major parties.

It is possible to respond by saying that Perot's slide in the polls had less to do with a resurgence of partisan loyalty than with the spate of negative news coverage that began to surface in June (Perot III) and with the mistakes Perot made. In this view, if Perot had only been a better candidate and avoided his "unforced" errors, he might have succeeded in remaining viable and keeping it a three-person race. But even this line of thinking, which we find quite plausible, does not fully support the "death of party" thesis. Is it not possible to think of third-party candidates in previous campaigns who, if they had run a flawless campaign, could have remained viable and kept it a three-person race? Certainly FDR feared that Huey Long had this potential. And—to look at the same point from another angle—consider just how many flaws the two major-party candidates were able to overcome and yet hang on to finish far ahead of Perot.

Finally, many prominent analysts touting the scope of the Perot phenomenon were not exactly disinterested observers, but had ulterior motives. The "Perot phenomenon" served as a convenient rhetorical battering ram in a long-standing campaign to undermine the two-party system. At the forefront of this movement in academia stands Theodore Lowi, who has identified the two-party system as "a nineteenth century relic confined largely to Anglo-American tradition [that] has failed to adjust to the requirements of modern twentieth century democratic government."[25] Among experts from the political elite who were often cited in the press is former presidential candidate John Anderson, who is "frustrated with a two-party duopoly," and for whom its demise would retrospectively vindicate his own role as an independent candidate in 1980 and qualify him as the prophet of a new era, a John the Baptist to Ross Perot's mission of redemption.

CONTEXTUAL CAUSES OF THE PEROT MOVEMENT

If we resist the idea of a massive Perot phenomenon caused by a collapsed party system, we must still explain an important Perot movement in the spring and a significant Perot vote in the fall. Two types of causes can be identified: contextual factors and political factors. The contextual factors—lowered institutional barriers for new parties, easier media access, and money—come to light in comparing Perot's campaign with other recent third-party candidacies and observing certain advantages it enjoyed.

First is an easing of the legal barriers to the entrance of a third-party candidacy that has taken place over the past quarter century. To meet Perot's February challenge of being put on the ballot in all fifty states (plus the District of Columbia) required no small amount of organizational effort and money. Still, Perot's task here was not as demanding as that faced by George Wallace in 1968 and John Anderson in 1980. A large part of the early effort and money of those campaigns was devoted to getting on the ballots (which at the time was more difficult) and to engaging in protracted legal battles and constitutional challenges to some of the states' highly restrictive ballot access laws. Perot was freed of such efforts. As John Anderson noted, "My 1980 campaign was obliged to use its front-end money in legal battles to simply get on the ballot. These battles were won and the precedents stand, helping future candidates. . . ."[26]

A related issue, having implications of institutional access, was Perot's inclusion in the presidential debates. Perot was the first third-party candidate to appear in a presidential debate with both other major-party candidates. (Anderson appeared in one debate, but only with Ronald Reagan.) It is questionable whether Perot met the bipartisan debate commission's stated criterion of having a reasonable chance to win, but the real reason he was invited was a political judgment on the part of the Bush campaign that it wanted him there.

A second contextual cause that contributed to the Perot vote is a transformation that has taken place in the structure of the media since 1980. With the advent of cable television and the proliferation of "infotainment" talk shows that feature interviews and discussions with prominent individuals, there are more opportunities for a prominent personality to reach the American public. These shows served as Perot's early primaries or caucuses. Perot's rating "victories" then gave him the momentum to appear on the major network infotainment shows, such as *Good Morning America* and the *Today Show*, which in one instance allowed him a full two hours to answer viewer questions. Access to the public in the media is no longer controlled, as it once virtually was, by the major news journalists, who stood like self-appointed gatekeepers between the candidates and the public. This new "channel" of access presumably will remain open to other major third-party candidates in the future.

A third factor is money—in the form of personal wealth. Ross Perot, of course, has lots of money, and he ended up spending what (for any ordinary mortal) is an incomprehensible sum—about $60 million. Because he was not in the final campaign nearly as long as the other candidates (and spent very little traveling around and organizing rallies), Perot was able to concentrate his resources and outspend the other two candidates by a considerable margin at the end of the campaign.

Perot's personal wealth obviously gave his campaign an enormous advantage over the campaigns of George Wallace and John Anderson. Perot was freed from soliciting money and thus could avoid the role of appearing to be a supplicant to any special interests. By the use of his personal funds, Perot, under the terms of campaign finance legislation, also disqualified himself from accepting public funds after the election, as well as from receiving any public funding for the 1996 election. This refusal of public funding keeps the "movement" very much in his own hands.

The importance of Perot's private wealth for the success of his campaign, though considerable, was not as great as one might think. Neither Perot's standing in the polls during the spring, nor his vote in the fall, was bought. In fact, during the period of Perot's spectacular rise in the polls in the spring, he spent—relatively speaking, of course—very little money. His wealth at this point helped him less because he was spending it than because he had made it himself (which was a leading point in his personal biography) and because he had it (which convinced others that he would have the staying power to run a "world-class" campaign, rather than a shoestring operation). Perot's access to the public at this time came entirely from the huge chunks of free television time and press coverage he received. Perot found booking national talk shows no more difficult than—well—Mickey Mouse tossed salad.

Perot's spending paradoxically increased after he withdrew from the race in July. Much of his funds at this point went to financing the volunteer organization *United We Stand, America*, headed by Orson Swindle. The main idea at this point seemed to be to keep the cause alive, if not also to silence criticisms that he had betrayed the volunteers. But Perot was also keeping the campaign going, and a good deal of money was spent on completing petition requirements in some of the states, particularly New York. Indeed, during this time, the whole organization was being tightened and made more dependent on Perot's financial support. As one report commented, "the grass roots of Mr. Perot's campaign are heavily watered by Mr. Perot himself."[27]

Even in the fall campaign, however, Perot's resurgence was not mainly attributable to the money he spent, at least not initially. Once again it was the free television, especially in the presidential debates, that was most important. It was not until after the debates, in the last two weeks of the campaign, that Perot opened the flood-

gates and began his massive spending campaign in the national media—
evidently with some success.

Perot's huge spending at this point ironically belies many of
the usual charges associated with the use of big money in political
campaigns. For many, the very mention of the words "media" and
"money" conjures up the idea of slick ads that unfairly discredit
opponents, appeal to emotions, and rely on subliminal reactions. Perot's
half-hour and hour-long programs, during which he personally lec-
tured the public on the nation's problems, were the antithesis of this
model. Even his short spots, which consisted of nonpictorial textual
statements read by a narrator, appeared to be paragons of rational
persuasion. Although some complained that Perot's media campaign
was in fact the ultimate ad trick—a scheme that avoided slick when
slick was "out" and that merely stated problems without ever developing any solutions—the fact remains that Perot's ads met and surpassed all the "external" criteria for rational persuasion that good
government groups propose to clean up campaign advertising.

THE POLITICAL FACTORS

Although contextual causes facilitated Perot's rise, the main
sources for Perot's support were found in three political factors: the
low standing of the major-party candidates; the existence of gridlock
(in conjunction with a weak economy); and a fertile ground for an
appeal to outsiderism. The first of these causes is short term and
situational. The gridlock may dissipate, if not disappear altogether,
with the election of a Democratic president to go along with a
Democratic Congress. The strength of the last cause, which is politically determined and thus contingent, holds the key to the future
of the Perot movement.

The first political factor, the condition of the standing of the
major candidates, calls attention to certain very strong parallels between
the elections of 1980 and 1992. In both election years, there were
incumbents who by April were viewed as ineffective—Carter overall (and perhaps especially in foreign affairs) and Bush in regard to
the voters' dominant concern about management of the economy.
For voters inclined to reject the incumbent, the normal two-party
system thus offered only one option for change. In both elections,
there was considerable feeling early on that the choice of the out-
party candidate (Reagan and Clinton) was weak or unacceptable. As
Thomas Edsall remarked in July: "The ratios of voters' negative to

positive evaluations of the two major party choices, President Bush
and Arkansas Governor Bill Clinton, are worse at this stage of the
campaign than in any other presidential race in the history of polling."[28] In short, in 1992 as in 1980, there was a "space" for a third
candidate. This space was not ideological, but provided opportunities for a candidate who could offer the hope of supplying more
effective leadership and taking on the "system." Perot stressed his
personal ability to "get the job done" and "to clean out the barn."
To the extent, obviously, that the perceived weakness of the major-
party candidates was the cause of the independent vote in both 1980
and 1992, there is a question about the future prospect of the Perot
movement. By 1984, with Ronald Reagan having proved his competence, John Anderson vanished as an option.

The second political factor that contributed to the Perot movement was the existence of "gridlock." Gridlock refers to a situation
in which the federal government seems unable to take decisive action
of any sort because of fundamental differences between the president and Congress. Gridlock in this sense has been a major concern
of political analysts since 1981, especially on matters of budget politics
and management of the economy. But the matter became important
to the general public during the period of extended economic weakness in the Bush presidency, when action of some kind was widely
seen to be needed. While President Bush did not always have a coherent
plan on the table (and then did not always vigorously support the
plans he had), it was still the case that Congress almost uniformly
blocked his programs from mid-1991 on. Frustration at inaction was
reflected in opinion poll after opinion poll, and in the speeches and
comments of more and more politicians.

The possibility (though not the necessity) of gridlock inheres
in our constitutional scheme of separation of powers, in which the
policymaking power is divided between the president and the Congress. Overcoming gridlock therefore depends on the president being
compatible with a majority in Congress on the general direction of
public policy. This compatibility is possible with a president working with the other party, but is more easily achieved when the same
party controls both branches. Reversing this proposition, a short-
hand statement for the cause of gridlock is "divided government,"
a situation in which the president and Congress are in the hands of
different parties. In this circumstance, the engines of partisanship in
each branch have a vested interest in preventing action and annoy-
ing and embarrassing the other branch, beyond what is entailed by

their real policy differences. Gridlock, in this view, is almost always a partisan phenomenon.

When Republicans began planning the campaign in 1991, they had high hopes that gridlock could be used as a major theme. The cause of gridlock, in the Republican view, was the Congress, specifically the Democratic majority in Congress which had been there too long and was guilty of serious abuses of privilege. The object was to end gridlock by ending divided government. When Ross Perot emerged as a force in the spring, relying on public frustration with gridlock as one of his main springboards, Vice President Quayle took a calculated risk and sought to defend the quasi-constitutional status of the two-party system—Democrat as well as Republican—against Perot's independent challenge. According to Quayle, the best solution to gridlock—indeed, the only solution—was for citizens to vote for the same party to control both the presidency and Congress, whether Republican or Democratic.

The changing fortunes of the campaign, however, soon made this argument untenable for the Republicans. By late summer, it had become clear that the Democrats would probably control the Congress, no matter what happened in the presidential race. To persist in Quayle's argument would thus implicitly be to argue for a vote for Clinton. While speakers in the first three days of the Republican national convention continued the Quayle line of attack, Bush himself began in his acceptance speech to modulate the Republican position, arguing that gridlock was only partly "partisan" in character. It was related to a particular configuration of Democrats in the Congress, and the large number of new members to be elected, Republican or Democrat, would help end it.

Bill Clinton also spoke of gridlock, naturally blaming it more on the presidency and (since he wasn't part of it) on "brain-dead Washington politics." Yet Clinton was even less anxious than President Bush to identify gridlock purely with "partisan" gridlock, for he did not wish to tie himself too closely to the Democratic party, especially its congressional wing. Though nominated by the Democratic party, Clinton was also running during much of the early part of the campaign for the nomination of the outsider party. However much Clinton in the end might eventually need to govern with congressional Democrats, for the moment they had to be kept at arms length—or beyond.

Despite the efforts of both major parties to capture this issue, it was Ross Perot who made the most of gridlock. What Perot could offer, far more even than Clinton, was his distance as an outsider.

If gridlock was caused by Washington politics and the constant bickering of the two parties, then by definition a candidate not only from outside Washington, but from beyond the two parties, was not responsible. As an electoral appeal, certainly, this innocence was reason for many to think that Perot would be the best person to resolve the problem. Yet how he might resolve it was never quite as clear. Perot's answer—not entirely implausible—was that the way to end gridlock was to go beyond partisanship. His own election would be such an extraordinary event that members of Congress would be unable to miss the signal. "Elect me," as Perot loved to say, "and you will see Congress and the White House dancing like Ginger Rogers and Fred Astaire used to dance." And there was no question about who would be taking the lead.

The third and most important political cause of the Perot vote was his ability to tap into the loose and vague "outsider" sentiment. This sentiment could clearly be connected to the frustration with gridlock in 1992, but it goes beyond it. Outsiderism as an appeal fosters the image of a governmental system flawed in its structure, its personnel, and its spirit. Government has lost touch with the people as a result of some form of corruption, whether it stems from a selling out to special interests and foreign governments or from the use of government privileges to keep and hold office. The only way the system can be saved is by a movement or crusade from the outside that "cleans the barn." Being on the outside is thus a moral position more than a political one. It is this position that reassures people that the outsider can be trusted to "just do it," even if he cannot say exactly how. The central appeal of such a campaign must thus be to reinforce continually the symbolic point of being different and unconventional.

Even though the problem of gridlock and the problem of insiderism are not the same, it is still possible that ending gridlock might succeed in muting the appeal of outsiderism. If people come to believe more in party accountability and have the sense that they can blame a party and hold it responsible for failure, then perhaps this feeling will help absorb some of the animus against insiderism. Only time will tell.

But a remedy in any case is not the same as a cause. And there is no question that Ross Perot's appeal in 1992 was founded on his "outsider" theme. Perot became the nominee of the outsider party, evoking a modern tradition of outsiderism that can be traced back to Jimmy Carter's 1976 campaign. It is not by accident, then, that the three horsemen who helped devise Carter's 1976 campaign all felt a strange attraction to Ross Perot. There was Patrick Caddell, Carter's pollster and the patron saint of angry outsiderism and alienation. Caddell gave Perot a very close look-see, but then decided not to bite, casting his lot instead with Jerry Brown. There was Gerald Rafshoon, Carter's media adviser and master promoter of soft-sell outsiderism. He worked a while for Perot but left the campaign early, frightened off—or so he claimed—by aspects of Perot's character. Finally, there was Hamilton Jordan, Carter's campaign manager and the tactical genius of outsider warfare. Jordan became one of Perot's two official campaign managers in the spring campaign.

Just in case the connection between these two "outsider" movements escaped notice, Gerald Rafshoon decided to point it out for the sake of history in a *Washington Post* op-ed:

> Like Jimmy Carter, I thought, Ross Perot was nonideological, essentially moderate, pragmatic. . . . A lot of people who rang doorbells for Jimmy Carter were circulating petitions for Ross Perot 16 years later. Hell, the two men even looked alike.[29]

The look-alike claim may be an exaggeration, unless you can equate teeth with ears.

Ross Perot was the last and the purest of the outsiders of 1992. For Perot was the only candidate not burdened at all with having had a political career, the only one therefore who could truly claim to step in from the outside and heal the process. Up to Perot, outsiderism was bipartisan, having a home in both the Republican party (Duke and Buchanan) and the Democratic party (Tsongas and Brown). Perot made outsiderism nonpartisan, or rather transformed it into a movement beyond the insider dimension. As the pure outsider—outside the parties altogether—Perot at his rare best also knew how to give effective expression to the plain, commonsense voice of the people in a way that contrasted with the wooden jargon of the policy wonk ("grow the economy"), and the pompous eloquence of the speech writer ("a thousand points of light").

PEROT: AN OUTSIDER FIGHTING TO GET IN

As much as Perot benefited from being an outsider, it nevertheless seemed to him and his campaign in May that the key to winning the presidency was to modify his outsider image. If pure outsiderism gave him his initial boost, it also imposed a ceiling on how high the campaign could go. For as much as people may prefer an outsider, they also want assurance that the outsider would in fact be able to accomplish something once inside—that he had the steadiness, reliability, and skills of a politician, without being a politician. Perot's basic strategic challenge during the spring campaign thus became, at a certain point, the opposite of Bill Clinton's. Clinton was an insider seeking to get outside, whereas Perot was an outsider seeking to get inside.

The importance of "getting in" explains the most fateful decision of the Perot campaign, one which was responsible for taking it to its heights and, at least indirectly, of bringing it crashing to the ground. This was the announcement on June 3 that Perot was hiring as campaign managers two persons recognized as major insider players: Republican strategist Ed Rollins and Democratic strategist Hamilton Jordan. News of this bold move sent tremors through the political establishment in Washington, as many now for the first time took seriously the possibility of a Perot presidency. The aftershock Washington then feared was the naming of a major political figure as a vice-presidential candidate, someone who would give the campaign new respectability. Many names were bandied about in the press— Jeane Kirkpatrick, Colin Powell, and even Jack Kemp. But Perot never succeeded in landing a true candidate before the campaign collapsed—a failure, incidentally, that probably imposed a ceiling on the fall campaign.

The collapse of Perot's campaign in July, insofar as it was due to self-inflicted causes, involved the very professionals who had been hired to guide it to victory. By the middle of June, as the negative image (Perot III) began to take hold inside the media, Rollins (with Jordan's concurrence) insisted it was now time for the professionals to actively assume "normal" campaign control to save the campaign: Perot must not permit himself to be defined by the media, he had to define himself—or rather his campaign had to define him. The key element of Rollins' plan was a major ad campaign in July produced by ad man Hal Riney, who had done the Reagan "feel good" Morning in America commercials in the 1984 campaign. Rollins also wanted to screen Perot's appearances and determine his schedule. In a word, Rollins now wanted to institute "managed outsiderism," reining in an insurgency campaign with traditional techniques.

Perot, however, balked. He followed his own instincts, rejecting the Riney ads as too expensive (meaning, probably, too "professional" or "inside"). As Rollins later complained, "He wouldn't use the tools everyone else used. When we tried to explain those tools and explain you couldn't get there without them, he just couldn't go forward."[30] Perot's rejection of Rollins' plan (which had been presented to Perot as an ultimatum) led Rollins to resign, which in turn led to Perot's withdrawal. At the time, with Perot's standing in the polls rapidly declining anyhow, success seemed impossible. If there was uneasiness in the public about an unproven outsider being able to manage the government, surely it was confirmed by Perot's inability to manage his own campaign.

Rollins, out of a job he had taken at great risk to his insider career, immediately sought to write the history of the Perot campaign to his own advantage. Perot failed because he would not "come inside." It was at this point, too, that Perot IV emerged and that commentators began publicly to assail "amateurism" and "outsiderism" and contrast them unfavorably with "professionalism" and being "inside." As Molly Ivins wrote, "Watching someone without political skills try to run for public office sure as hell increased my respect for political skills."[31] Ross Perot, who had just taken outsiderism to its summit, now seemed responsible for burying it.

At least at the tactical level, however, there is a question about whose judgment at the time was better, Rollins' or Perot's. Think of this: How would people have reacted to glossy image commercials produced by the same ad man associated with one of the "emptiest" of all national campaign appeals? Perot's invaluable outsider image rested on his vaunted ability to "tell it like it is": "If you ever see me doing photo opportunities, have me led away." Perhaps Perot's closest adviser in the spring campaign, Thomas Luce, had it correct: "I'm not convinced ads will do that much. . . . I'm not discounting the importance of what Ed Rollins and Hamilton Jordan can do, but I really believe that if this is a unique time in American history, Ross will be president, and if it's not, he won't be."[32]

This whole issue of the best tactics remains moot. On the one hand, when Perot came back into the race in October, he proved that it is possible to run a nontraditional campaign quite effectively. (His key mistake—the wedding conspiracy charge—was not related to his outsider appeal, although it did reflect a campaign wanting in professional political judgment). But on the other hand, the fall campaign really was never more than a third-party campaign seeking to make a good showing. Rollins and Jordan in June had been interested in winning, not in beating Teddy Roosevelt's mark in 1912.

The main point, however, is not whether Perot or Rollins was right in late June or early July. It is that Perot had put himself in a no-win situation: keeping Rollins was for him impossible, while firing him would destroy the campaign. As Jim Squires, Perot's media adviser, so aptly put it, "The Perot presidential express was in effect undone by a Trojan horse of his own making."[33] Perot, in short, did not have an effective strategy for making the transition from pure outsider to a viable politician with an outsider appeal. Such a transition, admittedly an enormously difficult (if not impossible) political tightrope act, proved a feat well beyond Ross Perot's abilities—an assessment shared by both his supporters and his detractors. Ambition should be made of sterner stuff.

PEROT AND THE MEDIA

Few candidates complained more about the media than Ross Perot. Yet perhaps no candidate ever benefited so much from it. Perot's hostility toward journalists was never very far beneath the surface. He seemed to relate to members of the Fourth Estate about as well as Richard Nixon did. Near the end of the campaign, he told reporters: "You guys hate that I'm in the race; you're acting like jerks."[34] He was probably correct on both counts.

Perot's relationship to the media is important not just from the standpoint of its political impact on the 1992 campaign, but from a longer-term—some prefer to say "institutional"—perspective. For whatever the political effect of the media on any particular campaign, it will be around as a major player in future elections. Its importance, at least as some judge it, is summed up in the following comment of James David Barber: "The media in the United States are the new political parties."[35]

As some grammarians like to point out, "media" is a plural, not a singular, noun (a technicality we have chosen to ignore). But this point at least serves as a reminder that the media contains different "channels" of communication to the public. In the case of presidential politics, there are two such channels, which we distinguish by their function in the campaign, not by the technology employed (e.g., print, radio, or television). Channel I is the medium through which the candidates communicate more or less directly with the American people. It includes the debates, paid advertising, the airing or printing of the candidates' speeches (as at the convention), and interviews (especially talk show interviews that allow the candidate a very broad range). Channel II consists of the presentation and interpretation of the candidates and the campaign in the news, news analysis, commentary, and editorials. This channel is distinguished by the fact that the information does not come directly from the candidates, but is mediated by someone else. Traditionally, this mediating function has been performed by the nation's major mainstream journalists from the networks and the nation's main newspapers and news magazines, although this year there was more internal competition inside this channel from the tabloids (print and TV), from local reporters, and from radio talk show programs. (The tabloids laundered the Gennifer Flowers story for the mainline media, while Rush Limbaugh and other radio commentators challenged the previous monopoly of the prestigious media "tribunes.")

What occurred in 1992 was not a lessening of the power or influence of the media—far from it—but a shift in the relative importance of the two channels in favor of Channel I. Those who lost power, accordingly, were the mainstream journalists, who were also under greater pressure from competition inside their own channel. Ross Perot (along with Bill Clinton) helped lead this shift to Channel I, and Perot's campaign in particular benefited immensely from this new point of access. Channel I allowed Perot to take his campaign to the people against the establishment, which included the media elite.

As significant as this shift in influence was, however, it is still limited. Channel II—the "mediated" channel of news and interpretation—still commands most of the attention, and the media tribunes remain at the center of media power. The story of Perot's relationship to the media, therefore, must include a discussion of his treatment on Channel II.

The mediating function of Channel II has two major properties. The first flows from the activity of producing and disseminating news. The selecting, processing, and presenting of information by the news is not neutral, but reflects a bias of what is important or newsworthy. According to Thomas Patterson, "Press values produce their own news agenda."[36] Foremost among these "news values" is the premium placed on what is new—on an event or occurrence that deviates from a usual pattern or previous expectation.[37] It is all the better when this event or occurrence does not happen all at once, but unfolds over time, allowing news and news commentary to play a role in moving and shaping the event. The news becomes part of its own story.

News thus emphasizes or favors movement or change, albeit movement and change in no particular direction as measured by any substantive standard. News has a mildly provocative quality and effect. Although the tone of tightly controlled hysteria projected by certain

American network anchors goes beyond what the function of news requires, news, virtually by its very nature, imports a different set of values or biases into any political process in which it comes to play a prominent role. Herein, in fact, lies the deepest effect of the media on the political system: As news coverage gains in influence over the processes of decisionmaking in any particular institutional setting, its biases replace those that were there before. In the electoral process, the replacement of party decisionmaking by a system deeply affected by news is one of the causes for the emergence of "outsiderism." Electoral institutions traditionally promoted stability by imposing barriers against those who would seek to ride to power on a temporary wave of opinion. As the media displaced parties, these barriers have been weakened.

Ross Perot was the new story par excellence of 1992. What else could one mean by labeling his campaign a "phenomenon"? Day after day, this story unfolded and gathered momentum, preoccupying all of the serious analysis, defying all odds, and building on itself. It was perfect news. Oddly enough, however, the press never had "fun" with this story. Many journalists sensed that Perot as the outsider and declared foe of the press was usurping some of their own authority in American politics, which relies on some characteristics of outsiderism.

The second property connected with the activity of the press in the presidential selection process today pertains to the "responsibility" they have (or are imputed to have) to screen the candidates. According to two leading experts of the media, "The media have moved well beyond the role of simply providing information, especially in the long, drawn-out contests for presidential nominations. Their reporting of such events has become increasingly interpretive and judgmental. Reporters now perform the once quintessential party tasks of evaluating the candidates, appraising their suitability and setting standards of success and failure."[38]

While some in the media embrace this "responsibility," others disclaim playing any such role, other than as it may flow incidentally from their reporting the news "as it is." The difference here cannot be resolved by saying that deliberate screening should be restricted to editorials. In reality, the greatest source of the journalists' power comes through news and news analysis, not through editorials and commentary. It is the news story, not the editorial, that every candidate fears. For when presenting a story, journalists (ostensibly) are not just speaking in their own name, but purport to report some objective truth.

Reporting, unlike editorializing, must be bounded by the facts of a story, which constrain the journalist. Still, "going with a story" involves a good deal of discretion. If, collectively, journalists select stories at least partly with a view to hurting certain candidates and promoting others, doing so because of their assessment of the qualities of the candidates, they are then using the news as an instrument to "filter" or "screen" candidates in some meaningful sense. After all, this was the meaning of filtering and screening when it was exercised previously by party leaders: they made judgments about the candidates and then used their power to apply those judgments.

It is on this score that Ross Perot believed he had a quarrel with the media. For there is no question that, after the happy days of Perot I, most media tribunes had come to the conclusion that Ross Perot was not temperamentally fit to be president. Many of them said so. As their scrutiny began in earnest, they found the stories to corroborate this view (and they arguably did not even begin to scratch the surface). Yet Perot was no doubt correct in sensing that the journalists were looking to get him—to find the stories that would confirm their judgment. At the same time Perot was enjoying the attention of the media as the "phenomenon" of 1992, he was also becoming a target—or so he thought—of the journalists' collective judgment that he was dangerous. One notices here a clear difference between the press's treatment of John Anderson in 1980 and Ross Perot in 1992. John Anderson, mini-phenomenon of 1980, was a favorite of the media, while Ross Perot, mega-phenomenon of 1992, was intensely mistrusted.

Perot used his access to Channel I (direct communication) to deflect these attacks from Channel II (mediated news), seeking to inoculate himself from any negative stories by alleging a conspiracy by the media (duped by the Republicans) to destroy him. This strategy worked for some time, to the frustration of many media tribunes. At one point Sam Donaldson reportedly told Larry King, "Once I get Perot, I'll destroy him." King replied "Sam, if you destroy him, he'll go up 20 points. The media will help him by knocking him."[39] The success of Perot's tactic of outflanking the media tribunes prompted one political scientist to observe, "Perot is doing to the media, with the aid of the media, what the media have done to the political parties."[40]

THE FOURTH ESTATE: BYE-BYE?

The extensive development in 1992 of Channel I has led some analysts to intensive soul searching about the role of the media as an "institution" in American politics. What worries some is that a dangerous candidate can now circumvent one of the last remaining screens or filters in the presidential selection system (the "responsible" press) and take his case directly to the people via "infotainment" programs. While one might applaud this sentiment, it is hard to take seriously the idea that the "responsible press" in fact performs a screening or filtering role, or that if it does, it performs this role in a defensible way.

The press cannot really perform a screening role effectively because its chief instrument of power is reporting the news, which on the whole tends to favor outsiderism and soft popular leadership. To the extent that media tribunes may attempt to go further and handicap candidates by selecting news stories in a way that favors good candidates and damages dangerous ones, their judgment is subject to question. The same power that they may use to strike at dangerous candidates can also be used to undermine legitimate ones. The same thing, of course, might be said of any "elite" group that plays a screening function—for example, party leaders at the conventions of years gone by. But unlike the party bosses, no political process selected the press corps, and at least half the public, including most conservatives, believes that the press corps cannot be trusted to use its "discretionary" authority fairly. Conservatives are virtually unanimous in thinking that the press corps uses its discretionary authority on balance against their viewpoint, commonly identifying conservative candidates as extreme or dangerous.

The media may have taken the place of the parties, but that does not mean that the media can perform the function of parties. When parties lost out to the media, something of institutional value was also lost to the American political system. The same cannot be said for the decline of the media tribunes' power. On balance, then, there is probably more to applaud than to lament in the opening up of Channel I. Admittedly, this channel provides a new point of access that may give a dangerous candidate a voice he or she might not otherwise have. The risk is that this access is granted without having to pass any threshold other than piquing the fascination of some talk show hosts, who already have more airtime on their hands than odd or unconventional guests to fill it. But Channel I also provides a check on a press corps that has no legitimate claim to exercise any institutional role as a "screen."

Even if one rejects this view, however, the press corps' previous screening role cannot be saved. For the press corps owed this role to the accident of occupying a particular position at a particular stage in the technological development of communications. That stage is now passing. No one ever "founded" the press corps as a political institution. Nor does this institution have any real constituency, other than some reporters, big networks, and certain schools of journalism. No one is going to fight to maintain the institutional prerogatives of the press corps. No candidate would hesitate going around and undermining this "institution" if it suited his or her interests. The media became an institutional player by virtue of a technological circumstance, a circumstance that can now be modified as easily as adding twenty channels to the cable TV menu.

THE PEROT CANDIDACY AND AMERICA'S ELECTORAL INSTITUTIONS

Perot's candidacy was often praised during the spring, even by detractors, for sending the "message" that something was radically wrong in American politics. Yet if Perot deserves credit as the messenger of dissatisfaction, does it follow that the electoral institutions should reward the messenger with the keys to the realm?

This is the direction in which many would take us, either deliberately or inadvertently. For example, when Ross Perot began his campaign, John Anderson led a familiar assault on the electoral college system for its alleged unfairness to third-party candidacies:

> Frustrated with a two-party duopoly, many feel that they are without real choices and real voices; they wonder what to do next. It doesn't have to be this way. We could make it simpler for new candidates like Ross Perot to run and to allow supporters of these candidates to vote their true beliefs. . . . In 1980 I ran for president as an independent . . . for a time my standing in the polls was 20%. Yet in the end I only received about 7% of the vote. It wasn't because all those voters stopped supporting me. It was because many calculated that I couldn't win and that a vote for me would be wasted.[41]

Others, concerned more about the difficulties connected with an electoral college deadlock and a House election, appeared before a Senate committee in the summer to propose "simplifying" the entire system. A frequent suggestion was to abolish the electoral college and select the president by a direct popular vote, with a runoff election if no candidate receives more than 40 percent in the first round.

What so many were forgetting in their concern for "fairness" or "simplification" is another objective of the presidential selection system. Traditionally, that system—meaning the institutions for both nomination and election—has been asked to perform a moderating role in American politics. It has done so by placing temporary hurdles in the way of new movements founded on recently discovered currents of opinions, and by erecting barriers against candidates who indulge in demagogic appeals and employ what the founding fathers contemptuously referred to as the "little arts of popularity."

How far the presidential selection system can and should go in performing this moderating function, and what methods can be employed to do it, have long been issues of dispute. Because the selection process is not a formal governmental institution (like Congress), but a looser set of arrangements that manage an election, the tendency has been to argue that the screening prerogatives of electoral institutions should be limited. After all, the purpose of an election is not so much to restrain as to reflect. Elections are the appropriate occasion for the public to express its will and to give voice to sentiments for change and renewal. Nevertheless most still hold that there is a legitimate, if modest, role for electoral institutions to play in "structuring" and moderating this whole process.

The two key elements in the system that have provided a moderating influence have been the two-party system and the electoral college. The party system has served to screen candidates in the nominating phase and to channel national political conflict inside two known and "safe" institutions, with allowances made for third-party options. (In rare instances, of course, one party or another may make a major break with its traditional position.) The electoral college as it has evolved has played an important role in maintaining two-party competition. As there is nothing to be gained by finishing third in any state, voters have been reinforced in their normal inclination to stay with one of the major parties.

The presidential campaign of 1992 illustrates the wisdom of these elements of moderation. The two parties managed in the end to select two able candidates, who both espoused safe and "mainstream" positions. The main justification of the electoral college, as it now functions, is to slow down a candidate like Ross Perot and minimize his influence. In the end, it served just this function, as Bill Clinton won the presidency on his own with a comfortable *electoral* majority. If one imagines a race in 1992 conducted under the direct election plan, it is easy to think of how different matters could have been. Perot down the stretch would no doubt have appealed to voters to send the election to a second round, where he and his volunteers could then have played a deciding role.

The case in favor of maintaining the existing influences for moderation ought to be relatively uncontroversial, just because their role is now so minimal. Only the most fastidious can complain that the electoral system is closed to new candidates or outsiders. The reforms in the nominating processes of the major parties in the 1970s eliminated most of the capacity of parties to screen or filter candidates, to such an extent that journalists now openly speak of their "duty" to perform this role. (A few rule changes in recent years have returned to the parties a few prerogatives, and the long series of primaries at least allows for a good look at the candidates.) As for third-party candidacies, many of the legal barriers—quite rightly— have come down. And the Perot candidacy demonstrated that many of the biases against third-party candidates, such as a systematic deficiency in media attention and exposure, no longer necessarily apply. No one, for example, can possibly say that they did not see or hear enough of Ross Perot in 1992.

In defending a moderating role for the electoral process, it is unnecessary to indulge in gratuitous charges of demagogy against Ross Perot. In its strongest sense, a demagogue refers to an individual who (usually knowingly) raises and manipulates the darkest kinds of passions, with the end of climbing to a position of power. Anger and fear on the right, envy and class hatred on the left, are the classic tools in the demagogue's repertoire. Demagogy in the strongest sense does not fit Ross Perot. He used few if any such appeals, and in many respects deliberately shunned anything resembling classic demagogy. For example, it was Perot by the end who called for sacrifice and additional taxes, thereby preaching an ethic of restraint or responsibility; and it was Perot who aired what at any rate appeared to be the serious ads that addressed the public's reason, not its passions.

There is, however, a "softer" style of demagogic politics—perhaps we should call it a politics of popular leadership—that represents a greater danger today than the harder variant. The line between this kind of politics and legitimate politics has admittedly been increasingly blurred, which is only another way of indicating the extent of the current danger. Perot's campaign illustrates three characteristics of this sort of politics, and the "space" he opened, if maintained, lends itself to an increase in popular leadership.

1. *The "riding" of a mood or humor.* Ross Perot, though not responsible for creating outsider sentiment in 1992, rode it with all the zeal of the real cowboy he always yearned to be. Time and again during the campaign he promised to be "outside," "different," or

"unconventional," which may well be a qualification for some things, but which, with its emphasis on novelty, contradicts the original idea of filling the presidency with a person "of whom the people have had time to form a judgement and with respect to whom they will not be liable to be deceived."[42]

This is not a statement against third-party candidacies, which form an important part of the American system, but a statement in favor of maintaining barriers that compel them to prove themselves in the face of some institutional resistance. There is, in this respect, an important difference between the Ross Perot candidacy of 1992 and a possible Ross Perot in 1996. In the 1992 campaign, the American people really did not know Perot very well. By 1996, Perot will be less a phenomenon than a fixture. If Perot's movement survives and grows, it will have overcome the only sort of barrier that democratic electoral institutions can legitimately erect.

2. *An absence of any content.* One must distinguish here between Perot's first and second campaigns, although the difference is not as great as many suppose. The impression of Ross Perot today derives mostly from the second campaign, when he flooded the airwaves with what looked like substantive discussions and when his campaign book, *United We Stand*, full of bar graphs and issue positions, was published and available. But during the whole first campaign in the spring, Perot avoided taking a stand on nearly every issue. Time and again, when asked to spell out his program or even approach, he would promise only to get the best experts together, sit down in a room and analyze the problem, come up with options, and then decide. When Perot took to the hustings in June, his rallies were based on a content-less can-do theme. In Sacramento, appearing with a huge flag in the background and with the *Chariots of Fire* theme song to introduce him, Perot declared, "We can fix it, as long as you're sick of it. . . . It's time just to go out and do it."[43]

Some compared Perot's appeal to Ronald Reagan, no doubt because of the folksy homilies, the cowboy image, and, yes, even the mistakes in detail. Yet a comparison of the two is more instructive for its contrast than its similarities. Whatever one may say of Reagan's style, the main element of his appeal was his espousal of a certain set of ideas and a public philosophy. Reagan's "outsiderism" was subservient to, or controlled by, the content of his appeal. The opposite was true of Perot. Others compared Perot to Jimmy Carter, for both men, as engineers (and Annapolis graduates), liked to begin a discussion by implying that there was a "scientific" approach that should dictate the solution: You take a look at the issue, break it down, study the options, and arrive at an answer. Yet here again the contrast between the two men is more noteworthy than the similarity. For in Carter's case, anyone who heard him speak in the 1976 campaign will recall that he not only made use of the formulas of the engineer, but he also applied them. Carter had tremendous knowledge of the facts and an extraordinary grasp of the issues, enough to bore many audiences to death. By contrast, Perot in the spring of 1992 had mastered very little, and people had no notion of where he wanted to lead the nation. His statements about balancing the budget "without breaking a sweat" told the story that he had not yet done the necessary homework.

The major point here is not that Ross Perot was less knowledgeable than others who have sought the presidency, but that, in the absence of a connection to a political party, his lack of content left people with no chance of knowing where he was going. Parties provide a general idea of what the candidates stand for without consulting each and every detail of their position. The party philosophy situates the candidates. It does so even when a candidate makes a point of saying that he or she will be a new kind of Republican or Democrat, for then we are alert to how the candidate may wish to move in relationship to an established position. None of this could be said of Ross Perot. People had very little idea of what they were buying, and Perot had every reason early on not to bother telling them.

3. *A populism without forms.* Forms and procedures are central in securing orderly consultation with the public in any democratic system. The Perot campaign made a mockery of the idea of forms, with its "rigged" phone polls and its phony claims of key decisions being made by volunteers. Of course these kinds of ploys are usual for political movements, which obviously cannot be held to the same standards as established institutions. What modern political movement has not stressed, in an exaggerated way, its intimate connection to the will of the people?

The real danger, however, was found in Perot's suggestions that these formless populist "principles" be carried over into how the nation is governed. Thus, in the quest for yet another "unconventional" idea, Perot proposed instituting oxymoronic "electronic town halls" as a means of governing. Somehow or other—in a way he never quite specified—these "meetings" would be used as a supplement to (or substitute for) normal deliberative processes inside Congress. Again, Perot, who likened his role in relation to the volunteers as that of a "servant," promised to carry that idea into the White House, declaring that he would resign the presidency if the people did not want him.[44] The idea of "serving" so conceived directly contradicts the classic idea that the president should possess "courage and magnanimity enough to serve [the people] *at the peril of their displeasure*," defending the public's interest over its inclination.[45] By undermining these forms, Ross Perot's politics in 1992 threatened to move the political system further along a dangerous road from representative democracy to pollocracy.

NOTES

1. Theodore Lowi, "Three-Party Politics: A Natural Order," *Campaign*, vol. 6, no. 8, August 1992, p. 48; Alan Brinkley, *The New Republic*, July 27, 1992; George Will, "The Veep and Blatherskite," *Newsweek*, June 29, 1992, p. 72.

2. The second statement was made during an appearance on NBC's *Today Show*, on September 18, when Perot was contemplating reentering the race. *Los Angeles Times*, September 19, 1992, p. A17.

Incidentally, Larry King was prepped for his question. Perot had given a similar response in a question-and-answer session in Nashville early in February. A Tennessee businessman, John Jay Hooker, heard this response and—seeking to encourage a Perot candidacy—had the answer phoned to Larry King by a friend. See Jim Squires, "How Ross Perot's Campaign Came Apart," *Rolling Stone*, October 1, 1992, p. 52.

3. *Washington Post*, May 5, 1992, p. A5. In comparing himself to New Hampshire, King was casting a faint echo of the boast of Louis the Fourteenth, the last monarch to bestow on himself state-like qualities when he declared: "L'état, c'est moi."

4. Walter Mondale, "Primaries are no Test of Character," *New York Times*, February 26, 1992, p. A21.

5. William Raspberry, "Perot: Don't Run," *Washington Post*, April 3, 1992, p. A21.

6. Connally managed but one delegate for his efforts, in part because he was viewed as attempting to purchase what should never be for sale. John Connally, incidentally, served as an adviser to Perot during the active phase of the latter's campaign. Both men, in addition to their cultivated images as can-do tough guys, shared a genuine antipathy to George Bush, whom they regarded as not being a real Texan.

7. *Los Angeles Times*, October 1, 1992, p. A19.

8. David Broder, "The Washington in Perot's Mind," *Washington Post*, June 28, 1992, p. C7.

9. *Washington Post*, June 25, 1992, p. A1.

10. *Washington Post*, June 25, 1992, p. A18.

11. David Broder, "The Washington in Perot's Mind, *Washington Post*, June 25, 1992, p. C7.

12. Harvey Mansfield in "Only Amend: Perot vs. the Constitution," *The New Republic*, July 6, 1992, pp. 13-14.

13. *Washington Post*, June 25, 1992, p. A18.

14. *Washington Post*, July 19, 1992, p. A1.

15. *Time*, July 27, 1992, p. 32.

16. *USA Today*, July 24, 1992, p. A6.

17. *Washington Post*, July 17, 1992, p. A17.

18. *Washington Post Weekly Edition,* October 12-18, 1992, p. 37.

19. Observation of Mr. Cary Federman.

20. See Daniel Boorstin, *The Image: A Guide to Pseudo-Events in America* (New York: Harper & Row, 1964).

21. Wick Allison, "How Bush Can Win," *National Review*, July 6, 1992, p. 37.

22. *New York Times*, June 9, 1992, p. A27.

23. Earl Shorris, "Market Democracy," *Harpers*, November 1978, pp. 93-96.

24. Martin Wattenberg, *The Rise of Candidate-Centered Politics* (Cambridge, Mass.: Harvard University Press, 1984), p. 2.

25. Theodore Lowi, "Three-Party Politics: A Natural Order," *Campaign*, vol. 6, no. 8, August 1992, p. 46.

26. John Anderson, "Can any independent win the presidency?," *USA Today*, July 20, 1992, p. 9A.

27. Tim Noah, "Perot Waters His Grass Roots Heavily," *Wall Street Journal*, September 30, 1992, p. A18. Of the fifty state coordinators still working in September, at least ten were being paid by Perot.

28. Thomas Edsall, "Party Coalitions and the Perot Factor," *Washington Post*, July 12, 1992, p. A13.

29. Gerald Rafshoon, "Why I Left Perot," *Washington Post*, July 16, 1992, p. A23.

30. *Washington Post*, July 19, 1992, p. A1.

31. *USA Today*, July 20, 1992, p. 9A.

32. *Washington Post*, June 25, 1992, p. A16.

33. Jim Squires, "How Ross Perot's Campaign Came Apart," *Rolling Stone*, October 1, 1992, p. 52.

34. Reported on ABC World News, October 20, 1992.

35. Cited by Gary Orren and William Mayer in "The Press, Political Parties, and the Public-Private Balance in Elections," in Sandy Maisel, ed., *The Parties Respond: Changes in the American Party System* (Boulder, Colo.: Westview Press, 1990).

36. Thomas Patterson, "The Press and Its Missed Assignment," in Michael Nelson, ed., *The Elections of 1988* (Washington, D.C.: Congressional Quarterly Press, 1989), p. 107.

37.   See Harvey Mansfield, *America's Constitutional Soul* (Baltimore: Johns Hopkins University Press, 1991), pp. 164-67.

38.   Gary Orren and William Mayer in "The Press, Political Parties, and the Public-Private Balance in Elections," in Sandy Maisel, ed., *The Parties Respond: Changes in the American Party System* (Boulder, Colo.: Westview Press, 1990).

39.   Cited in Howard Kurtz, "Press Faces Enigma in Non-Candidate," *Washington Post*, May 5, 1992, p. A5.

40.   Harvey Mansfield, "Only Amend: Perot vs. the Constitution," *The New Republic*, July 6, 1992, pp. 13-14.

41.   John Anderson, "Break the Political Stronghold," *New York Times*, July 24, 1992, p. A25.

42.   *The Federalist*, number 64.

43.   *Washington Post*, June 19, 1992, p. A24.

44.   These points are discussed by Harvey Mansfield in "Only Amend: Perot vs. the Constitution," *The New Republic*, July 6, 1992, pp. 13-14.

45.   *The Federalist*, number 71.

CHAPTER FIVE

The 1992 Congressional Elections

At the end of the summer, as the 1992 congressional elections approached, the reputation of Congress stood at a low point, the rate of congressional retirements (and thus open seats) was extraordinarily high, and Congress itself, as an institution, had become a major issue not only in congressional races but in the presidential campaign as well. Congress seemed poised for a major change.

For years, the United States Congress has been the bastion of the Democratic party. Democrats have controlled the House of Representatives continuously since the elections of 1954 and for all but four years since 1930. Having enjoyed the considerable advantages of incumbency during this period, now Democrats were saddled with its growing liabilities. The Senate has been more closely contested in recent years. Republicans actually captured control of the upper chamber from 1981 to 1986, but Democrats won it back in the 1986 elections and have held it since.

Republicans began the decade of the 1980s with high hopes of recapturing the House, just as they had won the Senate. These hopes were dashed, however, after only modest gains in the Reagan landslide of 1984. If the Republicans could not capture the House with this kind of presidential victory, then their best chance for ousting the Democrats would be an election under a different set of constituencies. Thus, the GOP began concentrating its plans and pinning its new hopes on 1992, the first election that would occur after the redistricting of 1990. These hopes grew in the wake of the Persian Gulf War, which produced a double boon for Republicans: high ratings for President Bush, which seemed to presage easy reelection, and additional liabilities for Democratic incumbents, most of whom had voted against the war. In the fall of 1991, the Republican plan was to use President Bush to spearhead a huge national party campaign targeting the Democratic Congress. The plan was for a campaign based on "Quotas, Kuwait, and Congress." It might not look so good, but it sounded right.

Republicans obviously had their hopes dashed again. Although they picked up ten seats in the House and maintained an unchanged, cloture-proof contingent of 43 in the Senate, their gains were much smaller than they (and many Democrats) had expected, and the Democrats retained solid majorities in both houses. Their problem, of course, was not just that they lost their issues, but that they lost a popular president to lead them. Given their defeat in the presidential race, the Republicans' modest gains in Congress stood in contrast to the pattern of most of American history, and could be counted something of a minor achievement. Still, while this gain cast doubt on claims of a "mandate" for Bill Clinton, Clinton did possess at least modest coattails, which were hidden because they were offset by other factors like redistricting. Divided government was ended by the Clinton victory, and the Democratic majority in the Senate, if not the House, tilted further to the left.

While the traditional partisan dimension of congressional elections showed little change, the elections were heavily overlaid by the same inside-outside dimension that affected the presidential race. Outsiderism was a major theme in congressional campaigns throughout the year, and it influenced congressional elections much more than one would imagine by looking just at partisan shifts. Fourteen states approved congressional term limitations; 19 House members were defeated in primaries; 110 new representatives and 12 new senators were elected to the 103rd Congress, the most since 1948; and voting for candidates from third parties rose to record rates for modern times. In addition, a record number of minorities won House seats, aided by what amounted to the institutionalization of a new principle of descriptive representation. A record number of women, many using gender as another indicator of outsiderism, were elected to both the House and the Senate. Of course, it is still an open question—and a very important one—whether outsiderism will prove more powerful to these new members than their traditional partisanship.

REDISTRICTING

The results of the congressional elections were affected by some important background factors, beginning with the process of reapportionment and redistricting. A key to Republican hopes for the

House in 1992 lay in the decennial reapportionment mandated by the Constitution, and in the process of redistricting that is governed by Supreme Court rulings and recent civil rights legislation. Reapportionment allots representatives to each state on the basis of population as determined by the census (though every state receives a minimum of one seat). After the 1990 census, the Census Bureau under congressional statute determined that House seats should be allotted on the basis of one seat for approximately every 550,000 inhabitants.

The census data confirmed a forty-year trend of relative population shift from the Northeast and Midwest toward the "sunbelt" states of the South and West. Thirteen states lost one or more representatives, including New York (three) and Illinois, Michigan, Ohio, and Pennsylvania (two each). Eight states gained representatives, most notably California (seven), Florida (four), and Texas (three).

Critics of the counting procedure used by the Census Bureau challenged the results in the federal courts. Small states with declining populations sued to prevent the transfer of their seats to growing states. Montana, which fell 12,000 people short of being entitled to keep both its seats, lost its case before the Supreme Court and is now the most populous congressional district in America, with nearly 800,000 residents. The major controversy, however, was not primarily inter-state, dealing with reapportionment, but intra-state, dealing with redistricting. Some brought suits arguing that particular segments of the population (particularly urban dwellers) were systematically undercounted, thus skewing the drawing of district lines. Large cities, heavily urban states, and minority groups sought an adjustment in the census, but Commerce Secretary Robert Mosbacher permitted the original numbers to stand.

Table 5-1
Apportionment of Congressional Seats by Region

Region	1910	1950	1990
South	104	106	125
Border	47	38	32
New England	32	32	23
Mid-Atlantic	92	88	66
Plains	41	31	22
Rocky Mountains	14	16	24
Pacific Coast	19	43	69

Source: Vital Statistics on Congress.

Overall, Republican strategists were heartened by the seat shift from the "rust belt" to the "sun belt." Nevertheless, the shift was not in itself sufficient to produce a more Republican Congress without some success at the next stage of the process: redistricting *within* the states. The politics of redistricting in 1992 were unlike anything anyone had ever experienced before, due largely to stunning advances in technology. The redistricting process has led to greater and greater technical innovation by both political parties, which utilize an array of computers and consultants to fine-tune the art of "gerrymandering," or maximizing the party's seats through the most efficacious drawing of district lines. Furthermore, with the ready availability of personal computers, virtually anyone with an interest in redistricting could design a plan and offer it as an alternative. As a result, a variety of interest groups joined political parties in devising redistricting schemes.[1]

Because redistricting is ultimately the responsibility of state governments, the first battles over redistricting were fought in the gubernatorial and state legislative elections of 1990. California, Texas, and Florida—the three largest gainers of congressional seats—each elected a governor in 1990. In each case the races were hotly contested, with the national parties taking a keen interest in the results. In the end, the Republicans narrowly won California but lost Florida and Texas (after leading by a wide margin).

The Republicans enjoyed surprising successes, however, in many of the rust belt states that were losing congressional seats. These were almost as important as the states gaining seats, as all the district lines had to be redrawn, inevitably eliminating the districts of some incumbents. In the gubernatorial races, Illinois remained Republican, while Ohio and Michigan shifted from Democratic to Republican governors.

In the nation as a whole, Republicans and Democrats each had a net loss of one governorship (as two independents took office). In the battle for the control of state legislatures, Republicans suffered net losses of six state senates and one state lower house. The Democrats thus bolstered their already large advantage nationwide.

When the states completed their redistricting, Republicans at the national level were highly satisfied with the results. Indeed, many felt that they had won the redistricting war more clearly than would have been expected on the basis of the mixed outcomes of the 1990 state elections. Near the end of the redistricting process, Republican National Committee Chairman Rich Bond argued that redistricting had succeeded in making 80 previously Democratic House seats competitive. Key Democrats disputed the magnitude of Bond's claim, but not the direction of the shift, stating that they expected to lose 20 seats due to redistricting and for another 30 to 40 to remain competitive. In the eyes of some Democrats, the results of redistricting were "a disaster for the party."[2]

One of the main factors that explained the Republicans' unexpected success was the unprecedented interjection of the federal courts into the redistricting process. Not until 1962 did the Supreme Court accept that the courts had a major role in congressional redistricting. In a series of cases from 1962 to 1964, the Court established the "one man one vote" principle (now amended to read one person one vote), declaring that both federal and state election districts violated constitutional guarantees of equal protection if they contained unequal populations.[3] By 1983, the Supreme Court was overturning congressional redistricting plans that deviated from equal population by as little as one-seventh of 1 percent.[4] And in 1985, the Supreme Court held for the first time, though in very tentative fashion, that partisan gerrymandering was a justiciable question.[5] Combined with this greater propensity on the part of the federal courts to interject themselves into redistricting questions was an open invitation for even more judicial influence in the form of the Voting Rights Act Amendments of 1982.

The Voting Rights Act Amendments of 1982, as interpreted by the federal courts and administered by the Justice Department, appeared to bolster Republican prospects in 1992. The Voting Rights Act Amendments of 1982 required states to make the maximum possible effort to ensure that some legislative districts contained a majority of racial minorities. Section 2 of the Amendments called for a result, rather than merely an intent, standard when judging the existence of racial discrimination in the drawing of district lines. This controversial standard was upheld by the Supreme Court in 1986 in *Thornburgh v. Gingles*.[6] For those states falling under the Voting Rights Act's Section 5 preclearance requirement, the Justice Department must approve redistricting plans by this criterion before they go into effect. In 1991 and 1992, the department rejected plans from several states under the preclearance provision. Beyond the preclearance provision, district plans for all of the states are subject to legal action under Section 2 of the law. What all this legislation meant in practice was that each state began its redistricting process by first carving out all plausible minority-based districts before proceeding to draw the remainder of the district lines.

Republican political strategists were frequently tempted to invoke the Voting Rights Act Amendments, even if it conflicted with the scruples some had about the resulting judicial interference and racial balkanization. The temptation proved stronger than the scruples, and the Justice Department became an active advocate of minority-based redistricting. Blacks and, to a lesser extent, Hispanics form a crucial part of the Democratic coalition. As a result, it was to the Republicans' advantage to concentrate those voters as much as possible in the same districts (the old gerrymandering practice of "packing") rather than permitting them to be distributed widely enough to tip the balance in several districts. Thus, both nationally and at the local level, the Republicans made tactical alliances with minority groups seeking majority-minority districts. These odd coalitions, often backed by the Justice Department, frequently defeated the plans of the white Democratic establishments.

When no satisfactory plan was forthcoming from the states, the federal courts were empowered to draw the district lines. Plans were ultimately produced by the federal judiciary in nine states with 95 congressional districts, including Alabama, Arizona, Florida, Illinois, Kansas, Michigan, Minnesota, Oregon, and South Carolina. State courts dictated districts in California and Pennsylvania, with another 74 seats. Republicans clearly benefited in most of those cases. The judges were, at a minimum, more evenhanded than the Democratic legislatures, and in some instances even appeared to tilt toward the Republicans.[7]

Beyond the partisan implications of redistricting, there was a broader—and ultimately perhaps more important—consequence. For the first time, the concept of descriptive representation—a view that the key to representation lies not in a delegation of decisionmaking authority or in congruence of opinion but in similarity of characteristics—was legitimated and enforced by federal edict. The Voting Rights Act Amendments of 1982, and the interpretation of that legislation by the federal courts and the Justice Department, is essentially based on a view that blacks can only be properly represented by blacks, Hispanics by Hispanics, Asians by Asians, and so forth (although the courts have not yet gone so far as to explicitly maintain that whites can only be properly represented by whites).

Connected loosely to this legal endorsement of descriptive representation, the "spirit" of the idea also gained ground in the form of an increased emphasis on gender politics. Dozens of women candidates were swept to victory in the primaries and general election because they convinced large majorities of female voters that "women's interests" could only be understood and protected by women.

This rise of the concept of descriptive representation was welcomed by some as the only avenue for diversifying American political institutions. Others, looking across the sea, feared the long-term effects of racial, ethnic, and gender polarization inherent in descriptive representation. The term "balkanization," after all, has regained some of its currency as an epithet.

CONGRESSIONAL REPUTATION

At the same time districts were being redrawn, Congress as an institution experienced a sharp and continuing decline in public esteem. This problem was the result of three factors: continuing gridlock in government, a growing public conviction that Congress was out of touch with the average American, and a series of embarrassing congressional scandals.

Perhaps the most common explanation for the apparent rise of governmental gridlock holds that gridlock has been primarily the result of persistent "divided government" or control of the presidency and Congress by different parties. Presidents Reagan and Bush adopted this view, as have many academics (especially among what has been called the "responsible party" school).[8] In this view, divided government makes agreement on coherent policies unlikely, as no one is willing (or required) to accept responsibility for the direction of government; and there are positive incentives for each party (and thus each branch) to seek to harass and embarrass the other.[9] Others argue that gridlock is the symptom of a much deeper sclerosis, in which the excessive insinuation of special interests into the political process has made needed innovation impossible, regardless of party control.[10] Finally, others attribute gridlock to the entrenched nature of incumbency, which insulates Congress from demands for change. Supporters of congressional term limitations are among the foremost proponents of this view. In any case, it seems clear that Americans have become increasingly concerned in recent years about the apparent inability of Congress to act. Ross Perot's appeal was based at least as much on an attack against "gridlock" as on an attack against the debt, and 1992 was the first year in recent history in which more poll respondents believed divided government to be a problem than not.

The second reason for the declining confidence in Congress was the growing perception that Congress was out of touch with the concerns of ordinary Americans. That perception was fed most prominently by repeated pay increases voted by Congress for itself in the late 1980s (congressional pay now stands at $125,000). One instance provoked a firestorm of public opposition, when radio talk show hosts encouraged listeners to send tea bags to their congressmen in remembrance of the Boston Tea Party. Citizens were sufficiently agitated to complete ratification in May 1992 of a constitutional amendment which had languished for nearly two hundred years prohibiting congressional pay raises from taking effect until after an election had intervened. Concerns were also widespread over congressional perks like free mailings and travel. In April of 1992, 82 percent of respondents to an ABC poll agreed that "those we elect to Congress in Washington lose touch with the people pretty quickly."[11]

Finally, the public's negative view of Congress was greatly reinforced by a series of ethics scandals. The first of note came in George Bush's first year, when Speaker of the House Jim Wright resigned in disgrace, followed weeks later by House Majority Whip Tony Coehlo. The savings and loan crisis damaged Congress generally, but specific ethics charges were brought against only five senators (four Democrats and one Republican). In the end, only Democratic Senator Alan Cranston of California, who was retiring, was reprimanded.

Perhaps the most damaging scandal, however, burst forth when it was reported by the General Accounting Office in the fall of 1991 that hundreds of members had written overdrafts that were covered by the House Bank. In an attempt to control the damage, Speaker Thomas Foley closed the bank. However, House Republicans, led by a group of seven freshmen (dubbed the "Gang of Seven") kept the spotlight on the scandal some called "Rubbergate." A House Ethics Committee investigation found 19 current and five former members to have seriously abused bank privileges, including one Arkansas Republican who had written 996 bad checks in 39 months and a New York Democrat who had written 980.

Sensing a vast political opportunity, Republicans utilized public pressure to force the Democratic leadership to support a resolution requiring full disclosure of all 355 current and former representatives who had written bad checks during the 39-month period in question. House Sergeant-at-Arms Jack Russ, whose office ran the bank, resigned, and a special counsel was appointed by Attorney General William Barr to investigate possible criminal wrongdoing in relation to the scandal. While some key Republicans like Mickey Edwards and Vin Weber were affected, Republican strategists clearly viewed the check-kiting scandal as "the weapon to end perpetual

Democratic control of the House," a means of overcoming the well-known tendency of voters to despise Congress while liking their congressman.[12]

Simultaneously, there were reports of $700,000 in unpaid bills at the House restaurants, and four employees of the House Post Office were charged with embezzlement while one was accused of selling cocaine. Democratic Senator Brock Adams of Washington was charged with allegations of sexual misconduct. Rumors circulated that House Speaker Thomas Foley's wife, who works on his staff, was implicated in the Post Office scandal. By the end of March, the National Republican Congressional Committee was running television advertisements citing the bank scandal as emblematic of the Democrats' mishandling of power.

The cumulative effect of these factors was a growing conviction among voters that change was needed. One form this conviction assumed was a desire to change the members of Congress. Anti-incumbent sentiment had begun to emerge in 1990, but failed to change the final outcome of many congressional elections. Only one Senate incumbent and 16 House incumbents were defeated. However, incumbents' margins of victory declined by an average of 4 percent, and in some individual cases much more dramatically, providing a warning shot. This anti-incumbent sentiment continued to grow over the next two years. In 1990, 56 percent had agreed that Congress was doing a bad enough job that "it's time to turn most of the rascals out." By 1992, 76 percent agreed. Overall, only 18 percent approved of the way Congress was doing its job. Throughout most of 1992, 55 to 60 percent of respondents agreed that it was time to give a new person a chance in their congressional district.[13] Anti-incumbent sentiment was also revealed by the fact that there were only one-third as many uncontested seats in 1992 as in 1990 (15 as opposed to 45).

The second form voter dissatisfaction took was a desire to change Congress itself as an institution. In 1990, California, Colorado, and Oklahoma all adopted term limitations for their state legislatures, Colorado even attempting with uncertain constitutionality to limit congressional terms. Only in Washington state in 1991 was a federal term limits proposal turned back, but proponents succeeded in placing it back on the ballot in Washington and in 13 other states in 1992. Conservative columnist George Will, who had once strongly opposed congressional term limitations, came out in favor of them, and the idea seemed to gain in popularity throughout the country.[14] Congressional term limits preventing anyone from serving more than six House terms and two Senate terms were supported by approximately two-thirds of Americans according to polls, with virtually no differences by party, region, or gender.[15]

CONGRESSIONAL RETIREMENTS

Adding to the volatility of the congressional elections was another factor: the large number of senators and representatives who chose to retire rather than face reelection in 1992. Some, like Senators Warren Rudman and Kent Conrad, left out of frustration over governmental gridlock (although Conrad later returned in a special election in December). Some, like Vin Weber, retired when it became clear that their check-bouncing records would make reelection too difficult. Some retired due to redistricting, many in order to avoid having to run against another incumbent into whose district they had been thrown. Many undoubtedly calculated that the anti-incumbent tide was too strong to fight. Finally, according to a congressional ethics law passed in 1989, 1992 was the last year that retiring members could keep leftover campaign funds. Most retiring members denied any intention of keeping such funds, but once all the other reasons for quitting were considered, this little inducement was not always overlooked.

By the end of summer, the announced retirements of 52 House members and seven senators had far surpassed the post-World War II records; in addition, nine House members were leaving to run for higher office. Since open seats are almost always more competitive than races against an incumbent, and since almost twice as many of those retiring were Democrats than Republicans, Republican strategists believed they had an additional reason to hope for further gains in November. In reality, the retirements may have been a mixed blessing for the Republicans, insofar as many vulnerable Democratic incumbents had been replaced in primary elections by fresh faces who could now run as outsiders.

THE PRESIDENTIAL RACE

The final background factor affecting the 1992 congressional elections was the presidential race. Traditionally, presidential elections have had an important impact on congressional races. In 1992, the congressional races could be influenced by four possible two-way relationships—both congressional parties in relation to the major-party nominees—as well as by their relationship to Ross Perot's candidacy.

　　Congressional Republicans. Presidential relations with Republicans in Congress were strained following the tax reversal in October 1990. Most congressional Republicans voted against the budget agreement and viewed it as not only philosophical but political treachery. It had cut the ground out from under numerous Republican Senate and House candidates in the 1990 elections. Nevertheless, from March 1991 on, congressional Republicans clearly hoped that George Bush's revived popularity, together with a weak Democratic candidate, would add the final element needed for heavy Republican gains in the upcoming congressional elections—a major coattail effect.

　　As Bush's popularity began to nosedive in late 1991, congressional Republicans sought to help him regain the momentum. Conservative congressional Republicans advocated adopting an activist economic agenda and a confrontational stance against congressional Democrats. They were rebuffed, however, on at least two important occasions—in the fall of 1991, when action might have reversed Bush's image of domestic languor, and in the spring of 1992, when Bush's own March 20 deadline for congressional action on his economic proposals was allowed to pass without an energetic presidential response. Only at the Republican convention in late August was the congressional theme made a centerpiece of the Bush effort. And even then the President himself tempered the attack, introducing the argument that gridlock could be solved through general congressional turnover, making partisan control unnecessary.

　　Bill Clinton had no need or reason to attack the Republican congressional contingent, since they were the minority and had little power over policy. Indeed, Clinton ran a remarkably nonpartisan campaign in this respect. Nor did congressional Republicans threaten Clinton, except peripherally. The most visible and controversial exception was Congressman Robert Dornan of California, who in October took to the floor of the House during special orders period to attack Clinton's draft record, trip to Moscow, anti-war demonstrations, and other indiscretions. Whether this series of attacks in the end hurt Clinton—rather than Bush—is highly questionable. The questioning of Clinton's Moscow trip, taken in "the dead of the winter," suggested something ominous for which there was no proof. When Bush foolishly mentioned the trip, Clinton counterattacked and—

now occupying the high ground—avoided even responding to any of
the other charges.

   Congressional Democrats. The relationship between Bill Clinton
and his party in Congress was perhaps the most complex and important of the four. Each was reluctant to embrace the other. Congressional Democrats understood their own vulnerability, and they remained uncertain of Clinton's electability long after the Gennifer
Flowers and draft stories surfaced. On at least two occasions—immediately prior to New Hampshire and from late March until early
April—many congressional Democrats were privately hoping that
one of their own (especially Richard Gephardt or Lloyd Bentsen)
would enter the race to save the party from Clinton. As a result, most
congressional "superdelegates" remained uncommitted long after it
became clear that Clinton had defeated all of his announced opponents.

   Similarly, while Clinton clearly wanted the votes of the
superdelegates and while his program was closer to the position of
congressional Democrats than those of his major opponents, he also
wanted to maintain distance from an increasingly unpopular Congress. The inside-outside dimension predominated, at least for a time,
over the partisan dimension. Clinton needed to look like an outsider
much more than he needed to look like a Democrat. Thus, a "summit
meeting" with Democratic congressional leaders that had been proposed in early June to discuss a common agenda was canceled. Even
further, extraordinary efforts were made to conceal those leaders at
the Democratic national convention in July. Clinton took pains in his
acceptance speech to disassociate himself from Congress, calling
for an end to the "brain-dead politics in Washington"—presumably
at both ends of Pennsylvania Avenue.

   Despite their mutual desire for distance, Clinton and congressional Democrats also needed each other, and in fact aided each other
in more subtle ways. Those in Congress took the lead in confronting
Bush and helping to establish the Democratic theme of economic
action and middle-class tax relief that Clinton subsequently rode with
great success. Long before their party's nominee was known, congressional Democrats embarked on a strategy of using legislative
fights to establish the Democratic agenda and to draw policy distinctions with Bush. The Democrats deliberately set up vetoes ex-
pecting that they would prove embarrassing for the President later.
This was, in essence, a strategy of "one step back, two steps forward," conducted in the belief that there are times one must lose in
order to win.

This strategy focused on a combination of economic and social issues. A number of veto-provoking bills were passed throughout 1992, including a middle-class tax cut financed by higher taxes on upper-income taxpayers, an urban aid bill also containing higher taxes on the wealthy, several abortion provisions, and a family leave bill. Congressional Democrats were thus very successful in setting a negative agenda for the campaign.

As Clinton proved to be a formidable candidate, he protected the position of many Democratic incumbents who would have been much more vulnerable had a Walter Mondale or Michael Dukakis been at the top of the ticket. At the very least, congressional Democrats (and other Democratic officeholders) were spared the all-too-familiar discomfort of having to run away from their presidential ticket.[16] As the election drew closer, Clinton became a positive asset. While he never chose to align himself with Congress, by November 3 many congressional Democrats sought to align themselves with him.

As for President Bush, he approached the Democratic Congress with the same wavering purpose that characterized so much of his presidency. After spending three years compromising with Congress, he attacked it in fits and starts in 1992. He was unafraid to continue wielding the veto, but could not or would not sustain any positive assault. The best example was the March 20 deadline for action that he set in his State of the Union Address. When the deadline arrived, the President gave a speech and demanded 68 spending rescissions (out of over 1,300 that congressional Republicans wanted him to use). The deadline was never heard of again. In the end, Bush proved extremely reluctant to make the sorts of consistent partisan attacks on Congress that might have worked to his (and his party's) benefit. After four days of partisan Congress-bashing in Houston, public opinion had shifted. According to CNN polls, prior to the convention voters overwhelmingly preferred to solve divided government by electing a Democratic president. By the last night of the convention, a small plurality preferred to solve divided government by electing a Republican Congress.[17] Yet this theme was dropped, replaced with the nonpartisan promise of generic change.

The Perot Factor. Finally, Ross Perot's presidential meanderings introduced a wild card into the congressional elections. In the spring of 1992, as Perot's popularity rose, some analyses showed him contesting enough electoral votes to deny any candidate a majority of the electoral college. In that event, the presidential election would have been decided in the House, with each state having one vote.

This prospect threw Congress into quiet turmoil for several weeks. Members of Congress had to deal with two unfamiliar problems. First, House members would have had to decide for whom to vote and on the basis of what criteria, a decision not nearly as easy as one might think. Party alone, while a powerful factor, might not be a sufficient guide. If one's district or state voted another way, there would be a powerful temptation to abandon the dictates of party in favor of protecting one's own position in the eyes of one's constituents.

Second, the presidential race could have a much more direct impact on congressional elections than usual. Voters in a close three-way presidential race might demand in advance to know how their congressional candidates intended to vote in a contingency election. Such a race could even have had the effect of turning the congressional elections into a parliamentary-style election, in which voters chose their congressional candidate on the basis of presidential preference. Indeed, there was speculation that Perot himself might recruit supporters to run for Congress. When Perot announced in July that he would not run, this danger passed, and his reentrance in the fall never posed a threat of sending the election into the House.

THE CONGRESSIONAL PRIMARIES

The initial stage in the congressional elections was the nomination of party candidates, which in the vast majority of states is accomplished through a primary election. The congressional primaries in 1992 revealed two major trends.

The first, which came as no surprise, was a much greater than normal anti-incumbent vote. The post-World War II record of defeated House incumbents was broken, with 19 members denied renomination, compared with only one in both 1990 and 1988. Furthermore, 29 more incumbents were held to vote totals below 60 percent, compared to eight and four in the previous two elections. Most of those experiencing electoral difficulties during the primaries were Democrats. In the Senate, three-term incumbent Alan Dixon of Illinois was defeated for renomination. Scandal played a large role in the anti-incumbent tide during the primaries: of the 19 House members who were defeated, 14 had appeared on the check-kiting list.

The second trend was an influx of minority and women candidates, though it partially overlapped with the first trend. Unprecedented numbers of minority and women congressional candidates received major-party nominations. Because of the redistricting imperatives of the Voting Rights Act Amendments of 1982, more majority-minority districts were created. This led to primary (and later, in most cases, general election) victories by black and Hispanic candidates. For example, longtime Representative Stephen Solarz of New York, one of the Democratic party's premier foreign policy experts, was defeated in his primary race partially because he was running in a district redrawn to ensure a Hispanic majority. (He also just happened to be guilty of 743 House Bank overdrafts.)

The primaries also saw a substantial increase in the number of women candidates. Many of them won their primaries, prompting pundits to declare 1992 "The Year of the Woman" in politics. This designation was perhaps an exaggeration, since 1990 had seen nine female Senate candidates (six of whom were Republicans). What perhaps justified the label, however, was that more women in 1992 were in a position to win in November. Senate races received the greatest attention, with 11 women winning nominations, many in upsets over established male opponents. For example, political neophyte Lynn Yeakel of Pennsylvania defeated Pennsylvania Lt. Governor Mark Singel. Cook County Recorder of Deeds Carol Moseley Braun defeated Dixon in Illinois. Similarly, an unprecedented 106 women in 35 states won House primaries; the previous record had been 69 in 1990. Overall, in congressional and gubernatorial primaries without an incumbent, women actually had success rates 77 percent higher than men; as late as 1988 they had only drawn even.[18]

Several theories were advanced for the success of women candidates. First, while a large majority of women as well as men had supported Clarence Thomas' nomination to the Supreme Court in 1991, the episode had the effect of mobilizing the feminist minority. Yeakel and Braun both cited the Thomas-Hill hearings as reasons for their candidacies. Second, feminists were also increasingly mobilized by the Supreme Court's decisions in *Webster* (1989) and *Casey* (1992) permitting states greater leeway in regulating abortion. Third, a number of women's organizations like the National Women's Political Caucus, EMILY's List (leaning Democratic), and the WISH List (leaning Republican) had formed. By 1992, these organizations (sometimes called "the old girls' club") had reached sufficient maturity to direct substantial organizational and financial resources toward women candidates with compatible positions on women's issues. Fourth, the reduced importance of national security and foreign affairs and the concomitant rise of domestic issues like health care worked to the advantage of women candidates. Finally,

women held the advantage of being viewed by many in the electorate as "outsiders" in a year when it was very good to be one. Polls
showed that voters thought women to be more honest and upright
than men in politics.[19]

Thus, both the anti-incumbency sentiment and the influx of new
kinds of candidates in the 1992 congressional primaries opened the
possibility of sweeping changes in November. While both factors
benefited outsiders, the two worked at cross-purposes in partisan
terms. If for no other reason than that so many more incumbents
were Democrats than Republicans, Republicans stood to gain the
most from anti-incumbency sentiment. But Democrats stood the most
to gain from the success of minority candidates, and from the year's
large crop of women.

THE CONGRESSIONAL ELECTION RESULTS

When the ballots were finally counted, this promise of change
was only partially fulfilled. There were 110 new House members
and 12 new senators. Aided in most cases by a substantial "gender
gap" among voters, five of the 11 women Senate candidates won,
tripling the number of women in the Senate. In the House, female
representation increased from 29 to 47 voting members. There were
also 12 more black representatives (there had been 26), seven more
Hispanics (there had been 12), and two more Asians (there had been
three). At the same time, however, there was little change in the
partisan balance. Democrats made no gains in the Senate, remaining
at 57 seats. The Republicans gained ten seats in the House, which
was far smaller than they had hoped for in September, when Chairman Vic Fazio (D-Calif.) feared the loss of 25 to 35 seats, but far
better than one would expect historically given the presidential results. There were virtually no partisan shifts in open seats in either
the Senate or the House. The benefits to Republicans from redistricting were greatest in the states most affected by the Voting Rights
Act Amendments. In the 13 states that elected minority members to
the House in 1992, the Republicans made a net gain of 22 seats.
Thus, the deal made during the redistricting process between the
Republicans and minority groups bore fruit for both.

There were also relatively few incumbents who were defeated.
A total of 24 House incumbents lost, 16 of them Democrats, leaving
an incumbent reelection rate of 93 percent. Republicans beat Democrats in three of the four races that pitted incumbent against incum-

Table 5-2
Blacks and Women in Congress (1969–1993)

Session of Congress		House Blacks	House Women	Senate Blacks	Senate Women
91	(1969)	9	10	1	1
92	(1971)	13	13	1	1
93	(1973)	16	16	1	1
94	(1975)	16	19	1	0
95	(1977)	15	18	1	0
96	(1979)	15	16	0	2
97	(1981)	17	19	0	2
98	(1983)	20	22	0	2
99	(1985)	20	22	0	2
100	(1987)	22	23	0	2
101	(1989)	23	25	0	2
102	(1991)	26	29	0	2
103	(1993)	38	47	1	6

Source: Vital Statistics on Congress; Roll Call.

bent because of redistricting. Only four Senate incumbents were defeated, two Democrats and two Republicans.

Still, there were some other signs of outsider strength. Following a trend begun in 1990, incumbent reelection margins were reduced, and there were 47 races nationwide in which the winning incumbent had 51 percent of the vote or less.[20] Furthermore, there was a striking increase in third-party activity in congressional races, which is an indicator of voter sentiment against the "inside" parties and politics as usual. In 1992, there were 73 districts where the minor-party vote totaled 5 percent or greater. This compared to 51 such districts in 1990; 23 in 1988; and 39 in 1980, a year comparable in many respects to 1992.

Most congressional incumbents were able to ride out the storm by aligning themselves with the outsider mood of the country. As they campaigned, they echoed presidential candidates in their call for change, describing their frustrations with Congress as an institution and speaking of the need for congressional reform. Few incumbents actually ran as incumbents, although they certainly took advantage of the superiority in resources they enjoyed. As of mid-1992, only one Senate challenger (Dianne Feinstein) had raised more money than the incumbent, and the top 50 fundraisers among House candidates were all incumbents.

The high rate of incumbent victory on November 3 is also explained by the earlier retirements and defeats of the weakest and most vulnerable members. Thus, the incumbent reelection rate of 93 percent overstates the security enjoyed by incumbents in 1992. As in the primary season, most of the defeated House incumbents were tainted by scandal; 18 of the 24 were on the check-bouncing list, meaning that a total of 77 of the 110 House incumbents who graced this honor roll did not return to Washington in 1993. As one analyst noted, "If you're an incumbent and you know you've got a serious challenger on your hands . . . and you haven't done anything illegal or sleazy, then you should be able to keep your seat."[21] Still, many incumbents were destroyed in 1992 by indiscretions that they would probably have survived in past election years.

Many congressional campaigns focused on the "issue" of outsiderism versus insiderism. Unlike recent years in which local concerns dominated congressional races, a national concern dominated in 1992. It was not a normal or traditional issue at all, but rather the institutional question of congressional reform. Challengers talked about it, sensing in voters' dissatisfaction a tool with which to pummel incumbents. Incumbents, sensing the same danger, talked about it to immunize themselves from the nation's angry mood. Those running for open seats talked about it, hoping to capitalize on the issue. Term limits, congressional perks, scandals, reforms like the line item veto and committee rotation, and general institutional renewal became commonplace themes across the nation. The 1992 congressional elections were more focused on institutional questions than any congressional elections in recent memory.

While the presidential candidates made some effort to discuss policy issues, congressional candidates spent comparatively little time and resources dealing with traditional national issues. The Persian Gulf War, which Republicans had hoped would serve as a potent campaign theme, made virtually no impact except in a few select races. To the extent that national issues were important, it was the domestic agenda that dominated discussion. As with the presidential election, the issue of greatest importance was the state of the economy, followed by health care, education, and the deficit. Incumbents used their positions as far as possible to address the question of jobs. New York's Senator Alfonse D'Amato, in the midst of a brutal reelection fight, kept the Senate in session all night in a filibuster to save 875 jobs in a New York typewriter factory planning to move to Mexico.[22]

In addition to the economy, one other national issue had importance for several congressional races: abortion. This issue was pushed from both sides, as many female candidates sought to make abortion the central question in their campaigns, and almost two dozen anti-abortion candidates pioneered the use of graphic television advertisements depicting the results of abortions. These advertisements stirred controversy in many communities where reluctant television stations were ordered by the Federal Communications Commission to air the ads to comply with federal election guidelines. While all the candidates utilizing these advertisements lost (only two survived the primaries), political victory was not their chief objective. For many, spreading their message on the airwaves was the very purpose of their campaigns.[23]

Finally, while congressional campaigns remain much more individualistic and candidate-centered than thirty years ago, the political parties nevertheless retain an important role in congressional elections. In 1992, that role manifested itself in the redistricting process, the recruitment of certain candidates, assistance of state and local parties, and fundraising and other assistance from the national parties, mostly from each party's congressional campaign arm. Historically, however, the greatest impact of party on congressional elections has come in the form of the partisan coattails of the victorious candidate.

BILL CLINTON'S COATTAILS?

A paramount question in all presidential elections is whether the presidential victor aids his party at lower levels. Indeed, the degree to which winners are deemed entitled to claim a mandate has historically depended on their ability to enlarge their party's congressional contingent. In the 11 presidential elections from 1948 to 1988, the presidential victor's party averaged an increase of nearly 17 seats in the House and two seats in the Senate. Democratic winners outperformed Republicans, averaging 24 House seats to the GOP's 12, and a fraction better than two Senate seats to the GOP's even two. By this standard, Bill Clinton, like George Bush and John F. Kennedy before him, had "negative" coattails.

Recent elections have shown an increasing tendency toward split-ticket voting. In 1920, only 3 percent of House districts voted for a president of one party while electing a congressman of the other party. Since 1956, the percentage of split-voting congressional districts has never fallen below 26 percent, reaching a high of about

45 percent in both 1972 and 1984.[24] This tendency has produced years such as 1988, when Bush won the presidency but lost two House seats, and 1984, when Ronald Reagan's 49-state landslide dwarfed his party's minimal 14-seat House pickup. Clinton's victory continued in that pattern, in the loss of ten seats in the House and no gains in the Senate. Two-thirds of defeated House incumbents were Democrats. Clinton entered the White House with fewer Democrats in the House than any Democrat since Harry Truman. The Democratic House contingent of 258 members in the 103rd Congress was well below the 295 enjoyed by Lyndon Johnson and the 292 that accompanied Jimmy Carter.

Table 5-3
Presidential Coattails, 1948–1992, Net Seat Shifts

Year	President's Party		House	Senate
1948	D	(Truman)	75 D	9 D
1952	R	(Eisenhower)	22 R	1 R
1956	R	(Eisenhower)	2 D	1 D
1960	D	(Kennedy)	22 R	2 R
1964	D	(Johnson)	37 D	1 D
1968	R	(Nixon)	5 R	6 R
1972	R	(Nixon)	12 R	2 D
1976	D	(Carter)	1 D	0
1980	R	(Reagan)	33 R	12 R
1984	R	(Reagan)	14 R	2 D
1988	R	(Bush)	2 D	0
1992	D	(Clinton)	10 R	0

A more detailed analysis shows that in the 19 victorious Democratic Senate races, Clinton lost the state in five instances and finished with a larger margin of victory than the Senate candidate in only four. Furthermore, at lower levels, Clinton's influence seemed minimal or nonexistent. While Democrats picked up two governors, their gubernatorial victories seemed unconnected to Clinton's success.[25] At the same time, Republicans actually made substantial gains in state legislatures.[26] Tart-tongued Representative Patricia Schroeder (D-Colo.) remarked in 1988 that "Bush had no coattails; he had a bikini!"[27] If that was true, then—at least by the traditional measurement of coattails—Bill Clinton had come dangerously close to indecent exposure.

Yet a more nuanced approach to the question of coattails is in order when one takes into account the degree of noncomparability among districts from 1990 to 1992. The nation's elections by and large did not take place in the same constituencies. If Democratic House seat losses defy historical coattail patterns and lay bare the tenuousness of Clinton's "mandate," it is also true that Clinton probably saved the Democrats from even greater losses. Beyond the statistical conception of coattails lies a broader question: did he help or hurt his party, all other things being equal?

From all appearances, Clinton's strength and Bush's weakness worked to help Democrats. Certainly those in the political arena believed this to be the case. In mid-September, *Congressional Quarterly Weekly Report* remarked that "for the first time since Jimmy Carter ran in 1976, Democratic House candidates across the country are embracing their national ticket and even have reason to hope for a 'coattails' effect."[28] While Clinton kept some distance from the congressional Democrats until near the end of the campaign, after the Democratic convention Democratic candidates were increasingly anxious to tie themselves to Clinton. Conversely, as early as July, Republican candidates were deeply concerned about Bush's possible negative effects on their campaigns, believing that the economy and Bush's unpopularity and political errors could bring them down, too.[29] In the fall, columnists Rowland Evans and Robert Novak warned that GOP candidates were "burdened by the dead weight of George Bush." Republicans avoided mention of President Bush, and some like Illinois Senate candidate Rich Williamson explicitly disassociated themselves from him.[30] Rather than rely on Bush, many Republican challengers sought to attract Perot voters.

More specifically, observers pointed to the beneficial effects of Clinton at the top of the ticket for Democrats in the South and on the West Coast. Democratic officeholders in the South, including a number of senators targeted by the Republicans for having opposed the Persian Gulf War, considered Clinton a great asset. In the end, only North Carolina's Terry Sanford lost—after suffering a heart attack weeks before the election. Georgia's Wyche Fowler also lost, but not until a runoff three weeks later in which Clinton was not on the ballot. And Clinton's effect on lower races in California and Washington may have saved two Senate seats (Boxer of California and Murray of Washington both won by substantially smaller margins in their states than did Clinton) and numerous House seats. Indeed, it was unexpected Democratic successes in the new California House districts and the open seats in Washington state that deprived the

Table 5-4
Presidential Coattails in 1992 Senate Races

Margin of victory or defeat in percent,
Clinton and Democratic Senate candidates

State	Clinton	Candidates
Alabama	−7	+32
Alaska	−9	−14
Arizona	−2	−24
Arkansas	+18	+20
California	+15	+5 (Boxer)
California	+15	+17 (Feinstein)
Colorado	+4	+10
Connecticut	+6	+22
Florida	−2	+32
Georgia	+1	+1 (defeated 11/24 in runoff)
Hawaii	+12	+31
Idaho	−14	−14
Illinois	+13	+10
Indiana	−6	−16
Iowa	+6	−44
Kansas	−5	−32
Kentucky	+3	+28
Maryland	+14	+42
Missouri	+10	−8
Nevada	+3	+11
New Hampshire	+1	−2
New York	+16	−2
North Carolina	−1	−4
North Dakota	−12	+20
Ohio	+1	+10
Oklahoma	−9	−11
Oregon	+11	−4
Pennsylvania	+9	−2
South Carolina	−8	+2
South Dakota	−4	+33
Utah	−19	−16
Vermont	+15	+10
Washington	+12	+10
Wisconsin	+4	+6

Republicans of much larger national gains.[31] The almost total lack of a Republican presidential campaign in California thus cost the party dearly.

One other piece of empirical evidence lends indirect support to the proposition that Clinton aided his party in the congressional races. Surveys indicate that voters' inclinations to vote Democratic in congressional elections paralleled precisely the rise in Clinton's fortunes over the five months prior to the election. Just before the Democratic convention, when Clinton was locked in a three-way tie, voters expressed a preference for Democrats in Congress by approximately a five-point margin. Immediately after the convention, when Clinton was surging to a 2 to 1 lead in the presidential race, the preference for Democrats in Congress reached double digits. That margin was up to 17 points in October.[32]

In sum, despite redistricting, retirements, scandals, and having opposed a popular and successful war, Democrats managed to minimize their losses and retain comfortable control of both houses. The variable that most sensibly explains this outcome was the effect of the presidential race. Of course, the other way of looking at the situation is to say not that the Democrats were saved from greater losses by Clinton, but that the Republicans were saved from losses by redistricting and an "outsider" year.

TERM LIMITATIONS

Outrage at Congress manifested itself less through the congressional elections in November than in numerous state referenda. Curiously, at the very same time that voters were returning 93 percent of the incumbents who survived to run in the final elections, proposals designed to limit congressional terms were approved in all 14 states where they were on the ballot. Thus, the outside party won its greatest victory where no actual seats were at stake. All of the proposals limit senators to two six-year terms. Eight of the 14 limit representatives to three two-year terms; four limit them to four terms; and two limit them to six terms.

Term limits measures received at least 60 percent support in 11 of the 14 states. The only state with a positive vote below 55 percent was Washington, which had defeated a similar proposal in 1991. Columnist David Broder called the collection of initiatives "the closest thing to a national referendum ever held in the United States."[33] The 14 states join Colorado, which passed such a measure in 1990.

The term limits movement gained substantial momentum as a result of the 1992 elections. Approximately one-quarter of the Senate and one-third of the House are now serving from states that have passed term limits, although no candidate would be prevented from running until 1998. The term limits movement is also having an effect on state politics, where a number of states (among them, California) now have limitations on the number of terms individuals may serve in the state legislature. Even without national term limits, the state term limits should have an important, indirect impact on congressional elections. The usual source for serious challengers in House races is the local state representative or senator. More of these politicians will now be available as challengers for House seats.

Table 5-5
1992 Term Limits Initiatives

State	% Support
Arizona	74
Arkansas	60
California	63
Florida	77
Michigan	59
Missouri	74
Montana	67
Nebraska	68
North Dakota	55
Ohio	66
Oregon	69
South Dakota	63
Washington	52
Wyoming	77

Source: New York Times, November 5, 1992, p. B16.

The wisdom of term limitations is uncertain. Proponents make the Jacksonian argument that periodic rotation in office is necessary to restore popular control over the institution, and to ensure that it remains in touch with the problems and aspirations of the American people. The "citizen legislator" of the early republic is held up as a model, and those concerned with high incumbency reelection rates point to term limits as a way to ensure a steady stream of open seats and new blood.

At this point the arguments for term limits point in two slightly different directions. On one side, some emphasize that the representatives will now be closer to the people and follow more directly their wishes. This represents the Jacksonian or anti-federalist argument for term limits. On the other side, some advocate term limits in order to increase the likelihood the members of Congress will actually exercise discretion and deliberate about the public good. Only when freed from the constant campaigning and fundraising endemic today can representatives look to the future in a statesmanlike manner. In this view, we need what looks like a populist reform to serve a more constitutional or "federalist" objective.

Opponents respond that term limits are undemocratic. They also hold that limits may bring unwanted consequences, such as increased power for unelected congressional staff members and bureaucrats who would possess the expertise that can only be matched by years of service in Congress. Although forced retirements would increase, incumbent reelection rates may also increase; "strategic politicians" may calculate that their best chance lies in waiting for the inevitable open seat. Legislative accountability would be reduced, actually increasing the tendency toward shortsightedness. And the goals of term limits proponents might be achieved with less drastic, subconstitutional changes, like campaign finance reform, strengthening of the parties, and reduction of congressional perquisites like free mailings. In short, to opponents, the best way to limit terms is to vote against your incumbent.[34]

Aside from the merits, the constitutionality of the term limits measures is dubious. The federal Constitution stipulates eligibility requirements for federal offices. It is questionable whether states can add requirements beyond the age, citizenship, and residency requirements constitutionally specified for members of Congress. Proponents argue that Article IV of the Constitution, which gives states the power to regulate the "time, place, and manner" of congressional elections, includes the power to limit the number of terms legislators may serve in Congress. This issue will be decided in the federal courts, although perhaps not until a member of Congress can claim standing to sue after being prevented from running.

Nevertheless, if state measures are overturned as unconstitutional, the term limits movement is unlikely to disappear. Some advocates of term limits concede that the state initiative route is unconstitutional. In their view, it nonetheless remains politically valuable to highlight the issue, thereby giving impetus to a drive for a constitutional amendment. Americans to Limit Congressional Terms, the organization which spearheaded much of the term limits drive in the states, claims to have 300,000 members, and they are already pressing Congress for such an amendment. Should that fail—and, given the nature of Congress' interest in this subject, this is likely—there remains the constitutional convention route. State legislatures could bypass Congress and call directly for an amendment to be considered at a constitutional convention.

It is too early to predict the final result of this agitation, but it is clear that term limits have enormous appeal. Term limits serve as a proxy for irritation with Washington in general and might be only the vanguard of a broader movement to reform American institutions. Voter dissatisfaction in 1992 was more institutional than partisan in nature; the term limits drive succeeded where individual challengers failed. In the 15 states that have passed term limitation initiatives, only six of 121 incumbents were defeated. At the least, then, term limits initiatives provided an outlet which diverted anti-incumbent sentiment away from actual incumbents.

THE MEANING OF THE
CONGRESSIONAL ELECTIONS

While Congress received a major facelift in 1992, it remains to be seen whether the voters achieved anything more than a cosmetic alteration. Institutional reform was at the forefront of many campaigns, and the 103rd Congress has more new members than any Congress since 1948. Yet it is far from clear what effect a turnover of nearly one-quarter will have. Will the outsider-insider axis develop into as powerful a force in Congress as it was during the campaign, or will the traditional partisan and ideological axes remain dominant?

Some congressional leaders expressed concern before the 103rd Congress even met for the first time that the 122 new members could be "bombthrowers" with a reform agenda all their own. Democrat Leon Panetta explained that fears centered on the possibility that "a class like that develops a dynamic of its own. . . . That's the unknown quotient that's scaring the hell out of everyone."[35] Others, including outgoing Representatives Vin Weber (R-Minn.) and Dennis Eckart (D-Ohio), predicted that new members would arrive in Washington full of grand ideas, then quickly assimilate into the status quo, distracted by the time-consuming imperatives of seeking reelection.

Whatever institutional change the incoming class may or may not produce, one thing is certain: institutionally, the congressional elections of 1992 left an enormous vacuum. Some six states lost over 100 years of seniority (New York lost 217 years), and 21 state delegations began the 103rd Congress with at least 20 percent new members. The Arkansas House delegation is 75 percent new, Georgia 64 percent. Altogether, the House lost more than 1,500 years of seniority and the Senate nearly 140 years. While the Democratic leadership survived intact, three members of the Republican House leadership did not return. One-third of both the House Ways and Means Committee and the House Appropriations Committee members also did not return. Which members and what ideas fill this vacuum will affect Congress for decades. The Watergate generation has been supplanted by the Rubbergate generation.

At the intersection of the institutional and the partisan, the retention of Democratic control of Congress coupled with Bill Clinton's victory means the end of divided government, or at least a respite from it and all its real or imagined evils. Indeed, numerous post-election analyses argued that Democratic losses in Congress were minimized partly because the public had at long last grown weary of divided government. Political scientists and ordinary citizens will have an opportunity to test the proposition that government works best when it is under unified party control.

Unified government, and more specifically the unified government produced by these elections, will present not only opportunities but dangers to the Democrats. The opportunities are obvious. Programs long desired by the Democratic Congress can be enacted without as great a risk of presidential veto. And Clinton himself will possess a legislative partisan base, at least some of which probably owes its electoral survival to him.

There are also many dangers. The first comes from the reality of unified government itself. There is no longer an opposition president to blame. As New York Senator Daniel Patrick Moynihan remarked, "My God . . . now it's *our* deficit."[36] Failure to produce to the satisfaction of the country could lead to loss of control of both branches. In 1990 and 1992, the predicted anti-incumbent tide was largely deflected by congressional Democrats toward an uncooperative president; that tactic is no longer available.

The second danger comes from the composition of the unified government. Bill Clinton was elected not only as an outsider, but as a "different kind of Democrat" who perceived the need to reformulate the Democratic party along centrist lines. If he proves to be serious about that task, he will discover that he faces a Democratic congressional majority whose left wing was strengthened in the 1992 elections. New Senators like Barbara Boxer, Carol Moseley Braun (who advocated defense cuts four times deeper than Clinton's), Russ Feingold (who advocated tax increases twice as great as Clinton's and proposed a resolution in the Wisconsin state senate at the height of the Persian Gulf War calling for unilateral American withdrawal), and Dianne Feinstein will join Tom Harkin and Paul Wellstone on the left of the Senate. The growth in the number of minorities and pro-abortion women will almost certainly also tilt the House contingent further to the left.[37] As a result, Clinton may find himself relying to an uncomfortable degree on Republican votes on issues such as crime, welfare reform, and foreign intervention.

Paradoxically, it is also possible that a number of new Democratic members may make fiscal restraint a higher priority than Clinton. Incoming members seemed to place a greater emphasis on the deficit than the current leaders or members, and an alliance with Republicans on many budget and fiscal issues is a strong possibility. Thus there are at least two emerging and potentially hostile centers of Democratic congressional power. The first consists of the refortified liberals, the second of the conservative/moderate bloc.

Bill Clinton, a more skilled politician than Jimmy Carter, will almost certainly have greater success with Congress. He is an instinctive deal-maker, not prone to hand down solutions from on high; if anything, his weakness lies in the other direction, of accommodation to the point of losing form. Democrats in Congress are anxious to avoid the mutually destructive relations of the Carter era. Nevertheless, it is likely that Clinton will at some point run afoul of doctrinaire liberals, whom he cannot thwart without endangering his standing in the party but cannot accommodate without endangering his position with the electorate. It is also likely that Clinton will at some point run afoul of the deficit cutters, whose help he needs to remake the Democratic image but whose imperatives threaten the myriad programs that he has promised but cannot pay for.

The Republicans also face dangers and opportunities. The greatest danger may be that potential candidates and contributors, having seen an extremely promising year end in a mere ten-seat gain in the House, will conclude that Democratic congressional control is a part of natural law that Aquinas forgot to transcribe. The other key danger is that Republicans will mishandle their role as the opposition by compromising either too much or too little. An ongoing debate is assured between the confrontationist and accommodationist factions of the congressional party. In any case, the Republicans can now adopt the role of pure opposition, no longer tied to a White House that many Republican members considered a drag. The congressional party will thus be freed to act as it did during the Carter presidency, as an incubator of ideas and a definer of partisan differences. Senate Majority Leader Bob Dole wasted no time in appointing himself spokesman for the 57 percent of American voters who had voted against Bill Clinton, and promised to be the "chaperon" at the presidential "honeymoon."

Already strengthened by ten seats in the House, the Republicans can probably hope to gain some additional seats in the 1994 elections. In every midterm election after 1934 the party in control of the White House has lost seats, and the high number of current Democratic seats means even greater exposure to risk. Additionally, while Republican gains from redistricting were much more limited than the party hoped in 1992, redistricting did make a number of formerly uncompetitive districts potentially winnable for the remainder of the decade. Thus, some analysts have speculated that redistricting may yet hold the promise of a "timed-release" effect favorable to the Republicans in future years.[38]

Significant gains in 1994 could put the Republicans within reach of a working or even outright majority in 1996, if Clinton is vulnerable and the top of the Republican ticket is strong. It may have been necessary for the Republicans to lose the White House in order to make serious gains in Congress.

CONCLUSION

The congressional elections fit in well with the general oddity of the 1992 election year. The year started with scandal and numerous retirements. It was spiced with the vagaries of a redistricting process made even more convoluted than usual by the Voting Rights Act, the courts, and the Justice Department. It proceeded to a primary season which saw a postwar record for incumbents defeated, and records for minority and women nominees. It ended with a general election in which the presidential winner lost seats in Congress but probably had coattails anyway; in which that winner ran on a platform of centrism while the most liberal elements of his party bolstered their position on Capitol Hill; and in which voters in 14 states approved term limits proposals by huge margins while the national electorate returned 93 percent of the incumbents running.

The 1992 elections mean the end of divided government. There is continued potential over the long term, however, for conflict between president and Congress, on policy, ideological, and even institutional grounds instead of partisan grounds. Finally, Republican presidential defeat paradoxically carries with it the potential for a reinvigorated congressional Republican party.

The partisan outcome of the elections—Republican gains despite a presidential defeat—could be accounted for by a combination of factors that include redistricting and the importance of outsiderism. The modest extent of those gains, however, also indicates the degree to which the old partisan axis was still operational and the degree to which outsiderism operated within certain limits. Voters were given three choices along the inside-outside spectrum: to leave Congress essentially untouched, to remove the worst offenders, or to endorse a wholesale remaking of Congress. In the end, the public forced a postwar record number of retirements, defeated a postwar record number of incumbents in primaries, and voted for moderate change in the general election, mostly in response to specific scandals. The call to "throw all the rascals out," though tempting to many Americans, was ultimately rejected. Indeed, the most extreme form of outsiderism to prevail was aimed not at the individual members of Congress but at the institution of Congress in the form of term limits, which were in many respects symbolic rather than substantive. Thus, as in the presidential race, the American people ultimately settled on a tempered form of outsiderism.

NOTES

1. See "Running Against the Computer," *Washington Post*, September 29, 1992, p. C5.

2. See "And the Winner Will Not Be . . . ," *National Journal*, September 26, 1992, p. 2161; Guy Gugliotta, "Blacks Join Forces With GOP on Remap," *Washington Post*, May 11, 1992, p. A4.

3. See *Baker v. Carr* 1962, *Reynolds v. Sims* 1964, *Wesberry v. Sanders* 1964.

4. *Karcher v. Daggett*, 1983.

5. See *Davis v. Bandemer,* 1985.

6. *Thornburgh v. Gingles*, 1986.

7. See Phil Duncan, "GOP's Remap Bounty Likely to Be Modest," *National Journal*, March 14, 1992, p. 682; Guy Gugliotta, "Blacks Join Forces With GOP on Remap," *Washington Post*, May 11, 1992, p. A4; Maralee Schwartz, "Michigan Delegation Caught in Redistricting Squeeze," *Washington Post*, April 21, 1992, p. A8.

8. This view is not held unanimously among academics, however. For example David R. Mayhew argues that gridlock is actually no worse under divided government than under unified government. See *Divided We Govern* (New Haven, Conn.: Yale University Press, 1991).

9. See, for example, James Sundquist, "The New Era of Coalition Government in the United States," *Political Science Quarterly*, Winter 1988-89.

10. See Jonathan Rauch, "Demosclerosis," *National Journal*, September 5, 1992, pp. 1998-2003.

11. *The American Enterprise*, November/December 1992, p. 83.

12. Rowland Evans and Robert Novak, "The Politics of Scandal," *Washington Post*, March 20, 1992, p. A25.

13. *The American Enterprise*, November/December 1992, pp. 82, 86-87, 90.

14. See George F. Will, *Restoration: Congress, Term Limits and the Rediscovery of Deliberative Democracy* (New York: Free Press, 1992).

15. *The American Enterprise*, November/December 1992, p. 92.

16. See Beth Donovan and Janet Hook, "Clinton and Democrats Plan to Touch Bases—Gingerly," *CQ Weekly Report*, April 25, 1992, pp. 1082-1086.

17. CNN, Republican National Convention, August 27, 1992.

18. Sandra Musumeci, "Primaries Herald La Belle Epoque," *Campaign*, August 1992, p. 1.

19. See Keith Glover, "After Years on the Outside, Women Find They're 'In' As Candidates," *CQ Weekly Report*, May 2, 1992, p. 1179; Sandra Musumeci, "Primaries Herald La Belle Epoque," *Campaign*, August 1992, p. 1; "Women's Campaigns Fueled Mostly by Women's Checks," *CQ Weekly Report*, October 17, 1992, pp. 3270-3273; Celinda Lakes, "Women Won on the Merits," *New York Times*, November 7, 1992, p. A15.

20. Of course, a 51 percent showing does not necessarily translate into a 2 percent or smaller victory, since there were some three-way races.

21. "Now It's Up To the Freshmen," *Roll Call*, November 5, 1992, p. 4.

22. "D'Amato's Pork Barrel Polka," *Washington Post*, October 19, 1992, p. B4.

23. Keith Glover, "Campaigning Crusaders Air Graphic Anti-Abortion Ads," *CQ Weekly Report*, September 26, 1992, pp. 2970-2972.

24. Gary C. Jacobson, *The Politics of Congressional Elections*, Third Edition (New York: HarperCollins, 1992), p. 158.

25. See Fox Butterfield, "Democrats Gain, No Thanks to Clinton," *New York Times*, November 5, 1992, p. B16.

26. Michael deCourcy Hinds, "Elections Change Face of Lawmaking Bodies," *New York Times*, November 5, 1992, p. B9.

27. Cited in Roger H. Davidson and Walter J. Oleszek, *Congress and Its Members*, Third Edition (Washington, D.C.: Congressional Quarterly, 1990), p. 99.

28. Dave Kaplan and Bob Benenson, "The Hot, Hotter, and Hottest of the November Contests," *CQ Weekly Report*, September 19, 1992, pp. 2836-2841.

29. See Jeffrey H. Birnbaum, "Republicans' Dream of Big Gains in House May End as Just That," *Wall Street Journal*, October 27, 1992, p. 1.

30. See Rowland Evans and Robert Novak, "Reverse Republican Coattails," *Washington Post*, October 5, 1992, p. A19.

31. See Ceci Connolly and Charles Mahtesian, "With Two Peers Leading the Ticket, South's Democrats Expect 'a Boost,'" *CQ Weekly Report*, July 11, 1992, p. 2019; Dave Kaplan and Bob Benenson, "The Hot, Hotter, and Hottest of the November Contests," *CQ Weekly Report*, September 19, 1992, pp. 2836-2841; David Rogers and Jackie Calmes, "Shake-Up of Congress Yields Big Coalition of Women, Minorities," *Wall Street Journal*, November 5, 1992, p. 1.

32. See Jeffrey H. Birnbaum, "Republicans' Dream of Big Gains in House May End as Just That," *Wall Street Journal*, October 27, 1992, p. 1.

33. David Broder, "Term Limits: The Movement Gathers Momentum," *Washington Post*, July 29, 1992, p. A23.

34. For the debate on term limits, see Morris Fiorina, *Divided Government* (New York: Macmillan, 1992), pp. 53-58; George F. Will, *Restoration: Congress, Term Limits and the Recovery of Deliberative Democracy* (New York: Free Press, 1992); Charles R. Kesler, "The Trouble with Term Limits," *Profile*, Fall 1992; Alan Heslop, "Time for Term Limits," *Profile*, Fall 1992.

35. "Visions of the Next Congress Inspire Reform Proposals," *CQ Weekly Report*, October 3, 1992, p. 3017.

36. David Rogers and Jackie Calmes, "Shake-Up of Congress Yields Big Coalition of Women, Minorities," *Wall Street Journal*, November 5, 1992, p. 1.

37. See Rogers and Calmes, p. 1; "Democrats versus Clinton," *Wall Street Journal*, November 5, 1992, p. A18; Helen Dewar, "Next President's Diplomatic Skill To Be Put To Test," *Washington Post*, November 5, 1992, p. A25.

38. Bob Benenson, "GOP's Dreams of a Comeback Via the New Map Dissolve," *CQ Weekly Report*, November 7, 1992, p. 3581.

The Presidential Election and the Future of American Politics

"The man with no ideas was running against the man of too many."
                    —Eugene H. Roseboom,
                    on the election of 1872[1]

Following the political volatility of the spring and summer, the nation appeared poised during the fall campaign for one last big surprise that might suddenly turn everything upside down. It never came. George Bush began the race behind, he stayed behind, and he finished behind. The issues and questions being discussed and debated at the end of August were the same as those being discussed and debated at the end of October.

There were two moments in this frozen campaign when there was at least a possibility of major change. The first came with the reentrance of Ross Perot on October 1. Bush, trailing badly, was prepared to welcome anything new—even his nemesis Ross Perot. As one high Bush campaign official noted, Perot might "at least change the dynamic of the race. . . . We were doing better when he was in there in June."[2] The last assessment also reflected regret inside the Bush camp at its decision in the early summer, when Clinton was a distant third in the polls, to attack Perot and help drive him from the race. What Bush strategists in their desperation now saw—and what they had not realized in June—was that while George Bush might be able to defeat Bill Clinton in a three-person race, he could not do so in a two-person race. The immediate effect of Perot's reentrance was slight, however, as he drew about an equal amount of support from both candidates.[3]

159

The second moment of potential change came at the conclusion of "debate week"—a period from October 11 through 19 in which four debates, three presidential and one vice-presidential, were packed together. Perot seemed now to have greater potential than anyone thought in early October, and Bush for a brief moment near the end appeared to rally. If the miraculous could somehow occur—a simultaneous rise of Perot's support at the expense of Clinton and a fall in Perot's support to the advantage of Bush—then maybe Bush could still see his way to victory. It never quite worked. While Perot in the end cut far more deeply into Clinton's support than most expected—and might have done so even more if he had waged an aggressive campaign *against* Clinton—it was not enough to spell Clinton's defeat. And George Bush was never really able to win back any more supporters, whether from Perot or Clinton. He never broke the 40 percent barrier under which he had hovered for most of the campaign.

CAMPAIGN STRATEGY AND THE 1992 ELECTION

Modern presidential campaigns use three kinds of strategies: one based on the geography of separate state races, a second on theme and issue appeals, and a third on appeals to groups. The first strategy asks "Where?," the second, "What?," and the third, "Who?"

State Strategy

The importance of a geographic strategy in presidential elections derives from the electoral college. Elections are won by electoral votes, leading campaign strategists to allocate resources inside the campaign on the basis of separate elections in each state. The importance of this fact often escapes pollsters, who like to treat national electoral data as a kind of homogeneous mass. In their view, an imaginary vote in Florida counts as much as an imaginary vote in Arkansas or California. Campaign strategists working under the logic of geography never see it this way. The value and meaning of a vote varies according to *where* it occurs. And that value is a dynamic fact that changes with events and decisions. Early on in a campaign, some states may be abandoned as lost, others counted as won. This process continues as the campaign proceeds. Once a state is abandoned, no more resources will be expended on it, and from the strategist's viewpoint, whether the defeat occurs by a small or a large margin is irrelevant.

A geographic strategy was central all along to Bill Clinton's campaign. From the outset, adversity proved a good teacher. The campaign began serious planning in May and June when Clinton was far back in third place in the national polls. There was no alternative but to concentrate on a strict geographic strategy. When Clinton pulled ahead to a huge lead in the polls in September, the campaign faced pressure of another kind: to abandon geography and go for a broad sweep to give Clinton a huge popular mandate. The campaign kept its head—and its geographic plan. That plan was always to target the states needed for an electoral victory. As political strategist Paul Tully kept reminding fellow Democrats, "Don't be greedy little pigs."[4]

Clinton's geographic plan received a tremendous boost in August when it became apparent that California and New York, the nation's two largest states with a combined total of 87 electoral votes, were already safely in the Democrats' column. The Republicans abandoned both by early September. Added to this base was a number of other surefire victories, including the District of Columbia, Minnesota, Massachusetts, and West Virginia. The Democrats' idea was then to break the Republicans' hold on some of the states in the South, to gather support in the far West and New England, and to prepare for a critical battle in some of the industrial states, such as Michigan, Ohio, Pennsylvania, and Missouri. The Republicans, having ceded so much from the outset, were reduced to a "tight" victory strategy with little margin for error.

The election results (see Table 6-1 on the following page) show the success of the Democrats' strategy. Clinton made important breakthroughs in the South (Georgia and Louisiana, plus the home states of the candidates, Arkansas and Tennessee); he won the far West and New England; and he kept enough resources at the end to wage an all-out battle in the industrial states, all of which he ended up winning. The Republican "lock"—an idea that any Republican candidate could count on 342 electoral votes—proved to be no more than a description of the past, not a deterministic prediction of an indefinite future.

Theme and Issue Appeals

The second kind of strategy is based on theme and issue mobilization. The electorate here is conceived as a mass of individuals, each of whom has a set of attitudes and preferences. In the case of a large number of voters, these attitudes and preferences can be affected

Chapter Six

Table 6-1

ɛsults of the Presidential Race, 1992

	inton	% Bush	% Perot	Electoral Vote
Ala.	41	48	11	9 R
Alaska	32	41	27	3 R
Ariz.	37	39	24	8 R
Ark.	54	36	11	6 D
Calif.	47	32	21	54 D
Colo.	40	36	23	8 D
Conn.	42	36	22	8 D
Del.	44	36	21	3 D
D.C.	86	9	4	3 D
Fla.	39	41	20	25 R
Ga.	44	43	13	13 D
Hawaii	49	37	14	4 D
Idaho	29	43	28	4 R
Ill.	48	35	27	22 D
Ind.	37	43	20	12 R
Iowa	44	38	19	7 D
Kans.	34	39	27	6 R
Ky.	45	42	14	8 D
La.	46	42	12	9 D
Maine	39	31	30	4 D
Md.	50	36	14	10 D
Mass.	48	29	23	12 D
Mich.	44	37	19	18 D
Minn.	44	32	24	10 D
Miss.	41	50	9	7 R
Mo.	44	34	22	11 D
Mont.	38	36	26	3 D
Nebr.	30	47	24	5 R
Nev.	38	35	26	4 D
N.H.	39	38	23	4 D
N.J.	43	41	16	15 D
N.Mex.	46	38	16	5 D
N.Y.	50	34	16	33 D
N.C.	43	44	14	14 R
N.Dak.	32	44	23	3 R
Ohio	40	39	21	21 D
Okla.	34	43	23	8 R

Oreg.	43	32	25	7 D
Pa.	45	36	18	23 D
R.I.	48	29	23	4 D
S.C.	40	48	12	8 R
S.Dak.	37	41	22	3 R
Tenn.	47	43	10	11 D
Tex.	37	40	22	32 R
Utah	26	45	29	5 R
Vt.	46	31	23	3 D
Va.	41	45	14	13 R
Wash.	44	32	24	11 D
W. Va.	49	36	16	5 D
Wis.	41	37	22	11 D
Wyo.	34	40	26	3 R
Totals	43	38	19	370 D–168 R

by arguments and symbolic entreaties in a way that can influence the vote decision. This point, which seems so obvious, has more significance than at first appears. It assumes, in line with the modern idea of a large floating vote, that the votes of many individuals are potentially "up for grabs" and that the purpose of campaigning is not only, as it may once primarily have been, to rally those who are already convinced, but also to win over many persuadable voters. Furthermore, in treating the electorate as a mass of undifferentiated individuals, this strategy recognizes that in today's electorate many people are not reached and mobilized as members of distinct groups or classes, but as parts of abstract attitudinal constituencies.

Examples of the logic of this strategy are contained in modern issues polls, of the sort that say, for example, that 43 percent of the electorate listed the economy and jobs as being one of the most important issues in the nation today, and of these, two-thirds preferred the approach of Bill Clinton. The different entities or "groups" identified here are not ordinary demographic groups, but categories defined by a common attitude. They cut across demographic groups and include Asians as well as whites, Northerners as well as Southerners, and Protestants as well as Jews.

The general objective of this kind of strategy is to focus the campaign on themes and issues which are judged to be important to a large number of people, and on which your candidate is judged

more favorably than your opponent. Of course, your opponent is
doing the same thing, so there must be a defensive as well as an
offensive strategy. In the end, the "theory" is that if you can focus
the campaign on themes and issues on which your candidate is judged
more favorably, you will be able to persuade more people to vote for
you. The only refinement is that, as the campaign goes on, it is not
the concerns of people in general that count, but the concerns of
those who are undecided or who might potentially be moved.

The categories on which theme and issue mobilization take place
usually include the following:

I.   Basic Theme
II.   Candidate Character
III.   The Major Issue Areas:
       1. Which candidate can best lead the economy?
       2. Which candidate can best promote domestic welfare and
          justice?
       3. Which candidate best safeguards basic values?
       4. Which candidate can best provide for the nation's security
          and promote its cause and interest in the world?

Basic Theme. The difference between the two campaigns on
this question was as simple as it was startling: Bill Clinton had a
general theme (change), Bush did not. The absence of a theme in
Bush's case summed up the essential problem of his campaign, if not
his presidency itself. It had no single positive message to stress. The
campaign's nearest thing to a slogan—the ungrammatical "Who do
you trust?"— was less a genuine theme than a reference to the character
question.

By contrast, the Democratic campaign was based on the theme
of "change," a word Bill Clinton and Al Gore pronounced so much
that it became a kind of campaign mantra. The Democrats controlled
the discussion of the basic theme, not because they were geniuses
in inventing something that did not exist, but because they found a
theme that was already present in the public mood. The theme of
change was connected for the Clinton campaign with the concrete
problem that most troubled Americans: the nation's economic conditions. But it did what every good theme manages to do—expand
from a concrete matter to connect with something broader, if more
vague. "Time for a change" tapped into the sentiment, felt especially strongly early on in the year, that there was something deeply
wrong with America—a compilation of economic decline, gridlock,

corruption, in short much that was in the "package" of outsiderism. And it connected to a sentiment that George Bush and the Republicans had been around too long, that what the country needed was something new and fresh.

The potency of the general theme of change was confirmed in the emergence of Ross Perot. In the eyes of almost every electoral analyst, Perot in the spring helped to activate a "pro-change constituency." Perot's pure outsider appeal can be viewed—symbolically—as a more extreme kind of change than Clinton's. Indeed, Perot often characterized his campaign as the only one that offered "real change." When Perot dropped out in July, his constituency, having been activated and cut loose from its place in a previous coalitional structure, shifted immediately to Bill Clinton, who was the more moderate version of the same thing—change without inhaling. The worry of the Clinton people in the fall was that Perot would again split this pro-change constituency.

Having no positive theme of their own, Republicans were forced into a defensive position. As a general rule of campaign strategy, the mere fact that you must wage a battle on your opponent's terrain means that you are already at a disadvantage. Still, there can be successful defensive strategies that cut into and undermine an opponent's strategy. Republicans sought to answer Clinton's change theme first by deflating its symbolic component and then driving the debate back to a discussion of particulars. The question Bush kept asking was not whether there should be change, but what kind of change there should be—change from what to what? Bush in the end had some success in suggesting that the Democrats' change meant more taxes and bigger government.

Second, Republicans tried to turn the theme of change back on the Democrats. Change means that one is not satisfied with what we have, and the advocate of change can therefore be accused of constantly running down America. Bush also tried using this tact against Clinton. The problem with this response, however, is that it pushed Bush into attaching himself too closely to the current state of affairs and exposed a fundamental dilemma of the campaign: whether to embrace the bulk of the status quo and run on it, or whether to repudiate it and blame it on the Democrats.

Finally, Republicans counted on the potential downside of the change theme, namely that people might find change to be too risky. The Bush campaign hoped that as election day approached the fear of change would grow, on the reasonable assumption that people are less averse to change when it is abstract and remote and more averse as the possibility becomes closer and more concrete. Part of this logic, however, depended on the structure of thought of the Cold War. As unpopular as he was in 1980, Jimmy Carter nevertheless profited from the idea that it was too risky to change, in large part because of the international situation. Gerald Ford had also used this theme in his campaign against Jimmy Carter in 1976. In 1992, it wouldn't work.

The results of the "change theme" were clear. Change was listed in exit polls as one of the most important general reasons influencing voters' decisions. The overwhelming majority of those voters chose Clinton.[5]

Character. The second category is the question of character. The "character issue" in the 1992 campaign was a mirror image in miniature of the thematic debate on change. Clinton did not want to talk about it, George Bush did.

The Republican campaign focused on what Quayle and Bush referred to in the debates as Clinton's "pattern of deceit" and "pattern of deception." The intent was not only to recall all the earlier accusations of which Clinton had been the target, but also to point to some of Clinton's "flip-flops" on the issues. It was designed, in part, to evoke Clinton's "slick" image as a deft politician who moved easily to one side or another to pick up votes. By depicting Clinton as just a politician, Republicans hoped this attack might also push him more to the inside. It might help turn an obvious Clinton strength— his ability to speak in full sentences (a quality Bush never mastered) and to connect with audiences—into a liability.

The character issue did not fail the Republicans, but it was not nearly powerful enough on its own to persuade very many voters. Bill Clinton had taken his "hit" in the spring, and perhaps the electorate had already discounted the character question. Nothing new or shocking was uncovered during the campaign, and unsubstantiated innuendoes about something Bill Clinton did on a trip to Moscow only gave Clinton grounds for counterattacking. Furthermore, in the second presidential debate in Richmond, ABC's Carol Simpson, who served as the moderator, virtually ruled the character issue out of bounds as not being what the people wanted discussed. Ross Perot concurred. And in the end, Clinton had effective ammunition of his own. Bush's broken promise on taxes qualified him as a world-class flip-flopper, which was the point of one of Clinton's most effective television ads. In addition, a last-minute "revelation" against George Bush on the Iran-Contra affair, contained in papers filed by special prosecutor Lawrence Walsh, brought that matter back into the public's mind in the final days of the campaign.

The Issues. The final category consists of positions on the major areas of public policy. The Republican campaign began with two of the four areas targeted to work to their advantage: taking care of the nation's foreign policy and safeguarding its basic ("family") values. Foreign policy worked dramatically in Bush's favor, but it was not regarded by many as a decisive question in determining their vote. Only 8 percent of the voters cited foreign policy as "mattering most" in their presidential vote, 87 percent of whom preferred George Bush. The controversial values question was also a reason cited by many for voting for Bush, but it is not clear here how many of the persuadable (as distinct from the converted) were won over by this appeal, nor how many others were driven away by it. The Republicans' stand on the issue of abortion posed a similar problem.

On the other two general issue areas, managing the economy and taking care of domestic policy, Clinton held a large advantage. The concern for improving the economy and promoting jobs was the most widely cited single voting factor among the specific issues listed in the exit polls, and Clinton was considered the candidate best able to handle these matters.[6] The related deficit question, also frequently cited, worked to the advantage of both Ross Perot and Bill Clinton. On domestic matters, Clinton profited from voters' strong concern about the issue of health care, which was at the top of the list of non-economic domestic issues, and also from attention to the issues of education and the environment.

The sum total of the issue questions tells a simple story. Clinton "controlled" far more of the issues that voters regarded as important than Bush. If you can imagine a fictional index comprised of multiplying importance times preference for each issue and then summing the total, Clinton came out far ahead. The response of voters to the specific issues reveals another interesting point about the Bush presidency. Bush, who often governed to the center, got very little credit for any of his centrist or liberal record. He may have claimed to be the environmental president and the education president, but the voters never bought it. (Indeed, moderates in many categories abandoned Bush at an even greater rate than the rest of the electorate.) Some might say that this was because Bush did not deserve any credit, but another explanation might be that, when it comes to distributing benefits, a Republican is always likely to be outbid by a Democrat.

The discussion of issues also reveals a curious conspiracy of deception that took place during the campaign. The actual similarities between Bush and Clinton on many issues were often obscured because both candidates had political incentives to accentuate their differences. Bush, knowing that he had been elected on a Reaganite platform in 1988, came to the conclusion that he could only be re-elected on one. He thus had enormous incentive to gloss over the four years between campaign 1988 and campaign 1992. Clinton, on the other hand, had to convince voters that he represented real change, which could not be accomplished if voters noted the similarities between his promises and Bush's record.

Group Appeal

The third general element in campaign strategy is that of group appeal and mobilization. This strategy is a supplement (or an alternative) to the last strategy of conceiving of the electorate in abstract categories defined only by their common issue positions. In a group approach, the strategist conceives of voters not as abstract points in an undifferentiated mass, but as whole persons whom we know and can imagine as having certain characteristics. The campaign then targets groups judged to be important for victory and sets about to appeal to that group in terms of its interest.

The categories involved here may be broad demographic classifications with no real conscious feeling of group identity, but which analysts believe to share certain concerns (such as suburban voters); or they may be categories in which a small percentage (but still a large number) may feel a group concern (such as the middle class or women); or they may be groups in which many members are highly conscious of a common identity and where there are recognized group structures, such as black voters, the Cuban-American community, or evangelical church groups.

The centerpiece of the Clinton group strategy—indeed the strategy of the DLC itself—was to shatter the Reagan coalition by going after the white middle-class voter, often the voter living in the suburbs. The way to capture more of these voters was to move closer to them on social issues such as crime and welfare—at least far closer than had been the case with "liberal" Democratic nominees in the past. Furthermore, in a weak economy, it would be possible to make a direct appeal to the middle class's threatened economic situation. (Recall here, too, that the character of the last recession was an unusually high loss of middle-class jobs.) The appeal to the middle class was the focus of Clinton's early primary campaign, which featured a middle-class tax cut, and it was central to his campaign acceptance speech, directed at "the forgotten middle class." The object of this strategy was not always to capture a majority of the groups, but to improve the Democrats' relative position. In addition, Clinton made special group appeals to women and to his home base, Southern whites.

A study of group voting in 1992 presents some serious difficulties because of the three-way character of the race. The overall dropoff in Republican strength from 1988 to 1992 was massive (from 53 percent to 38 percent) and was evident within every group and demographic category. But if one focuses on the Republicans' collapse alone, it is easy to forget that there was also a falloff in Democratic strength from Dukakis in 1988 to Clinton in 1992 (from 45 percent to 43 percent). This also showed up in most groups and demographic categories, where Clinton ran behind Dukakis. Because it was a three-person race, Bush's losses from 1988 were not simply Clinton's gains.

If one ignores the fact of a three-way race, the seriousness of the low scores for both Bush and Clinton can easily be exaggerated, and almost anything negative one wishes can be proved. It needs to be remembered that political campaigns are about winning election against someone else, not about beating a mythical candidate from four years earlier. The object of analysis therefore ought to be how the coalitions of the parties stack up relative to each other. Assuming a two-person race in 1992, and dividing Perot's votes evenly between the Republican and Democrat, Bush's and Clinton's results would both look much stronger. (Poll figures reveal, incidentally, that exactly the same percentage of Perot voters would have voted for Bush as for Clinton, if Perot had not been in the race.) On the other hand, if one assumes that there will be a strong three-person race next time, then it is not necessary to have a majority to win. One might win again very nicely, as Clinton did, with a lower share of the vote than Dukakis.

The real study of the coalitions and groups in each party should fix on their lineup in relationship to each other. Bush defeated Dukakis by 8 percentage points in 1988, and he lost to Clinton by 5 percentage points in 1992. This means a net swing of 13 percentage points. This swing put the Democrats ahead of Republicans among many voting groups in 1992, although Republicans still held an advantage in certain groups including white voters (especially Protestant white voters and born-again Christians), the wealthy, and married voters.

The most interesting point on which to focus in the data on groups is the question of where Clinton gained the most relative to the Republicans. A simple indication of the answer is provided by observing where Clinton actually had a higher absolute percentage of the vote than Dukakis in 1988. His major gains were among fairly highly educated white males, usually middle-aged and older, and among Southern whites. What we see here, then, is gains in support among the comfortable middle class. Clinton's strongest improvements came from within groups that often gave a plurality to Republicans in 1992. Clinton reduced the margin of relative strength among groups that are still overall more part of the Republican coalition than the Democratic. We can call them Clinton Republicans.

Table 6-2
Major Groups in Which Clinton Ran Ahead of Dukakis

Group	% of '92 Total Vote	% Dukakis in 1988	% Clinton in 1992	% Bush in 1992
College graduates only	24	37	40	41
Postgraduates	16	48	49	36
White born-again Christians	17	18	23	61
Jews	4	64	78	12
Republicans	35	8	10	73
Retired persons	13	49	51	36
Men 45–59	11	36	40	40
Men 60 and older	7	46	49	37
Male college graduates	20	36	40	41
Whites in South	24	32	34	48

Source: Voter Research and Surveys, New York Times, November 5, 1992, p. B9.

Ross Perot's constituency deserves a final word. Perot received about one-fifth of the vote, which was fairly evenly dispersed among most demographic groups. There were a few exceptions. Perot ran far better among whites than blacks and far better among younger people (18 to 29 years old) than among older people (60 and above). He did somewhat better among men than women, and his regional base was strongest in the far West and Midwest, and weakest in the South. As expected, he drew votes more easily from those with the weakest partisan ties. The Perot constituency reveals at one and the same time the possible strength and weakness of the movement. Given that Perot's voters look strikingly like the rest of America, there is no reason that his movement could not grow immensely. It is not confined to any particular group from which it would have to break free. For the very same reason, however, it is easy to imagine how this vote could reintroduce itself into the mainstream without leaving a trace of evidence that the movement was ever there.

VOTER TURNOUT

A major surprise of the 1992 election was a reversal in a steady trend of declining voter turnout that has been occurring since 1960 (see Table 6-3). Voting turnout jumped sharply from 50 percent of the eligible electorate in 1988 to 54 percent in 1992. Accounting for this change will no doubt be a long-term project, but the most likely starting point is to assume a reversal in one of the major causes leading to an increase in nonvoting. According to Ruy Teixeira, an expert in this field, the recent rise of nonvoters is due to "a decline of social connectedness" (social connectedness refers here to being married and a participant in community groups) and "a generalized withdrawal or disconnection from the political world."[7] Since there has been no improvement in social connectedness in the last four years, the decisive change must have occurred in the "psychological involvement" of voters and the feeling that their vote has some significance or benefit.

Table 6-3
Voter Turnout

Year	Eligible Population that Voted	Year	Eligible Population that Voted
1932	52%	1964	62%
1936	57%	1968	61%
1940	59%	1972	55%
1944	56%	1976	54%
1948	51%	1980	53%
1952	62%	1984	53%
1956	59%	1988	50%
1960	63%	1992	54%

Among the primary factors responsible for this change are, first, a major structural transformation in the political communication system. The campaign pervaded the airwaves and popular culture to a far greater degree than recent campaigns, which were restricted to the "serious" network news channels and to the ads of the candidates. But in 1992, as so many observed, politics was everywhere again: on radio talk shows, TV talk and entertainment shows, free video cassettes, and the tabloids. The 1992 campaign moved politics back in the direction of nineteenth-century campaigns, when political campaigns were part of the entertainment, with torchlight parades and mass mobilization.[8]

Second, there were more voting options than usual for the presidency because of the Perot candidacy. Perot presumably brought out voters who otherwise would not have voted. Fourteen percent of those who voted for Perot, or about 2.6 percent of the electorate, said that if Perot had not been in the race, they would not have voted.[9] The Perot voters also included a substantial number of occasional voters.

Third, there was a greater total mobilization effort by the presidential candidates. More money was spent on this election than on any other, in part because of the larger sums of soft money raised by the major-party candidates, and in part because of the large spending (more than $60 million) by Ross Perot.

Finally, there was much greater competition in congressional races in 1992. Turnout in American politics is not just a function of the races at the top, but of races up and down the line. More competition and more spending most likely brought more voters to the polls.

No one, of course, can say whether this increase marks a single aberration or a new trend in another direction. Oddly enough, however, some of those who have been the loudest in lamenting the previous decline were among the first to discount the significance of the rise, perhaps because they make a business of this misery. Curtis Gans, who heads the Committee for the Study of the Electorate, noted that "this turnout was about anger with the recession and had nothing to do with fundamental changes in our democracy."[10] In this view, what counts is not just the number of those who vote, but the purity of their motivation.

THE 1992 ELECTION AND THE
THEORY OF REALIGNMENT

The state of theorizing about elections is currently in disarray. Until recently, political scientists were in wide agreement on a schema for categorizing elections based on a broad theory known as "realignment." But in the last few years that theory itself has come under sustained attack for being unable to deal with modern electoral realities. As Everett Ladd has asserted, "The failure of realignment is manifest."[11] This attack on a cherished theory has brought forth just the kind of snide and indignant responses for which academics have become so justly known. Wading into such disputes goes well beyond our concern here; but we can speculate on where the 1992 election might fit into current election theory, trying first to place it into the categories provided by realignment theory and then to see whether the election provides evidence for a different approach.

According to realignment theory, there are three kinds of elections: realigning (or critical) elections, maintaining elections, and deviating elections. A realigning election is part of a broader realignment process in which the parties' old coalitions are permanently changed, often leading to a reversal of party dominance. A realignment process begins with the introduction of a powerful new issue or cluster of issues that polarizes the nation and that cuts across existing party coalitions. A realignment at this point may be averted if both major parties adapt to the new issue in the same way at approximately the same time. (This occurred, for example, in the progressive era after 1912 when both parties adopted a "reform" agenda.) Otherwise, a realignment will take place. In one case, both major parties try to avoid or straddle the issue, which leaves the way open for a third party that emerges to challenge and perhaps eventually displace one of the major parties. In another case, one of the major parties will adopt the issue (perhaps after heeding the warning signs from a third party) and the other will not. This situation leads to a realignment between the two major parties. Realigning elections are highly charged contests, in which the public becomes alert to current issues and in which voter turnout is accordingly high.[12]

Following the intense period of polarization that produces a realignment comes a much longer period of conciliation, in which the realignment is solidified by the gravitation of all major political actors toward a new political center. In this in-between period, there occur two other kinds of elections: "maintaining" or "deviating" elections. In a maintaining election, the long-term partisan alignment established at the outset prevails. The issues of the day (short-term forces)—foreign policy matters, scandals, economic performance, and candidate credentials—either are too weak to overcome long-term trends or they reinforce those trends. The situation is "normal," which generally helps account for a relatively low turnout. In deviating elections, by contrast, the short-term forces work against the dominant party, and it loses. Deviating elections generally occur at a time of greater (temporary) tension and dissatisfaction, which leads to higher turnout. But long-term political attachments remain intact.[13]

Since the establishment of consistent two-party competition in the 1830s, political scientists have identified three periods of realignment: (a) 1856–1860, when the Republicans turned from a third party into the dominant party on the basis of the slavery issue, which the two major parties had tried to straddle; (b) 1896, when the Republicans again moved from a position of rough equality to a position of dominance as the result of the Democratic party's leftward and pro-agrarian move, which was driven by the blossoming Populist party; and (c) 1932–1936, when the Democratic party claimed a position of national dominance as the result of the Great Depression.

Conditions since 1968 have puzzled political scientists, however, because the general voting pattern that held in earlier times no longer applied. Specifically, when voters realigned in the past, they did so across the board, voting for candidates for one party or another at all levels. After 1968, however (some put the date much earlier), this pattern of voting across the board broke down. Voting in presidential elections was unconnected with, or moved in a different direction from, voting for Congress (and for state offices). People voted mostly for Democrats for Congress, while favoring Republicans for the presidency, producing the modern norm of "divided government."

As occurs with the development of theories in most disciplines, the deviation of observed facts from a prevailing theory can lead to one of two responses. One is to abandon the theory as being no longer helpful or valid (a possibility discussed below). The other is to seek to amend it in such a way that it can take into account the discordant phenomena. Those who have sought to save realignment theory in this way have responded to the current problem by proposing the idea of distinct realignments occurring at different levels. In the jargon of the discipline, there can be a "split-level realignment," meaning a realignment for the presidency but not the Congress (or vice versa).

Specifically, in this view, the New Deal alignment persisted after 1968 in sub-presidential politics, as indicated by the fact that from 1968 until 1992, the Democrats remained in control of the House for all 24 years, the Senate for 18 of the 24 years, and dominated state and local politics.[14] At the presidential level, however, a Republican realignment occurred. From Richard Nixon's victory over Hubert Humphrey in 1968 through George Bush's defeat of Michael Dukakis in 1988, Republicans won five of six elections, four of them by electoral landslides. This chain of victories can hardly have been a fluke; the same issues consistently recurred, and the Republican coalition—both geographically and demographically—did not change, except to expand in the 1980s. Furthermore, Ronald Reagan in particular went far toward reorienting the national debate in a conservative direction. In this view, 1968 and 1972 could be seen as the critical elections (though some would say 1980). All other elections through 1988 would be considered maintaining elections except 1976, which represented a deviation.

Within the framework of split-level realignment theory, where can one place the 1992 presidential election? Since the election cannot be classified as a maintaining election (the Republicans lost), it must be either a realigning or a deviating election. In postelection analyses in the press, a case has been made for each possibility.

Thesis 1. The 1992 election marked the beginning of a realignment. The realignment will most likely lead to the dominance of the Democratic party at the presidential level; alternatively, it will eventuate in the triumph of a third party, most likely headed by Ross Perot, in 1996.

The argument for this view begins with the observation that the Republican coalition was successfully attacked and dismantled. Key groups of past Republican supporters, including suburbanites, white Southerners, and younger voters gave a much smaller proportion of their vote to Bush than to Republican candidates in the past. The "Reagan Democrats" were substantially brought back home by Clinton. A serious third-party candidate emerged and voter turnout increased substantially, consistent with the realignment thesis.

What were the potentially crosscutting and polarizing realigning issues? Here, one might mention the vague dimension of outsiderism as well as the more specific issues of the debt, trade, and abortion. In a slightly different way, the defeat of communism created a vastly changed issue environment by removing foreign policy as a major issue. Perot capitalized the most on outsiderism and the deficit, which provides an opening for him in 1996. If Clinton's mild outsiderism can't solve the problem of corruption in government or deal adequately with the debt, then maybe the real thing could. Such a scenario probably also requires a weak economy. If, on the other hand, Clinton is able to govern effectively and woo a substantial majority of the Perot voters, he could cement a Democratic majority coalition for some time.

The Democratic realignment thesis relies on a historical parallel between 1968 and 1992. In 1968, George Wallace abandoned the Democratic party to run as a third-party candidate, thereby helping to split the Democratic majority coalition. Richard Nixon won with only 43 percent of the vote in 1968, but the Wallace campaign served as a political "conveyer belt," helping to transport millions of Southern and working-class white Democrats into the Republican party's presidential coalition. If this parallel holds, Perot will do the same thing for Bill Clinton.

Thesis 2. The 1992 election was a deviating election in an era that remains Republican at the presidential level. Analysis of voting patterns reveals that Clinton won not so much because he added to the normal Democratic vote as because the Republican vote declined. In the end, Clinton won only 43 percent of the popular vote, less than Michael Dukakis in 1988 and not much more than Walter Mondale in 1984 or Jimmy Carter in 1980. Only in the District of Columbia and his own Arkansas did he receive 51 percent of the vote or more. Admittedly, a low plurality can still signal the beginning of a realignment—Lincoln won with only 39 percent and Nixon received only 43 percent in 1968—but Clinton's performance casts doubt on the breadth of his appeal. The high turnout of 1992 is also as consistent with a deviating election as with a realigning election.

Those who argue that 1992 was a deviating election find no basis in the kinds of issues involved for concluding that there was a realignment. From 1988 to 1992, there were no major observable partisan or ideological shifts in public opinion in favor of the Democrats. Furthermore, the issues that might theoretically spark a realignment were not the issues that decided the election, at least as between Bush and Clinton. In the campaign, Bush and Clinton ultimately agreed on the North American Free Trade Agreement; the deficit was a high priority for no one but Perot; and while abortion was an important issue to some voters, it was not central and it cut both ways.[15] The issue with the greatest realigning potential might have been the deficit and debt, which helped fuel Perot's rise. But a realignment based on that issue would work to the long-term advantage of the Democrats only if they adopt it first.[16] It is at least equally possible that the Republicans, as the party of small government and now the party with no governmental responsibility, will be first to attract the Perot vote.

As for the vague issue of "outsider" politics that helped propel Perot and Clinton, it can no longer help Clinton. Unlike partisan and ideological division, the outsider-insider axis is not capable of surviving success in its pure form. Outsiders who win power, by definition, cannot remain outsiders in the same way that, say, Democrats who gain power can remain Democrats. At best, they can attain a sort of middle ground—the inside-outside position that was much coveted throughout 1992. As a result, pure outsiderism is inherently unstable and must undoubtedly undercut itself for the incumbent. Ross Perot can still wear the outsider mantle in 1996, but the Republican nominee, whomever he or she may be, will have some claim to being on the outside as well.

Rather than strong issue polarization in 1992, the campaign was marked by considerable convergence. The Democratic party moved to the center, as Clinton ran as a "different kind of Democrat" who favored the death penalty, welfare reform, tax cuts, strong defense, 100,000 new police officers, and 100,000 fewer bureaucrats. To whatever degree Clinton was on the left, he had been preceded there on most issues by George Bush himself, not during his campaign but during his presidency. Hence the election was not a choice between black and white but between tan and beige.[17] The attempt to defeat the Republicans by looking more like them is consistent, not with the polarization that begins a realignment, but with the last phase of realignments, in which "conciliation" occurs in the newly defined center. The election of 1992 may not be so much the beginning of a new Democratic reign as proof that the Republicans have succeeded in moving the center of political gravity to the right. If economic and political realities force Clinton to curtail his most expansive (and expensive) promises, he may serve to consolidate Reaganism in much the same way that Eisenhower consolidated the New Deal by failing to reverse it.

The thesis that argues that 1992 is a deviating election finds a historical parallel not in 1968, but in 1912. In 1912, Theodore Roosevelt and the "Progressive" (or "Bull Moose") party rebelled against an unpopular "establishment" president, William Howard Taft, splitting the Republican party sufficiently to deliver the White House to Woodrow Wilson. But in contrast to George Wallace's voters in 1968, who migrated to the other party, most progressives returned to the Republican fold by 1916, and by 1920 Republican dominance had fully reasserted itself.

Thesis 3. Dealignment. Both of the theses set forth above take place within the horizon of realignment theory. There is, however, another possibility. It is that 1992 does not fit any category of elections under realignment theory, because realignment theory itself is outmoded. In this view, realignment is no longer possible, whole or split. The electorate has moved into a period of dealignment. Dealignment means that the electorate has been cut free from the moorings of solid partisanship and is thus capable of swaying to and fro with great volatility from one election to the next. Realignments can occur within segments of the electorate, but so many voters have been cut loose from party moorings that such changes do not come close to structuring the electorate as a whole. Elections are decided instead by the large floating vote, which is consistent with the volatile behavior of the electorate throughout 1992, as indicated, for example, in the wild swings in the polls throughout the spring and early summer.

The dealignment view is also consistent with the rise of a personalist third party and with the general phenomenon of outsiderism. Perot is not a conveyor belt to some new, long-term shift of partisan forces, because such shifts no longer occur. Instead, the Perot phenomenon is itself "permanent," not in the sense that Ross Perot and his organization will necessarily remain—they might—but in the sense that this kind of candidacy and party is an ever-present possibility in the new landscape of a dealigned electorate.

The mixed signals produced by the conjunction of the presidential and congressional election results also make sense in this interpretation. The dealignment theses, far from seeking to ignore the lack of a pattern in voting between president and Congress, use that fact as a piece of evidence in establishing the point that there are no realignments. The fact of divided government during this period is proof that voters are not tied to parties. Of course, it does not follow that there *must* be divided government, as it is about as likely that the same party will control both branches as not. But if "unified" (one-party) government occurs, it will be by accident, not because of a partisan vote or presidential coattails. Thus, in 1992, while voters elected a Democrat to the White House, they also strengthened his natural adversaries on the right by giving Republicans a ten-seat gain in the House. Voters were signaling in 1992 what some say they have been signaling now for years: they don't much care about party consistency, because they are not voting for parties.

According to this dealignment view, the historical parallel for the election of 1992 is neither 1968 nor 1912. It is 1992. No single election is really like any other, at least in the sense of being part of a cycle in which something inevitably leads to something else. If there is a new theory of categories, it is not based on any sequential pattern.

Which of these interpretations fits 1992? In some measure, electoral theories prove their worth not by their accuracy, but by the questions they force us to pose and the lines of analyses they open up. In this respect realignment theory, as the only fully developed theory available, continues to be helpful. Still, realignment theory has the curious quality of waiting to see what happens before it can explain what was has occurred; and for today's electorate, it assigns more weight to partisanship than it can possibly carry.

The theoretical position underpinning our approach in this book is an eclectic one that draws on some elements from the split-level view and others from the dealignment view. From the split-level theory we have taken the general insight that there can be different coalitions for different offices, as well as the more specific contention that these coalitions may have a substantial partisan component. From the dealigning view, we have taken the idea that there is a sufficiently large floating vote in the modern electorate to shift the outcome of any presidential election. This fact makes the "normal" situation in modern presidential elections unpredictable or volatile in the choice between the major parties. (It is another question, as yet unknown, whether and in what degree a floating vote implies regular candidacies from outside the two parties.) Finally, to this combination we add the idea that there can be loose "structures" that weakly constrain a substantial part of the floating vote at a given point in time. These structures consist of a likely set of voter responses to a likely set of arguments under a likely set of conditions.

In this view, then, the Reagan coalition combined a partisan base in the Republican party with a large segment of the floating vote that was mobilized by a certain set of arguments under a certain set of conditions. This coalition could be seen in the fact that the three elections from 1980 to 1988 all were essentially the same campaigns directed at winning a similar kind of coalition by making the same kinds of arguments. The negative symbols were George McGovern (a weak defense and cultural experimentalism) and Jimmy Carter (economic mismanagement and malaise); the positive themes were peace through strength, traditional values, and economic prosperity.

What happened to this "structure" in 1992? Because we are

speaking only of a loose structure, the question itself is partially misleading. The predominant fact of this situation is more the floating character of the vote than the weak structure that constrains it. Hence very little "happened" in 1992 that needs explaining from a theoretical point of view. In the voters' eyes, Clinton had more of the arguments on his side, and the floating vote floated to him. Yet, to answer the question more directly, insofar as there was a structure that had coherence, it was broken or interrupted in 1992. The opportunity for this break came from a weak economy, the emergence of the outsider-insider dimension, and the "collapse" of the foreign policy issue.

Admittedly, this is not much of a theory. In particular, unlike realignment theory, it denies that there is any automatic engine or driving force in electoral politics that mechanically works itself out in history and defines the place of a president even before he has assumed office and begun to govern. We doubt, in any case, whether an electoral theory can ever replace an analysis of governing, which must be considered on its own terms in light of the actions, successes, and failures of a president, Congress, and the leaders of the opposition party. The most that a study of elections can provide for governing is an analysis of the "strategic electoral situation," meaning the constraints and possibilities deriving from electoral considerations that impinge on political actors.

BILL CLINTON'S STRATEGIC ELECTORAL SITUATION

As President, Bill Clinton certainly will have the opportunity to cement the coalition that elected him, at least for the immediate future. His current strategic electoral situation does, however, contain certain difficulties.

First, Clinton's 43 percent victory means that, unlike most incumbent presidents, he cannot be assured reelection by simply holding his previous coalition; he must expand it. Only two presidents in American history—Abraham Lincoln and Woodrow Wilson—have taken office after receiving a smaller percentage of the popular vote. Furthermore, his margin of victory was provided by citizens voting against George Bush and the state of the economy rather than for Bill Clinton—an interpretation consistent with the view that presidential elections, especially those involving an incumbent, tend to take the form of a referendum on the incumbent's performance in which the "retrospective" element plays an important role.[18]

The second difficulty implicit in Clinton's electoral situation is that, as the head of a party that dominates both branches of government, he will be unable to escape responsibility for all of the nation's policies—from the deficit, to social policy, to economic performance. Presidents often live and die by the economy, which proved true for George Bush. Nevertheless, Bush had a plausible option to evade or limit this punishment—which he never consistently adopted—by blaming a Congress that would not pass his alternative economic program. (Ronald Reagan was able to remain partly an outsider by this technique, because, with a Democratic House, the government in Washington was never fully "his" government.) This option will not be open to President Clinton in 1996. From the moment he was elected, he could not escape his ironic fate as the ultimate insider president.

A third difficulty implicit in Clinton's electoral situation is the character of the ideological coalition that helped elect him. It contained two different groups: moderates who believed that the party had moved too far to the left after 1968, and liberals who, while recognizing the need of a more centrist appearance to win the election, wish to keep the party on the left in its policies. During the campaign, when only words had to be distributed, Clinton was usually able to bridge the gap between these two groups. When he is president, when the currency is deeds and decisions, the task will prove more difficult. If he is serious about recasting the Democratic party, he may have to disappoint the liberals sufficiently to provoke a challenge from the left; if he is too accommodating to the liberals, he faces a revolt of the Reagan Democrats in the general election. If he tries to split the difference, as Jimmy Carter did, he will face a challenge from the left in the spring of 1996 and from the right in November.

A final difficulty of Clinton's electoral situation is connected to his only real mandate, which was to not be George Bush. But this may be far easier said than done. Bush's preference for foreign policy can be reversed easily enough, but it may be much more difficult to convince the rest of the world not to intrude itself on a blissful domestic presidency, occupying not only the president's time and energy, but also driving the agenda of national politics. In domestic policy, some of Clinton's proposals are ideas that conservatives have pushed for years—from a limited capital gains tax cut, welfare reform, and enterprise zones—often blocked by a liberal Congress.[19] As for his more liberal proposals, they frequently differ from Bush's actual record (as opposed to his rhetoric) not in direction but only in magnitude.

George Bush signed a large tax increase, allowed spending to increase at the fastest rate in three decades, and permitted regulatory zeal to return to levels last seen in the mid-1970s. In all of these areas, Bill Clinton promises to do the same—only more so.

THE REPUBLICANS' STRATEGIC ELECTORAL SITUATION

The Republicans' strategic electoral situation is in many ways more complicated than the Democrats', and it has already become the subject of far more controversy within the party. This is usual for the losing party. But the problem has been aggravated by the fact that the Republican party has been a presidential party, not a congressional or state and local party. Having lost their only major institutional base, Republicans have less to fall back on and consequently feel that they have a smaller margin for error.

Moderates in the Republican party argue that Clinton's victory was a triumph of centrism that ought to be emulated, and they point to the conservatism exhibited at the national convention as an important reason for Bush's defeat (along, of course, with the economy). In this view, Bush lost the women, the suburbs, and the young because of the party's association with the "religious right," particularly on the question of abortion. The party will rebound only by adopting a more liberal (or libertarian) position on social and cultural questions to go along with (depending on which "moderates" one is speaking to) either a fiscal conservatism or a supply-side economic policy.[20]

Conservatives counter that Bush lost not because of the conservatism of his campaign, but because of the de facto liberalism and general indirection of his presidency (along, of course, with a stagnant economy). In this view, the lesson of the election is that the Democrats won by moving to the right, while the Republicans lost by moving to the left. Bush's policies destroyed the Reagan coalition piece by piece. If the convention was at times shrill, it was the consequence of having so alienated the party's base that the convention had to be used to resolidify it rather than reach out. Furthermore, conservatives say, the platform was no different in 1992 than in 1980, 1984, or 1988. The missing variable that accounts for the loss cannot be the platform, but George Bush's rejection of Reaganism in practice. The problem was not that Bush refused to buckle on abortion, but more accurately that abortion was the only thing he did *not* buckle on.

Conservatives will almost certainly prevail in this intramural skirmish, due to advantages in funding, organization, and intellectual candlepower. The more important question, however, is which kind of conservatism will triumph, for the differences among those claiming this label are substantial. Indeed, beyond a surface agreement about some of the faults of the 1992 Bush campaign, these differences are in certain respects far greater than those between some conservatives and moderates. (This fact is what gives moderates an important role in a situation that is not bipolar.)

Conservatives have been placed, perhaps too neatly, into three groups. One group, which has emphasized budget-balancing and deficit reduction, is led by Bob Dole and Warren Rudman (retired from the Senate but still active in politics); a second group, which has stressed the threat to traditional values and spoken of a "cultural war" in America, is headed by the two Pats: Buchanan and Robertson (who, however, are not necessarily allies); and a third group, which has emphasized opportunity, growth, and values, has formed around Jack Kemp, Bill Bennett, and Dan Quayle.

The 1992 Republican primary battle was an opening salvo in a contest between the last group and Pat Buchanan, in which George Bush and his renomination sometimes seemed an incidental sideshow. Buchanan lost that battle, and Kemp was the clear favorite for 1996 among the delegates at the national convention. Still, Buchanan compiled a list of contributors and volunteers who might be reactivated in 1996. Robertson and his forces, organized into a group entitled the Christian Coalition, are hard at work taking over the party at the local level in many states. And Dole and Rudman may be strengthened by connections to parts of the Perot movement.

The conflict that has sometimes erupted between Dole and Kemp is clear enough. Dole has held that many of Kemp's supply-side growth ideas would add to the deficit, while Kemp has argued that a growth strategy is the best way to eliminate the deficit. It is the difference between Buchanan's conservatism and that of Kemp and Bennett, however, that has been the most pronounced and sometimes the most incomprehensible to those outside the party. The foundation of this difference lies ultimately in a different grounding for conservatism. For Bennett and Kemp the values of which they speak—and Bennett has emphasized this theme more—are rooted in general philosophic principles and norms of Nature, accessible in principle to any ethnic or racial group. This fact explains the emphasis on inclusion and the celebration of the triumphs of minorities and immigrants in their rhetoric. For Buchanan, the values are rooted in the fact that "we" hold them and that they are ours. Who the "we" includes and excludes has been the issue. In his convention speech, Buchanan spoke of a "religious war going on in this country for the soul of America . . . a cultural war as critical to the kind of nation we shall have as the Cold War itself. . . . We must take back our cities, and take back our culture, and take back our country." Kemp referred to this speech as "divisive and exclusionary."[21]

The much-discussed "battle for the soul of the Republican party" is taking place in precinct caucuses, state and local party committees, think tanks, political action committees, the Republican National Committee and the Senate and House campaign committees, and Congress itself. Congress, which was the arena in which Republicans regrouped after 1976 to formulate a positive alternative program for the country, is likely to play an important role again. Yet the major Republican leaders this time—Kemp, Cheney, Bennett, Buchanan, and Robertson—are all outside of Congress and are likely to remain so for the next few years. This in itself will create a new kind of opposition politics, with some of the leaders being in the enviable position of having an established political record with no immediate political responsibilities.

CONCLUSION

The 1992 elections offered a spectacle of great volatility which ended with the long-standing Republican presidential coalition being shattered and with a large class of new members elected to Congress (though the Democrats maintained control of both houses). This volatility, however, was not simply random, but reflected the logic of a two-dimensional universe that dominated the politics of 1992. The key to understanding the twists and turns of this peculiar year lies in the interplay of a new, outside-inside dimension with the traditional partisan and ideological axes. This new crosscutting dimension put Ross Perot, Pat Buchanan, and Jerry Brown into the same camp on one side, and George Bush and the Democratic Congress into the same camp on the other side.

Much of the year can be explained by the scramble of political actors to get to the outside and their varying levels of success. The potency of that movement was expressed in the fact that an "outsider" third-party candidate for a moment shook the political establishment, finishing in the end with the votes of one-fifth of the electorate. Yet while outsiderism generally helped the candidates who could use it, it was no guarantee of victory. Radical outsiderism imposed a ceiling beyond which candidates could not go, whatever their other (and in many cases, serious) liabilities. Americans at virtually every juncture in the presidential contest chose the inside-outside option rather than the extreme outside. Bill Clinton, an insider-outsider, won the Democratic nomination against the insiders Kerrey and Harkin and the outsiders Brown and Tsongas. Then, operating from the same position, he defeated Bush to the inside and Perot to the outside.

Although Bill Clinton was advantageously positioned in relationship to both of his rivals on the inside-outside axis, his election over George Bush, even without this advantage, was hardly startling. For on the traditional dimension of American politics—partisanship and ideology—Bill Clinton was also well positioned. He took his own party to the center and was thereby in a good position to pick up the votes of his targeted forgotten middle class, who were unusually anxious about economic conditions. In a deeper sense, however, the economic anxiety and the appeal for change and outsiderism became possible because of a new (and favorable) state of affairs in the world brought on by the end of the Cold War. This state of affairs enabled Americans to indulge in the "luxury" of preoccupation with exclusively domestic concerns. Foreign policy—the important "issue" that never was—was thus the most important issue.

Free to cast off certain old restraints and experiment with something new, some voters took a chance on Ross Perot, and many more on the moderate outsiderism and political centrism of Bill Clinton. The inside in the person of George Bush was rejected, while the outside in the person of Bill Clinton was tempered to satisfy the need for competence and steadiness. The promise of change, sometimes almost for its own sake, beat a tired attachment to the status quo. In the end, the man with too many ideas beat the man with none.

NOTES

1. Eugene H. Roseboom, *A History of Presidential Elections* (New York: Macmillan, 1957), p. 231.

2. "Bush, Clinton Sending Envoys to Perot Meeting," *Los Angeles Times*, September 26, 1992, p. 1.

3. In hindsight, some might say that the perfect strategy for the Bush campaign would have been to help keep Perot in the race over the summer, but not allow him to get so strong as to beat Bush. But such a judgment

demands more refinement of campaign strategy than is possible. No campaign is in a position to calibrate the exact strength of another, turning it up or down like the volume on a compact disk recorder.

4. David Lauter, "Clinton's Strategy of Triage," *Los Angeles Times*, November 5, 1992, p. A1.

5. *The National Journal*, November 7, 1992, p. 2544. The data here are taken from the Voter Research and Surveys exit polls. The poll lists the following question: "Which candidate qualities mattered most in deciding how you voted?" Of the nine major possibilities offered, "Will bring about needed change" was the most frequently cited response.

6. "The Message Behind the Votes," *Los Angeles Times*, November 4, 1992, p. A11. Sixty-nine percent of the Clinton voters, 34 percent of the Bush voters, and 72 percent of the Perot voters cited jobs and the economy as being among the "most important issues in deciding how to vote." It was by far the most frequently cited factor, and it worked much more decisively for Clinton and Perot than for Bush.

7. Ruy Teixeira, *The Disappearing American Voter* (Washington, D.C.: Brookings Institution, 1992), p. 57.

8. Of course, the differences are notable as well. The nineteenth-century campaigns were collective, in the sense that they brought people together in groups, whereas modern campaigns are isolating, placing each voter before his or her television set. Furthermore, in the nineteenth-century campaign communication was controlled by parties, whereas today it is often in the hands of those having no connection to them.

9. "How the Nation Voted," *New York Times* (chart), November 5, 1992, p. B4.

10. "Turnout tops 100 Million," *USA TODAY*, November 5, 1992 p. 6A.

11. Everett Carll Ladd, "Like Waiting For Godot," in Byron Shafer, ed., *The End of Realignment?* (Madison: University of Wisconsin Press, 1991). This book contains a variety of views on the current state of electoral theory and provides a full bibliography of more than 30 pages of articles and books bearing on the subject. The very interested reader may wish to consult that list.

12. See James Sundquist, *The Dynamics of Party Change* (Washington, D.C.: Brookings Institution, 1973). Also Walter Dean Burnham, *Critical Elections and the Mainsprings of American Politics* (Englewood Cliffs, NJ: Prentice-Hall, 1963).

13. See Angus Campbell, "A Classification of Presidential Elections," in Campbell, Converse, Miller, and Stokes, *The American Voter* (New York: John Wiley and Sons, 1960).

14. What party identification means under split-level realignment theory is another contentious question. Does it indicate a presidential voting preference, or a congressional voting preference? In either case, movement

toward one party or another would still be a significant sign. It was not until the late 1980s that the Republicans began to draw close in voter identification.

15. Polls indicated that 12 percent of voters claimed to have made up their minds on the basis of abortion, the majority of them pro-life. But there may have been many other voters for whom the abortion issue was an important secondary factor, which in combination with other things determined the vote.

16. Clinton's economic team of Lloyd Bentsen, Leon Panetta, and Alice Rivlin indicates that he might move in this direction, but there are countervailing pressures as well.

17. Stephen Chapman, "Clinton's Victory Was Not a Vote for Change," *Denver Post*, November 8, 1992, p. D5.

18. See Morris P. Fiorina, *Retrospective Voting in American National Elections* (New Haven, Conn.: Yale University Press, 1981). In fact, on many of the policy preferences, even for the economy, voters were closer to Bush's program as stated during the campaign than to Clinton's (provided, of course, that voters did not know it was *Bush*'s plan).

19. Much of Clinton's campaign was directed at the task of emulating the Republicans and distancing himself from his own party. See Lars-Erik Nelson, "Clinton's moderate shield could deflect a GOP challenge for years," *Denver Post*, November 22, 1992, p. D4.

20. Governors Pete Wilson of California and William Weld of Massachusetts and former Labor Secretary Lynn Martin can be considered advocates of this line of argument. Weld, however, is a leading supply-side advocate and has formed important alliances with other conservatives on economic matters and questions of political empowerment. This shows that the lines in this struggle are fluid, with many points of divergence and intersection.

21. David Broder, "Jack Kemp, Heir Apparently," *Washington Post Weekly*, November 16-22, 1992, p. 2.

Index

About the Authors

James Ceaser is professor of government and foreign affairs at the University of Virginia, and Henry Salvatori visiting professor at Claremont McKenna College in California. He is the author of several books on American politics and American political thought, including *Presidential Selection* (1979), *Reforming the Reforms* (1982), and *Liberal Democracy and Political Science* (1991).

Andrew Busch is assistant professor of political science at the University of Denver. He is a graduate of the University of Colorado and received his Ph.D. from the University of Virginia in 1992.